FREEDOM IS
NOT
ENOUGH

FREEDOM IS
NOT
ENOUGH

BLACK VOTERS, BLACK CANDIDATES, AND AMERICAN PRESIDENTIAL POLITICS

RONALD W. WALTERS

ROWMAN & LITTLEFIELD PUBLISHERS, INC.
Lanham • Boulder • New York • Toronto • Oxford

ROWMAN & LITTLEFIELD PUBLISHERS, INC.

Published in the United States of America
by Rowman & Littlefield Publishers, Inc.
A wholly owned subsidiary of The Rowman & Littlefield Publishing Group, Inc.
4501 Forbes Boulevard, Suite 200, Lanham, Maryland 20706
www.rowmanlittlefield.com

P.O. Box 317, Oxford OX2 9RU, UK

Distributed by NATIONAL BOOK NETWORK

British Library Cataloguing in Publication Information Available

Library of Congress Cataloging-in-Publication Data

Walters, Ronald W.
   Freedom is not enough : Black voters, Black candidates, and American
presidential politics / Ronald W. Walters.
      p.   cm.—(American political challenges)
   Includes bibliographical references and index.
   ISBN 0-7425-3837-0 (cloth : alk. paper)
   1. African Americans—Suffrage.   2. African Americans—Politics and
government.   3. African Americans—History—1964–   4. United States. Voting
Rights Act of 1965.   5. United States—Politics and government—1945–1989.
6. United States—Politics and government—1989–   7. Presidents—United
States—Election—History—20th century.   8. Presidents—United States—
Election—2004.   9. Presidential candidates—United States—Biography.
I. Title.   II. Series.
JK1924.W343   2005
324.6′2′08996073—dc22   2005008343

Printed in the United States of America

♾ ™ The paper used in this publication meets the minimum requirements of
American National Standard for Information Sciences—Permanence of Paper for
Printed Library Materials, ANSI/NISO Z39.48-1992.

This work is dedicated to the
Rev. Joseph Lowery, who has given his life
to the task of empowering Blacks,
and through them all Americans,
by his indefatigable organizing to make the
Voting Rights Act come alive.

Contents

Contents

Tables

Tables

Preface

I open this book with a distinction, one based on the meaning of freedom to Blacks and whites in the context of American society, and one that should not be lost on the reader, because making this distinction is the fundamental purpose of the book. Freedom, to those who have power and citizenship, means the enjoyment of the absence of political restraint on the exercise of civil rights—one of the renowned features of American democracy. But as I point out, the meaning of freedom has differed for Blacks, and this should cause us to pause and question the status of freedom at every given era. I have chosen this era, the Fortieth Anniversary of the passage of the Voting Rights Act of 1965, to attempt to facilitate an understanding of the extent to which this intended instrument of Black political power, forged in the heat of previous civil rights struggles, has provided significant Black empowerment not only at the local level of government, but in the national political arena as well.

Achieving freedom has been a constant in the lives of Black people, from their first response to their manumission from legal slavery, to the civil rights marchers who sang songs like "Oh Freedom," "I've Got the Light of Freedom," and "Walking and Talking with My Mind (Stayed on Freedom)." These songs, sung with the desire of hope for full citizenship rights, will continue to energize successive generations of Blacks and all who share their aspiration for inclusion in American society.

With this in mind, I have dedicated this work to that generation of thousands of people, young and old, Black and white, North and South—the struggle generation—who celebrate what the Voting Rights Act has achieved thus far. They also share my concern, as indicated by the 2000 and 2004 presidential elections, that many of the old racial barriers to the unfettered right to vote, thought to have been weakened by the Voting Rights Act, still exist, while others have arisen with the use of the new electronic voting technologies.

Given the drama that has surrounded the quest to enhance the power of the Black vote, I focus this work on the mobilization efforts of the Black community because these efforts have been responsible for pushing the possibilities of the Voting Rights Act to the limits of its effectiveness with respect to voter turnout. In light of that fact, I have concentrated on the groups that have promoted and realized those efforts: Black labor, the Black church, and coalitions like the National Coalition on Black Civic Participation. And I specifically dedicate this work to the Reverend Joseph Lowery of Atlanta, Georgia, head of the Georgia Coalition for the Peoples' Agenda. He was a close associate of Dr. Martin Luther King Jr. and a cofounder of the Southern Christian Leadership Conference, a man who understood the mission of empowerment, and who at the age of eighty-three is one of today's most active leaders in the struggle to mobilize Southern Black voters. His long commitment and the success of his efforts should be an inspiration and lesson to future generations.

I would like to express my appreciation for assistance in the writing of this book to the Howard University Moorland-Spingarn Research Center's Voting Rights Act Documentation Project, which provided primary documents involving civil rights activists. Similar documents from the Civil Rights Oral History Project at the University of Southern Mississippi, and this author's long association with the culture and individuals of groups such as the Student Nonviolent Coordinating Committee, have also been invaluable. I would also thank the College of Behavioral and Social Sciences at the University of Maryland for awarding me sabbatical leave in the fall of 2004 to write the manuscript and my wife, Patricia Walters, for her support in believing that it would be possible to do.

In addition, I want to thank Professor Larry Sabato, director of the Center for American Politics at the University of Virginia, for inviting me to take part in this series on American political challenges, and the staff of Rowman & Littlefield, especially Jennifer Knerr, for her guidance in helping me turn an idea into an acceptable document for publication and to Janice Braunstein for her expert editing of the manuscript.

Chapter 1 of this review of the impact of the Voting Rights Act of 1965 revisits the culture of the civil rights movement, reminding us of the price paid and the objectives sought in acquiring an equal, unfettered right to vote. Chapters 2 and 3 reemphasize the contribution of the 1984 and 1988 campaigns of Rev. Jesse Jackson Sr. and summarize the influence of the Black vote in the presidential elections of 1992 and 1996. An examination of the midterm election of 1998 is included here to provide the reader with a description of the developing power of the Black mobilization activities that would come to bear on the 2000 presidential election. Chapter 4 asserts that the Voting Rights Act has been weakened both by recent Supreme Court decisions and by the politics of the dramatic end to the 2000 presidential election, and chapter 5 continues with an examination of the legacy of the 2000 election by discussing the various forms of Black voter disenfranchisement encountered, and recommending certain practical changes in voting law and practice. Chapter 7 analyzes the impact of Black mobilization on the 2004 presidential election and finds yet more new challenges to Black empowerment in the way in which the Democratic party and its major allied units implement voter turnout strategy. This then invites a discussion of the future impact of the Voting Rights Act and of Black voting rights in general, which leads us, finally, into a consideration of the tactics that have been used to enhance Black mobilization by controlling Black voter turnout, and of the politics of leverage by which that turnout delivers power to the Black electorate.

1

Black Empowerment and the 1965 Voting Rights Act

The Goal of Black Politics: Full Citizenship

The original national vision of freedom and liberty meant that the people of the United States were to be free of their colonial status and therefore free, with the power of governance in their own hands, to pursue their own destiny. As slaves, Blacks were not a part of that original vision, but had to seek a place in it, finding that the elements of the vision could not sustain their own freedom and that in fact, their status as slaves was a contradiction to the broader manifest goals of democracy. Sharing broad goals including "life, liberty and the pursuit of happiness" required the status of citizen, not slave. Thus, full citizenship became a valued goal for Blacks in the United States, a citizenship defined in part as the possession of the right to vote, with the vote conceived of as an instrument by which citizenship would be made meaningful.

It is ironic yet predictable that the group farthest down the ladder of American society should become the most vigorous proponent of the principles of democratic practice. The reason for this is that Blacks have always equated the ultimate fulfillment of their freedom with the achievement of equality with whites as part of a truly democratic society. The route to this status of citizenship for Blacks has been through the values and rights promised in the American Constitution to all citizens. Against this standard, the attainment of freedom from slavery was merely a prerequisite to a series of events that involved *the acquisition of citizenship rights, their fair implementation, and the use of those rights to achieve a dignified status in American society.* The objective of achieving full citizenship was a goal that characterized both the strategies and the ends of Black political participation. Blacks sought to develop and utilize the tools of participation in order to make their influence in governance felt, and in order to effect policies that were consistent with their quest for equality. Thus freedom, as the simple act of defining Blacks as non-slaves but citizens, was never enough.

If they were equal to whites Blacks would, in fact, possess the rights and resources that would enable them to exercise a sense of self-determination both corporate and individual. This absence of equality thus becomes an indicator of the degree of freedom. In an interesting discussion of the tension between equality and freedom, Alexis de Tocqueville appeared to be prescient about this matter in his view that "men cannot become absolutely equal unless they are entirely free."[1] It is in this sense that the nature of the quest for freedom by Black people in America is related to the quality of their rights, the substance and stability of which affect their status as citizens, a status which, in turn, affects their ability to maintain equality.

As the dominant route to freedom in America has been through the acquisition of American citizenship, the definition of citizenship historically has encompassed the possession of certain finite rights. But both the struggle for those rights and the subsequent status achieved by their possession has affected various groups in American society differently. This reality led Professor Linda Kerber to propose a concept of "braided citizenship" to explain that rights are elaborated within society by historical dynamics that are themselves comprised of competing pressures in the fields of economics, politics, and culture. It is these competing pressures that help to shape access to rights for certain groups or individuals under certain conditions and in a given era.[2] The progress of Black Americans toward full citizenship through the acquisition and maintenance of rights, and by a long and difficult struggle, is not only unique as a parallel to the progress and struggles of women, immigrants, and others—I also consider it to be a fundamental criterion by which the progress of real Democracy itself has been achieved in American society.

Given that some sectors of the majority group have been most ingenious in reinterpreting the law to construct new barriers, the goal of Black freedom through full citizenship has been a moving target that places a substantial emphasis on the reformulation of tactics and strategies in order to match the unique challenges that are present in various eras of history.

The vital importance of what can be achieved by the vote has always been at the heart of Black politics, as seen in the definitions proposed by two powerful Black leaders, Frederick Douglass and Martin Luther King Jr. I will argue here that the vision contained in those definitions of full access to this discrete right, envisioned by the Fifteenth Amendment to the U.S. Constitution and the 1965 Voting Rights Act, is not enough, but that the realization of that access by strong turnout, the ability to capitalize on that turnout by effective bargaining, and the mobilization of power by Black presidential candidacies are strategies that must be perfected. Just as it was not enough to be technically set free as slaves, so it is not enough to be given technical citizenship without its attendant rights; it is not enough to technically have the right to vote when that right can make no impact on the political system. At the dawn of the twenty-first century, it is not enough to have a theoretical status of freedom, and a defined, continuing disenfranchisement from effective political participation, which only yields a tainted status of citizenship.

Connecting Voting Rights to Freedom

Douglass Formulates the Vision

No one earlier or more often than Frederick Douglass, the great nineteenth-century civil rights leader, espoused the importance of the vote in achieving full citizenship for Blacks. Douglass began, after the Emancipation, to make obtaining citizenship rights his major point of agitation, and near the end of the Civil War, in April of 1865, Douglass gave a speech at a meeting of the Massachusetts Anti-Slavery Society in which he announced that he was for

> the immediate, unconditional and universal enfranchisement of the Black man in every State in the Union. Without this, his liberty is a mockery; without this, you might as well almost retain the old name of slavery for this condition; for in fact, if he is not the slave of the individual master, he is the slave of society, and holds his liberty as a privilege, not as a right.[3]

Frederick Douglass went on to set forth a series of reasons why Blacks should have the vote. He explained that the franchise was desired because it is the right of all citizens and that without it, Blacks were without status, a condition that would affirm to society that Blacks were unfit for equality. He felt that the elective franchise was necessary because of the uniqueness of America, a uniqueness based on the fact that the government was founded upon the "peculiar idea" of universal suffrage. Another important reason for the franchise, he believed, was that it signaled to the South that the sacrifice Blacks had made by turning against their former slave masters was both a just act leveled against the institution of slavery, and a reaffirmation of Black humanity.

Douglass enriched his theory for the acquisition of full citizenship with a point that would be used by Blacks in future generations, noting that just as it had in the Civil War, if America were in trouble again it would have to call upon Blacks to serve the country, and that they would be more amenable to serve if they possessed full citizenship rights. In this he drew considerable support from the views of fifty-nine Blacks who had been both former slaves and Union soldiers, who petitioned the Union Convention held in Nashville, Tennessee, on January 9, 1865, saying,

> We know the burdens of citizenship and are ready to bear them. We know the duties of the good citizen and are ready to perform them cheerfully, and would ask to be put in a position to discharge them more effectively. We do not ask for the privilege of citizenship, wishing to shun the obligations imposed by it. Nearly 200,000 of our brethren are here today performing duty in the ranks of the Union Army. Thousands of them have already died in battle, or perished by a cruel martyrdom for the sake of the Union, and we are ready and willing to sacrifice more. But what higher order of citizen is the soldier? Or who has the greater trust confided to his hands? If we are called to duty against the rebel armies in the field, why should we be denied the privilege of voting against rebel citizens at the ballot-box? The latter is as necessary to save the government as the former.[4]

Perhaps the most critical rationale for the Black vote was enunciated by Frederick Douglass in an article in the *Atlantic Monthly* of January 1867, in which he argued that while the fundamental basis for suffrage was the manhood of Blacks or the dignity of their humanity, the most important justification for suffrage was not philosophical, but practical, in that it could be used to strengthen society by empowering Blacks. He expressed it in the following manner:

> Give the negro the elective franchise, and you give him at once a powerful motive for all noble exertion, and make him a man among men.

In another place in this article he suggested:

> Give the negro the elective franchise, and you at once destroy the purely sectional policy, and wheel the Southern States into line with national interests and national objects.[5]

This position anticipated the attempt by the Southern states to maintain their conception of a weak federal government, and to enhance states' rights as the key to continued control over Black labor and social conditions. Douglass understood that the rights of Blacks were bound up in the outcome of the debate over the "realpolitik" of American federalism as a limiting context to Black empowerment.

True to Douglass's vision, the limiting context of states' rights crippled the implementation of the Fifteenth Amendment to the U.S. Constitution that explicitly gave Congress the power to protect Blacks from being denied by states the right to vote. By allowing states to deny Blacks the right to vote, a condition that lasted from the turn of the twentieth century until the passage of the 1965 Voting Rights Act, the initial freedom that Blacks had won from slavery, and even the authority vested in Congress to protect their right to vote, was not able to create a viable citizenship in the face of the raw, oppressive power of the Southern states. Black political participation was thus limited by the conservative context that dominated the political system at that time. In this sense, it would take much more than the Fifteenth Amendment for Black freedom to be attained, in a different context, in the twentieth century.

King Continues the Vision

The idea expressed by Frederick Douglass that the ballot for Blacks was central to the task of achieving full citizenship and empowerment was also one that Dr. Martin Luther King Jr. harbored as early as 1957. On May 17 of that year, he expressed himself on this subject in a speech at the Lincoln Monument at a mass gathering commemorating the third anniversary of the Supreme Court decision in *Brown v. Board of Education of Topeka, Kansas* (1954). He said, "Our most urgent request to the President of the United States and every member of Congress is to give us the right to vote."[6] And then he continued:

> *Give us the ballot* and we will no longer have to worry the federal government about our basic rights.
> *Give us the ballot* and we will no longer plead to the federal government for passage of an anti-lynching law; we will by the power of our vote write the law on the statute books of the South and bring an end to the dastardly acts of the hooded perpetrators of violence.
> *Give us the ballot* and we will transform the salient misdeeds of bloodthirsty mobs into the calculated good deeds of orderly citizens.
> *Give us the ballot* and we will fill our legislative halls with men of goodwill and send to the sacred halls of Congress men who will not sign a Southern manifesto because of their devotion to the manifesto of justice.
> *Give us the ballot* and we will place judges on the benches of the South who will do justly and love mercy, and we will place at the head of the Southern states governors who will, who love mercy and have felt not only the tang of the human, but the glow of the Divine.
> *Give us the ballot* and we will quietly and nonviolently, without rancor or bitterness, implement the Supreme Court's Decision of May 17, 1954 [emphasis added].

King's empowerment conception of the vote was vested in his

> firm conviction that if the Negro achieved the ballot throughout the South, many of the problems which we faced would be solved. I had come to see that one of the most decisive steps that the Negro could take was a short walk to the voting booth. Until we gained the ballot and place proper public officials in office, this condition would continue to exist.[7]

With this bold statement, he set forth his faith in the nature of the political system. With the opportunity provided Black people to participate in that political system, they might be able to play a self-determining role in the resolution of their own problems. Whether obtaining the right to vote has led to the fulfillment of King's empowerment goal for the Black vote is the key question raised in this work. But in the absence of a wide-ranging history of the Voting Rights Act, it is worth summarizing below the struggle to achieve voting rights, as a prelude to our concern in this work with the perfection of voting rights as a tool for the achievement of freedom in this age.

The Acquisition of Voting Rights

The Price of Voting Rights

The struggle to achieve voting rights involved and required the courage of local Blacks in a populist campaign, a fact that often lurks in the shadows of the larger myths of the Selma-to-Montgomery March and the exploits of Dr. Martin Luther King Jr. and the leaders and members of civil rights organizations. The voting rights struggle was all the more heroic because of the dangerous conditions under which Blacks lived against a backdrop of chattel slavery and peonage, a system of labor in which blacks were minimally rewarded financially and were controlled, in a manner resembling slavery, by ruthless criminalization, beating, murder, and other forms of violence that still reigned unchecked in many places in the South in the 1960s. The manner in which this danger was confronted forms the foundation of modern-day respect for the price of the Black vote—a vote tainted with the spilled blood of those who were killed, maimed, or otherwise challenged by a white supremacist culture led by the interlocking leadership of the Ku Klux Klan, the White Citizens Councils, and local police authorities.

One example of the fierce desire of Blacks to exercise the franchise was to be found in the tent cities of Fayette and Haywood counties in Tennessee. In many places in the South where the National Association for the Advancement of Colored People (the NAACP) was either banned outright or confronted with severe hostility, Blacks formed other organizations and leagues such as the Fayette County Civic and Welfare League, and the Haywood County Civic and Welfare League. The Civil Rights Act of 1957 authorized the Justice Department to sue to prevent prohibition of the right of Blacks to vote as result of intimidation or coercion. The Tennessee leagues, formed in 1959, attempted to register Black people to vote, but when the Democratic party excluded these would-be voters, the leagues filed suit, and the courts then validated the right of the prospective voters to register. However, Professor Allan Lichtman, a voting rights expert, says that enforcement of the act was limited by many factors, such as the strict criteria for bringing suit by the Justice Department, and the novelty of this responsibility for a Justice

Department which was, in many ways, simply an extension of the system of Southern states' control of Blacks.

The reaction of white Tennesseans was devastating, and they used their economic power to punish Blacks. One description is illuminating:

> Many [Blacks] lost employment, credit, and insurance policies. Whites refused to sell them goods and services. White physicians withheld medical care from their African American patients. Without notice in the winter of 1960, white property owners evicted more than 400 African American tenant families from their lands. The leadership of the Leagues did not capitulate to such unconscionable retaliation. Without hesitation and with the support of Shephard Towles, a self-determining African American property owner, they formed a makeshift community known as "Tent City."[8]

The families spent a hard winter in their tent cities made of surplus army tent material, but once their story was brought to public attention, the Justice Department filed suit against forty-five white landowners for violating the civil rights of Blacks attempting to vote.

The stark reality was that the situation in Tennessee was not unusual, even though some Blacks in the South managed to vote under the exceedingly difficult criteria enforced by local voting boards. In eight of the Deep South states covered by the Voting Rights Act in 1965, only 31 percent of Black people of voting age were registered to vote. For example, in the Alabama Black Belt of Lowndes and Wilcox counties, where Blacks were 80 percent of the population, there were almost no Black voters. In 1960, there were only 53,336 Black voters in the whole of Alabama, but after the enactment of the Voting Rights Act, the number rose to 537,285 by 1990.[9] This pattern was repeated in the other states of the old Confederacy, such as Mississippi, Louisiana, and Georgia where approximately 19 percent of all voting age Blacks were registered to vote in 1956, compared to 76 percent of whites. In Mississippi, there were thirteen counties without a single Black registered to vote, which together comprised 45.9 percent of the total voting age population in those counties. As a result of other suits lodged by the Justice Department pursuant to the 1957 Civil Rights Act, voter registration increased only slightly, as indicated by the record of hearings of the U.S. Commission on Civil Rights.

Table 1.1   Black Registration in Four Southern States, 1956 and 1964 (%, rounded)

States	1956	1964
Mississippi	5	7
Alabama	11	20
Georgia	27	27
Louisiana	31	32

Source: U.S. Commission on Civil Rights, "Political Participation: A Study of the Participation by Negroes in the Electoral and Political Processes in 10 Southern States since the Passage of the Voting Rights Act of 1965," Washington, DC, May 1968, 12.

Targeting the Right to Vote

The data in table 1.1 indicates, except for Alabama, the slow pace and ineffectiveness of the 1957 law. This stimulated the civil rights movement to focus more intensely on voting rights, and very often students were the foot soldiers. The Student Non-violent Coordinating Committee (SNCC) was born in 1960, and Lawrence Guyot, a SNCC activist and its Mississippi field secretary, said that the emphasis on voting began at a meeting of the SNCC in 1961 at Shaw University in North Carolina. At this meeting, Ella Baker, an adult advisor to the Southern Christian Leadership Conference (SCLC), helped to begin the organization and encouraged its members to forsake "the hamburgers" (lunch counter sit-ins) that had become so popular in 1960 and to select more political targets. She encouraged them not to merely follow the lead of their parent organization, the SCLC, but to develop their own strengths, saying, "strong people don't need leaders. Let's go find and facilitate leadership. And let's concentrate on the vote. And let's understand that we have too many leaders, but we don't have enough leadership."[10]

Meanwhile, Dr. Martin Luther King Jr. and his colleagues in the SCLC had become involved in the pursuit of a wider set of issues. From the bus boycott victory of the Montgomery Improvement Association in the late 1950s, the energy of youths coming to fuel the emergence of the sit-in movement, the Freedom Rides, and continued racism in public facilities such as libraries, bus and train stations, lunch counters, swimming pools, and other institutional or public centers began to absorb the attention of a civil rights coalition headed by such organizations as the NAACP, the National Urban League, the Congress of Racial Equality, the SCLC, and the SNCC. Therefore, the river of change that began to

9

flow from the 1954 Supreme Court decision in *Brown v. Board of Education* created the Civil Rights Acts of 1957, 1960, 1964, and 1965, all of which sought to prohibit the exclusion of Blacks from many areas of civic life.

The targeting by the civil rights movement of the right to vote was one of the most political of the movement's objectives. Locating the leadership for voting rights in poverty-stricken, racially oppressed communities promoted the goal of empowerment as well. However, these communities were also traditional bastions of Southern white domination, where brutal control was exercised over the lives of Blacks. Forging a movement under such conditions would therefore be extremely difficult, but also highly strategic.

In addition to the above, the focus on mobilizing to attain Black voting rights was an outgrowth of the larger civil rights movement that had, ironically, invited the involvement of then Attorney General Robert Kennedy. Kennedy feared that the mass mobilizations in the South, by challenging the social and cultural foundations of the Southern racial oligarchy, were not only dangerous for Blacks, but were making life difficult for his brother, President John Kennedy, who felt that he needed the South to enact much of his legislative agenda. So Robert Kennedy suggested that the civil rights movement in the South turn its attention away from directly challenging Southern whites to open up schools and public accommodations, and rather to pursue voter registration and civic education; he also enlisted the Field Foundation, an Illinois institution established by Marshall Field III, head of the retail store in Chicago, to provide financial assistance to this cause.

In 1961 the Field Foundation made a grant of $100,000.00, which was to be administered jointly by the United Church of Christ and the Southern Christian Leadership Conference, and the foundation appointed two young Black ministers associated with those churches, Rev. Andrew Young and Rev. Wyatt T. Walker, to manage the funds. The two ministers set up a center in Dorchester, Georgia, to promote voter registration and citizenship training, and before long, "Dorchester Centers" were established throughout Alabama, Mississippi, Georgia, South Carolina, and Virginia. These centers, however, were not able to empower Blacks to forge the strong patterns of political participation that would break through local white resistance.

A more promising attempt at this objective began in 1961 when Robert Moses, a teacher in the New York City school system, went south to join the movement. His practice of listening to local leaders and adopting their objectives was important in building respect for what would be accomplished by those who came south to help. It also built local leadership resources on the ground by involving these leaders in projects that would auger well for progress once the Northern volunteers were gone.

Robert Moses met individuals such as Amzie Moore, a local activist from Cleveland, Mississippi, who helped to acclimatize him to the Southern political environment and to orient him toward voter registration as a vital interest of Southern Blacks. Moses was also invited by C.C. Bryant, head of the McComb, Mississippi, NAACP, to come to McComb and set up a voter registration drive. The vicious climate in McComb and other parts of Mississippi was absolutely intolerant of Blacks attempting to vote: several people were killed and Moses himself was beaten badly on one occasion.

Nevertheless, in late March of 1962, with the additional support of several hundred thousand dollars from the Field Foundation, the Taconic Foundation and the Stern Family Fund, together with other liberal New York institutions, funded the Southern Regional Council and established the Voter Education Project. Wiley Branton, a well-known Arkansas Black attorney, was made president, and Bob Moses, executive director. Moses then moved his operation to Jackson, Mississippi, a city where he would have a much easier time mobilizing than in the rural areas of the state.

Mississippi proved difficult to organize because of the wanton violence visited upon civil rights workers, and before long Branton pulled financial support from Mississippi in favor of other sites in the South where the resistance was less formidable. Even so, Moses went on to develop the "Freedom Summer" project of 1963 that drew over one thousand youthful volunteers, mostly from the North, to Mississippi. The volunteers helped run freedom schools that taught citizenship and vocational skills as well as arts and crafts, promoted literacy, and of course conducted voter registration drives. By the end of the summer, the volunteers had successfully registered over twelve hundred new voters in Mississippi.

Fannie Lou Hamer

Fannie Lou Hamer was one of the local leaders who worked in the Deep South as early as 1962 to enfranchise Blacks. She was a determined and

11

charismatic leader who knew her citizenship rights and could effectively teach them to others. Her colleagues in the SNCC felt that she inspired people to challenge the social conditioning of inferiority and exclusion that Blacks experienced in the South, and that she exhibited a commitment to their rights with a "rock-hard" integrity. The comments of Professor Robert Jackall, an SNCC activist, about Hamer's charisma were typical of such feelings:

> It was something supernatural inside her. Like medicine men and miracle workers. She didn't appear on the stage, she arose. When she rose she spoke the words we hardly dared to speak to our own selves. She always touched the truth. It was the deepest truest truth which any of us knew. She went straight for the jugular, but not without compassion. She knew the heart and mind of the monster and it didn't frighten her, not even for a minute.[11]

In 1962, for attempting to register to vote in Winona, Mississippi, Ms. Hamer was arrested, thrown in jail, and beaten severely. She went on to be a leader of the Mississippi Freedom Democratic Party, which held the first widespread general election in Mississippi in 1964 to elect delegates to the Democratic National Convention. Doubtless this act of self-determination was crucial preparation for the exercise of voting for elected officials once the opportunity became a reality.

Most importantly, Fannie Lou Hamer's work was an embodiment of the ingredient necessary to realize the vision that King and Douglass had possessed: the recognition that only through access to political power could racism and poverty, especially in the South, be eliminated. Hamer as well as others liberally used the term "freedom" to explain their ultimate objectives, a reminder that although the dominating shackles of classic Southern slavery had loosened in the last century, the control exercised by whites over the political system still played a role in excluding Blacks from political power.

Overcoming Fear and Intimidation

We have mentioned some incidents of violence as a reminder of the price with which the franchise was won in the South. Although in the North Blacks were voting in some of the large cities, few were voting in the South given its legacy of repression. The primary reason was couched in the oral testimony of SNCC former activist Charles Cobb, who tells of the fear that decades of intimidation had visited on Blacks who dared to vote. As a volunteer, his responsibility was to go door-to-door to try to persuade people to register and vote. But he says they often had reservations born of the fear they faced.

> Many people said, "I understand what you are saying, except it'll get me killed and I'm not going to let that happen." People were receptive to the idea of it, but there were all kind of excuses why they couldn't do it. General excuses: "That's white folks business," or "I intend to make this crop on Mr. So-and-so's land," or there are all kinds of easily understandable reasons.[12]

It was then the role of the SNCC workers, as then SNCC president John Lewis confirmed, to help people overcome the "tremendous amounts of fear," and to mobilize them into making the sacrifice for the right to register and vote. It was up to the young people in the SNCC—who did not have loans, tractors, houses—to exhibit the quality of commitment that led people to actually believe that they were all in it together.

Lewis said that when the local people lost their fear, many of them became some of the best leaders, and that "it was best to have someone in the community, at the local level, saying to their peers, saying to others, 'It's ok. We can do this. We should be able to register and to vote.' It didn't make sense that in rural Alabama or rural Mississippi, where I grew up, to have people that had been very successful as farmers, as ministers, and at the same time been told that [they] could not register and vote."[13]

A famous incident occurred on April 9, 1963, when fourteen Black farmers went to Lexington, Mississippi, to register to vote. They arrived amid a tense situation, with a posse of thirty white men and FBI observers at the court house scene. When the sheriff, with his hands on his pistol, asked who would be the first, Hartman Turnbow stepped forward and said, "I will be first."[14] One week later his home was firebombed by night riders. Turnbow, however, emerged from his house, with guns blazing, and drove his attackers off in an action that saved his home. He was later accused by police authorities of bombing his own house.

Hartman Turnbow affirmed that the eventual passage of the Voting Rights Act was a monumentally positive development in the state of Mississippi:

> Anybody hadda told me 'fore it happened that conditions would make this much change between the white and Black in Holmes County here where I live, why I'da just said, "you're lyin'. It won't happen." I just wouldn't have believed it. I didn't dream of it. I didn't see no way. But it got to workin' just like the citizenship class teacher told us—that if we would register to vote and stick with it. He says it's gon' be some difficulties. He told us that when we started. We was lookin' for it. He said we gon' have difficulties, gon' have troubles, folks gon' lose their homes, folks gon' lose their lives, peoples gon' lose all their money, and just like he said, all of that happened. He didn't miss it. He hit it ka-dap on the head, and it's workin' now. It won't never go back to where it was.[15]

Turnbow's assessment is extremely illuminating, because it is the perspective of someone who lived through a nightmare of exclusion, violence, and intimidation in attempting to carry out his otherwise normal responsibilities as a citizen of the United States.

Nevertheless, by the November 1964 election, the Black vote had increased dramatically as a result of the Voter Education Project (VEP) of the Southern Regional Council, which in the period 1962–1964 put more than 700,000 new voters on the rolls in southern states. In Texas the Black vote went from 110,000 in 1962 to 375,000 in 1964; increases in both Georgia and Florida numbered an estimated 100,000.[16] Moreover, as a result of the general atmosphere of concentrating on increasing voter registration and participation, the Black voter turnout rate in the November 1964 elections was the highest it has ever been, at 58.5 percent, and the number of voters would continue to grow.

The Voting Rights Act Becomes Law

Realizing the necessity of having an additional civil rights law to enforce the Fifteenth Amendment did not come easily to President Lyndon Johnson, despite the depth of his grasp of what it would take for Blacks to enter into the mainstream of American society as equal citizens. Johnson had always been a superb politician who saw and understood the problems, and who also respected the art of the possible within a legislative context. Here he was confronted by a movement for civil rights that, as with most movements, did not respect the limits of its power and sought to acquire all that it could with the ferocity of its mobilization.

In 1964 Dr. Martin Luther King Jr. felt that the celebration and rejoicing at the enactment of the Civil Rights Bill had "curdled and soured." It had been replaced by a "frightening concern" that Senator Barry Goldwater, representing the "counter-forces of Negro Liberation," could run for president, "a Westerner from Arizona clasping the racist hand of Strom Thurmond."[17]

Martin Luther King Jr. was awarded the Nobel Peace Prize on December 10, 1964, and shortly after his return to the United States, Dr. King visited President Johnson. In the course of their conversation King brought up the necessity of a voting rights law. Johnson demurred, suggesting that he was attempting to pass other legislation related to his Great Society program, which he felt would do more to improve the lot of Blacks than voting rights. King replied that political reform was a necessary precondition to dealing successfully with other problems. Understandably, Johnson was rooted in a vision of what the power of the federal government could bring to bear on the problems faced by Blacks, while King wanted Blacks to obtain the power to find solutions rooted in the self-determined strategies of Black communities.

King evaluated Johnson's response as negative, thinking, "I left the mountaintop of Oslo and the mountaintop of the White House and two weeks later, went down to the valley of Selma, Alabama."[18] That "valley" for him and his colleagues meant places like the city of Selma, where there were fifteen thousand Blacks of voting age, but hardly any that were on the voting rolls, having been kept off by the likes of County Sheriff Jim Clark, who had earned a reputation as a ruthless enforcer of racial subordination. Here King and his colleagues would begin their drive to convince the nation, and through the nation, the government, that a new authority to establish the legitimate right of Blacks to vote was vitally necessary.

By working on the ground in the South, King understood something fundamental, observed by Frederick Douglass in the nineteenth century, which was that for the condition of Blacks to improve, and for the programs being designed and passed at the federal level to have their desired effect, Blacks ultimately had to take control of the local levers of power and become decision makers, or had to at least become significant participants in the communities in which they lived. In this King was mindful of the fact that without the power to vote and thereby the power to elect Blacks to office, or to influence the elected whites who implemented such programs, all of the intentions of the White House could successfully be thwarted. Johnson was in a position to provide the resources, but as a Southerner, King must have also understood that President Johnson would not long use federal power to implement programs upon unwilling whites at the local levels in the Southern states. Either the Black, Southern vote would be needed to elect Democrats, or white control of state and local government power would enable whites to effectively resist such programs.

In the spring of 1965, the drama of "bloody Sunday" and the subsequent Selma to Montgomery March converged to produce the climax of what would bring about a national consensus in support of a voting rights bill. The Voting Rights Act was passed on August 6, 1965, and in his remarks at the signing of the law in the Capitol Rotunda, President Lyndon Johnson observed that the intended effect of the law was to grant "every American Negro his freedom to enter the mainstream of American life."[19] Johnson also noted that "it is not enough just to give men rights. They must be able to use those rights in their personal pursuit of happiness." In other words, his point (which carried the title of this section of his remarks) is consistent with the perspective of this book that "rights are not enough."

This thought, that the exercise of freedom was predicated on the elimination of barriers, as well as on the provision of resources, was related to the famous theme that President Johnson presented at Howard University when the Voting Rights Act was nearing the legislative finish line in June of 1965. There, he defined freedom as follows:

> Freedom is the right to share, share fully and equally, in American society—to vote, to hold a job, to enter a public place, to go to school. It is the right to be treated in every part of our national life as a person equal in dignity and promise to all others.[20]

But then he continued:

> But freedom is not enough. You do not wipe away the scars of centuries by saying: Now you are free to go where you want, and do as you desire, and choose the leaders you please.
>
> You do not take a person who, for years, has been hobbled by chains and liberate him, bring him up to the starting line of a race and then say, "you are free to compete with all the others" and justly believe that you have been completely fair.

Thus it is not enough just to open the gates of opportunity. All our citizens must have the ability to walk through those gates.[21]

Johnson's parable was designed to deliver a common-sense rationale for special legislation necessary to engender freedom by ensuring the right to vote. It was a rationale that also sufficed to explain not only why the passage of the Voting Rights Act was necessary, but why his administration would take special action in calling a White House conference, "To Fulfill These Rights," that would invite scholars, leaders, and others whose task it would be to move beyond opportunity to the achievement of what could be called justice. In so doing, Johnson would operationalize his view that the enactment of a citizenship right was not sufficient until it was actualized through support by programmatic resources. This is the template that has undergirded one of the critical roles of Black politics.

Contents of the Voting Rights Act

To many in the South who supported the regime of Black racial subordination, the Voting Rights Act was regarded as a replay of how they conceived the Fifteenth Amendment. Because of fierce Southern resistance, the amendment was the subject of three additional pieces of legislation designed to implement it, which were in turn vilified by Southerners as the "force acts." These laws were intended to invalidate the "Black Codes" passed by Southern states after 1870 that had effectively eliminated the right of Blacks to vote. In that light, the Voting Rights Act of 1965 was considered by many whites in the South to be a twentieth-century force act that struck at the heart of their possession of absolute power in the region.

The Voting Rights Act explicitly suspended literacy tests and other devices as a prerequisite to voting, and Section 5 of the act covered states that maintained such devices or had less than 50 percent of the total voting age population actually registered or voting in the election of 1964. The states originally covered were Alabama, Alaska, Georgia, Louisiana, Mississippi, South Carolina, and Virginia, and twenty-six counties in North Carolina. These states were also subject to having federal examiners observe elections and register people to vote in the event that the local authorities refused to do so. The poll taxes passed by several states were not invalidated by the Voting Rights Act statute, because they had been addressed by the Twenty-fourth Amendment to the U.S. Constitution, ratified in 1964, for federal elections. However, it took several more rounds before these taxes effectively died. The Supreme Court in 1965 held that Virginia's poll tax was unconstitutional, and federal district courts struck down poll taxes altogether in 1966.

The action of the courts and the Congress in 1965, by eliminating further barriers to voting, made the application of the Voting Rights Act more powerful and set the stage for Black participation in subsequent elections, thereby promoting steady progress in registration and voting. The Joint Center for Political and Economic Studies has reported:

> The long term effect of the Voting Rights Act has been to gradually equalize the voting patterns between Blacks and whites in the South. According to the U.S. Census figures, Black registration in 1996 was actually higher than white registration in Arkansas and Texas.[22]

The pattern of progress in voting as illustrated in table 1.2 is striking. The table clearly shows what by now has become an historic fact, that there was a substantial jump in Black voter registration in a relatively short period of time, reflective of the reality that, given the opportunity, and through the reduction of barriers, Blacks would eagerly seek to participate in the institutions of government that determined their status in American society. These data reflect a 25 percent average difference in

Table 1.2   Passage of the Voting Rights Act

State	Pre-Act Registration	Post-Act Registration	Pre-Act %	Post-Act %
Alabama	92,737 (1964)	248,432 (1967)	19.3	51.6
Georgia	167,663 (1962)	332,496 (1967)	27.4	52.6
Louisiana	164,601 (1964)	303,148 (1967)	31.6	58.9
Mississippi	28,500 (1964)	263,754 (1967)	6.7	59.8
North Carolina	258,000 (1964)	277,404 (1967)	46.8	51.3
South Carolina	138,544 (1964)	190,017 (1967)	37.3	51.2
Virginia	144,259 (1964)	243,000 (1967)	38.3	55.6

Source: All pre-act registration statistics originate from the U.S. Commission on Civil Rights, and most are taken from the fall 1964 registration for the election. Other data for the post-act period are taken from estimates of the U.S. Department of Justice and from a survey by the Southern Regional Council report, summer, 1966; *Political Participation,* report, U.S. Commission on Civil Rights, Washington, DC, 1968, 13.

registration between the pre-act and post-act periods in the covered states. The situation in Mississippi especially provided the lowest point from which Black voter registration grew, but Blacks in that state also achieved the highest percentage of registration, among the covered states, in the 1968 election. The obverse was true in North Carolina, where twenty-six counties were covered by the law. Because Blacks here had enjoyed more access to the ballot, they were least affected by the passage of the Voting Rights Act.

The Yield of Southern Voting

In 1964 Blacks in the South voted at a rate of 15 percent less than Blacks in the North. Despite this disparity, dramatic increases in voting became the fuel that made possible the swift growth in the proportion of Black elected officials in the South. In 1970 the percentage of Blacks in Southern state legislatures grew from 1.7 percent in state senates and 2.4 percent in state houses to 6.5 percent in state senates and 9.3 percent in state houses by 1985. This was also facilitated by the Voting Rights Act, as the courts increasingly held that in order for the Black vote to register a Section 2 impact on the political system, single-member districts should be created, and at-large voting systems eliminated, to prevent dilution of the Black vote in Southern elections. Many of these districts had Black majorities that as a result elected Black officials, and the number of such districts grew by 45 percent between 1970 and 1985. Indeed, a testimony to the power of the Voting Rights Act was the fact that the states which had the largest number of Black elected officials in the nation by 2000 were Alabama (725) and Mississippi (850), places where Blacks had arguably been the most excluded and oppressed.

Black Empowerment and Voting Rights

Early Political Mobilization

The increase in Black voting was stimulated by the continued work of local voter leagues that had been in existence since early in the twentieth century throughout the South in cities such as Richmond, Virginia, and Atlanta, Georgia. As a new generation of elected officials came into office and began to use their own political organizations, some of the local voter leagues, such as the one in Atlanta, fell out of existence. The Richmond League, however, continued to function and to register and turn out voters for various elections, and it remains in existence at this writing. The voter leagues were important in providing mobilization support as well as funding for candidates running for office.

One of the earliest Black political action committees was the Southern Elections Fund (SEF). The fund was established in August of 1969 when Jack Chatfield, a field organizer for the SNCC, received an anonymous donation of $30,000 from someone who thought that the SNCC was doing a great deal to register voters but not much to fund the campaigns of candidates. The SEF began as a not-for-profit corporation that contributed vital financial assistance to Black candidates in eleven states in the South: Alabama, Arkansas, Florida, Georgia, Louisiana, Mississippi, North Carolina, South Carolina, Tennessee, Texas, and Virginia. A board of directors awarded grants ranging from $100 to $400 to candidates regardless of race, gender, religion, or national origin or political affiliation. The fund contributed both funding and technical assistance to the campaigns of over 800 candidates between 1970 and 1975 under the initial leadership of its chair, Julian Bond, and Antonio Harrison, its first full-time director.

I referred earlier to the role of the Voter Education Project (VEP) in helping to build the infrastructure for Black electoral participation. Founded by the Southern Regional Council in 1962, it was first headed by a lawyer, Wiley Branton, of Pine Bluff, Arkansas, then by Vernon Jordan of Atlanta, and then by John Lewis, the first president of the SNCC and a close associate of the Southern Christian Leadership Conference. Wiley Branton played a role in funding the early voter registration drives of the SNCC, but the VEP also made small amounts of funding available to candidates. The story of John Lewis, who as a young member of SNCC was beaten at the Edmund Pettus Bridge in Selma, Alabama, is well known. Far less well known is his role, as head of the VEP, in helping to establish the populist foundations of Black electoral power.

> We went all across the South when I was elected director, having what we called voter registration tours, and we would get some prominent figure and it was almost like a campaign. We would visit five and six counties in one day. I remember on one occasion in 1970, Julian Bond and I visited thirteen towns and counties in one day. It was like a campaign tour stop here and there, telling people [to vote]. Hundreds and thousands of people would show up. We

went into a cotton field in the Delta of Mississippi, convincing people why they should get registered.[23]

But as the freedom to vote began to produce results in the decades after passage of the Voting Rights Act, results evident in the election of Black officials and liberal white officials, that freedom was never safe from attempts to dilute it and suppress it, despite the Voting Rights Act's clout. Civil rights attorney Frank Parker said that the "massive resistance" of many Southern whites to the *Brown* decision in 1954 indicated that there would be an even larger resistance to Black voting. Even though there was a massive increase in Black voters in Mississippi in 1967, the first election after passage of the Voting Rights Act, only twenty-two out of one thousand elected officials were Black due to a massive white resistance strategy.

The various tactics employed by white officials in the Southern resistance campaign against Black voting have been listed in a report by the U.S. Commission on Civil Rights and include acts that resemble many remaining barriers today:

- raising the requirements, such as filing fees to get on the ballot
- changing formerly elective offices to appointive offices
- withholding pertinent information from Blacks
- omitting the names of officially registered voters from the rolls
- failing to provide adequate voting facilities in Black areas
- refusing to provide voting assistance
- moving polling stations without notice
- excluding boxes of ballots from Black precincts from the tally
- physically intimidating Black voters

The Shifting Sands of Legal Interpretation

The interpretation of the Voting Rights Act did remain stable. The courts in *Allen v. The State Board of Elections* (1969), a challenge to the Voting Rights Act by white Mississippi plaintiffs, held that only the changes a state made to its voter registration procedures were covered by Section 5 of the act and thus had to be cleared by the Justice Department. When this also was challenged, the Supreme Court decided in *White v. Register* (1973) that all voting procedures, including voter registration, were covered. The interpretation of the *White* case, however, lasted only seven years (1973–1980), being subsequently undone by the decision of a more conservative Supreme Court in *Mobile v. Bolden,* which said that it was necessary for a challenger to prove that a state "intended" to discriminate against Blacks by such changes.

Then there was the issue of whether Section 2 of the act, by prohibiting vote dilution, anticipated an attack on at-large voting systems or not. This was eventually answered by the courts in permitting the large-scale creation of single-member districts in the historic case of *Busbee v. Smith,* which grew out of the efforts of Julian Bond to create a Fifth Congressional District in Georgia. The result was that Blacks were successful in being elected to seats in city halls, county councils, state legislatures, judgeships, and the Congress of the United States. In fact, the creation of single-member districts continued through the administration of President George H.W. Bush in the late 1980s.

In 1982, Section 2 of the Voting Rights Act was amended to conform to the Supreme Court decision in *White v. Register* (1973), which found that at-large voting and multi-member districts diluted the Black vote. Section 2, therefore, prohibited the dilution of the Black vote and confirmed the trend by the courts to use race in drawing single-member districts to promote Black representation in legislative bodies at national, state, and local levels. Congress extended Section 5 in 1970 for five years, amended the act in 1975 for seven years, and then amended it in 1982, extending it for twenty-five years until 2007.

Presidential Politics

The foundation laid by the Voting Rights Act—the successive legal interpretations of it and the enthusiasm of Black voters, not only in the North, but especially the South—has been successful in creating a substantial number of Black elected officials. The total number of Black officials has gone from 1,469 in 1970 to 9,040 in 2002, and most of these serve at the local level. Nevertheless, Black federal, state, and local officials together comprise just over 2 percent of all elected officials. The Voting Rights Act has thus helped to influence the growth of Black elected officials, and the extent to which it removed barriers to Black voting has allowed a greater magnitude of turnout, positively affecting contests for president of the United States.

The dictum that "all politics are local" is true except when it isn't, which is to say that politics at the national level are often so decisive as to literally shape the form, the amount, and the style in which state and local resources are distributed. This understanding shapes the view that it matters who becomes president of the United States, of what his or her vision consists, and how he or she intends to govern. For disadvantaged groups such as Blacks, it matters even more because of the comparatively disproportionate extent to which they depend upon resources dispensed by the national government. These resources include rights that are guaranteed by the Constitution and its various amendments, as well as economic resources in programmatic form.

As one of the most disadvantaged communities in America, the socioeconomic status of the Black community is still such that, more than other groups, it needs government at the national level to provide substantive resources. Although much progress has been made since the passage of the Voting Rights Act, the National Urban League, a Black social service and research organization, produced an "Index of Inequality" in its 2004 report on the state of Black America that included the following highlights:

- Economics: Less than 50 percent of Black families own homes, versus over 70 percent of whites
- Homes: Blacks are denied mortgages and home improvement loans at twice the rate of whites (.45 index)
- Health: On average, Blacks are twice as likely to die from disease, accident, behavior, and homicide at every stage of life than whites; life expectancy for Blacks is seventy-two years versus seventy-eight years for whites
- Education: Teachers with fewer than three years' experience teach in minority schools at twice the rate that they teach in white schools
- Social Justice: A Black person's average jail sentence is six months longer than a white's for the same crime: thirty-nine months versus thirty-three months
- Civic Engagement: Military volunteerism in the Black community is substantially higher than in the white community[24]

This picture of the socioeconomic status of Blacks strongly suggests a community that needs to acquire resources in order to enjoy a freedom equal to that of other Americans. At the same time, it is true that in each of the categories listed above, the situation of Blacks in 1965 when the

Voting Rights Act was passed was worse than it is today. The question in this book is whether or to what extent Black participation in the electoral process might contribute to more positive change in the future.

Political scientists interested in this question have suggested the relevance of several theoretical concepts. For example, a well-known concept of Black politics is the "balance of power" theory in which the Black vote in presidential elections is considered to have provided the marginal number of deciding votes for Democratic presidential candidates who have won presidential elections. Professors Lucius Barker and Mack Jones would exact a tougher standard for evaluating the power of the Black vote than its balance of power role, suggesting that

> neither the election of Black officeholders nor being the swing vote which determines which white candidate will be elected is prima facie evidence that the Black vote has been converted into Black political power.[25]

They believe:

> In order to convert voting strength into actual political power a group must be able to maximize voter registration and voter turnout, develop institutional structures for recruiting supportive candidates for public office, and mobilize support for such candidates. Once supportive candidates have been elected the group must develop a system to hold them accountable to the group.[26]

Although this formulation would appear to be satisfactory, it is still consistent with the traditional influence of the Voting Rights Act in recommending what is required for the Black vote to gain power through electing *local Black officials*. Therefore, it leaves open the question of how the Voting Rights Act influences national elections where the Black vote seldom supports Black candidates for office. While retaining the general features of the Barker and Jones model, Professors Hanes Walton and Robert Smith believe that, in part, the balance of power theory works in national politics because although the theory assumes a strong Black voter turnout is necessary, it does not assume a majority position for the Black vote in a district. Rather, the theory, sees the Black vote as a unified vote in a national contest between two major political parties.

Both pairs of authors imply that it is necessary to go substantially beyond the mere balance of power effect of voting in order to determine what other forces contribute to accountability, an accountability defined as substantive political returns from voting. I suggest that a politics of "independent leverage" might suffice as a method of enhancing the balance of power effect, especially when considering Black presidential candidacies and the bargaining leverage they might achieve. Rev. Jesse Jackson Sr. implied the potential role of the Black vote in presidential politics in his often heard refrain that the "hands that picked cotton could pick a president." But he went beyond that to infer by his candidacies that the "hands that picked cotton . . . [could also be the hands of a president]." I argue here that what is important about the Jackson model was not only the quality of Jackson as a Black candidate, but the nature of the mobilization that stimulated his campaigns. I will examine both the movement aspect and their infrastructure as important factors in this mobilization.

Most presidential election cycles have no Black presidential candidate. In these instances, a Black infrastructure mobilizes the Black vote as a rich culture of participation by churches, student groups, civil rights organizations, labor organizations, and professional associations. This infrastructure becomes the foundation for whatever strategies are determined by Democratic party leaders to implement an effective voter registration and turnout. For Blacks, it is a vital coalition that is critical as a mechanism for extracting accountability to Black interests by enhancing the participation of Blacks in elections.

Conclusion

The primary subject of this work is directed at the way in which the Voting Rights Act has facilitated the ability of Blacks, in whatever state they reside, to vote for the office of president of the United States, and on how the strength of that vote has enhanced Black political power. Thus, a central theme in this work is the critical interplay between presidential politics and the nature of Black political mobilization. Since the major thrust of Black politics is most often provided by Blacks electing and supporting Democrats, this journey into the land of presidential elections will concern itself most frequently with the role of Blacks within the Democratic party.

In this work I employ the "Jackson model" to explain what is meant by independent leverage, as demonstrated when a Black presidential candidate seeks to achieve political goals for the Black community. In addition, I examine the role of the Black political infrastructure as a foundational factor in Black voter registration and turnout, both when there is and when there is not a Black presidential candidate. Furthermore, the elections of 2000 and 2004 have dramatically made the point that new issues of Black voter disenfranchisement pose new barriers to the Black vote. As a key process that regulates access to the ballot, voting systems help to shape the strength of voting, and as such affect the subsequent use of voter turnout as a political resource for bargaining leverage. This directs our attention to other contextual issues, such as the nature of election reform and the election strategies of key actors in Democratic party campaigns.

Reflecting on the voices of Frederick Douglass, Martin Luther King Jr., the SNCC workers, ordinary people in the Southern states, first-generation Black elected officials, and President Lyndon Johnson, it is clear that the Voting Rights Act of 1965 was essential to the political empowerment of the Black community. More specifically, it became the means by which Blacks began to influence national politics by making a difference in the selection of presidents of the United States. As such, this work is intended to examine how the Voting Rights Act, and newer legislation such as the National Voter Registration Act and the Help America Vote Act, might help to achieve the ultimate goals of freedom, by helping Black Americans exercise real participation in the political process as real citizens.

2

Leverage Politics and the 1984 and 1988 Jackson Campaigns

Summarizing the Jackson Campaigns

The presidential campaigns of Rev. Jesse Jackson Sr. represented an advance in American Black politics and as such deserve the kind of persistent scrutiny reserved for other classic campaigns in American history. In some ways these campaigns were a unique accident, bringing the personality of a charismatic Black leader with wide experience in social movement, together with the emergence of a threat to the forward progress of Blacks, to the use of electoral politics as a national agenda-setting strategy. Having achieved some success with presidential campaigns, the campaigns now became part of the existing repertoire of strategies available as tools for the empowerment of the Black community. In the sense that we discussed in the previous chapter, Black presidential politics has enhanced the ability of Blacks to participate in national politics and has enhanced the role of Blacks as citizens. I will briefly describe the 1984 and 1988 Jackson campaigns, but the reader should consult other works for the detail that it is not possible to entertain in this work.

The 1984 Campaign

The candidates in the Democratic primary election field in 1984 were former Vice President Walter Mondale of Minnesota, Senator Gary Hart of Colorado, Senator George McGovern of South Dakota, Senator John Glenn of Ohio, Senator Fritz Hollings of South Carolina, Governor Reubin Askew of Florida, Senator Alan Cranston of California, and Rev.

Jesse Jackson of Illinois. Hollings, Askew, and Cranston withdrew after the New Hampshire primary exposed the low level of their support. Senators John Glenn and George McGovern withdrew after the early March "Super Tuesday" primaries. This left Mondale, Hart, and Jackson still in the race, with Jackson showing surprising support in the South, but it was Mondale who became the ultimate winner of the nomination.

The Jackson campaign in 1984 registered nearly 2 million voters, both Black and white, and exit polls showed that as many as 12 percent of all Black voters were doing so for the first time. This resulted in 3.2 million voters for Jackson, just over half of them whites, in a campaign that raised nearly $2 million from largely small donations. The strength of the Jackson campaign carried over into the fall presidential election, and the 1984 vote for the Democratic presidential candidate shows that among Blacks, 90 percent voted Democratic, while the white Democratic vote was only 34 percent, marking 1984 as the most racially polarized election in modern history. This showing of the Black vote in 1984 was such that Black primary voters increased in states such as Alabama (87 percent), Florida (38 percent), and Georgia (14 percent). The fact that substantial increases in Black voting were also registered in New York City's minority communities, and that Jackson won the Virginia caucuses, facilitated subsequent victories by David Dinkins, who became the first Black mayor of New York City, and Douglas Wilder, who was elected the first Black governor of Virginia.

In addition, the Jackson campaign had a considerable impact on the election of other Black officials, as the number of Black mayors increased by thirty-one in 1984, the largest number in history, reflecting a change in the annual percentage increase in the total number of Black officials from 1.7 percent in 1984 to 6.2 percent in 1985.

The 1988 Campaign

The 1988 campaign by Jackson was stimulated by the fact that he began as the front-runner in 1987, once Gary Hart was eliminated from the field. As 1988 began, Jackson was running in another distinguished field of candidates that eventually was reduced to the governor of Massachusetts Michael Dukakis, Senator Al Gore of Tennessee, Representative Richard Gephardt of Missouri, Senator Paul Simon of Illinois, and former Arizona governor Bruce Babbitt. Because Jackson was so much better known, he was able to attract much greater support beyond the Black community and thus could broaden the scope of his campaign across racial lines and among Black leaders. His campaign raised nearly $7 million, attracted 6.8 million votes, and was even more successful than the previous campaign, winning twelve states (including the "Super Tuesday" Southern regional primary), as opposed to two states and the District of Columbia in 1984.

The impact of the Jackson campaign had continued after 1984, since the number of Black elected officials grew by 6.1 percent in 1986, but fell to 6.0 percent in 1987 and 2.2 percent in 1988. But despite the fact that Black voting fell by 4.5 percent in 1988, the 1988 Jackson campaign gave Jackson the stature of runner-up in the primaries, paralleling the growth of his stature in the Democratic party. Based on this substantial performance, Jackson was in an even better bargaining position in 1988 than he was at the end of the primary elections in 1984. As indicated by Professor Gerald Pomper, whereas Walter Mondale rejected Jackson's attempt to bargain in 1984, Michael Dukakis eventually agreed, and

> [Jackson was given] new institutional power within the party. Jackson clearly intended to renew his candidacy; modification in delegate-selection rules improved his chances in future elections. New seats were added to the Democratic National Committee for Jackson supporters, and he was promised financial aid in the fall campaign.[1]

Jackson had become the genuine leader of the party's progressive wing, and this role gave him access to all of the party leaders. And although, as I will note later on, the initial relationship between Rev. Jackson and Bill Clinton was tense, during the Clinton administrations Jackson served in a quasi-diplomatic post as special envoy to Africa, acted as a confidant to Clinton during Clinton's impeachment crisis, and saw to it that his own policy recommendations on retaining affirmative action and promoting inner-city economic development were seriously considered.

Creating a Balance of Power

As I indicated in *Black Presidential Politics in America,* the 1984 and 1988 campaigns of the Reverend Jesse Jackson were major attempts to implement a "balance of power" strategy from within the Democratic party. This strategy works most effectively when a Black presidential candidacy is adopted, and achieves a high level of turnout motivated by a social movement. The strength of Black registration, voting, and mobilization using the Jackson campaigns as a vehicle was important in building, during the primary elections, a magnitude of support that would have an impact on the eventual Democratic party nominee, the Democratic party platform, the party organization, and the agenda of subsequent Democratic presidential candidates. The basis of that strength has been measured by the standard elements of analysis, described by this writer and others, that include attention to policy issues, electoral successes and failures, the presumption of leadership credibility, convention delegate payoff, bargaining with the candidate, and the spoils of bargaining.

However, in keeping with the theme of this work I will attempt to illuminate the way in which mass Black participation—enabled by the Voting Rights Act—created a movement ethos in the Jackson campaign mobilization that resulted in the high turnout levels. Here I will pay more attention to the Black church and organized labor as the major institutions that mobilized such turnout. In the final section I will then revisit these campaigns to further characterize their political significance as an enduring paradigm of Black mobilization, and will use that paradigm in chapter 6 to evaluate the presidential campaigns of the Reverend Al Sharpton and Carol Moseley Braun.

The Social Movement Effect

The Turnout Anomaly

There is a very important anomaly that appears in the history of Black voting: the presidential election of 1964 showed a higher turnout of eligible Black voters than any other presidential election since that time. It was notable that this occurred the year before the passage of the Voting Rights Act and thus, one would have expected that the higher rates would have taken place after passage of the act. One reason for the high turnout in 1964 may be associated with a general political mobilization of the Black community that resulted from events that possessed a very strong motivational effect. The 1964 election was affected by the assassination of President John F. Kennedy in 1963, but Blacks were motivated also by the promise of the positive public policies that had been achieved under the leadership of President Lyndon Johnson, such policies as reflected in programs contained in the Great Society policy blueprint, and in the 1964 Civil Rights Act that prohibited racial discrimination in public accommodations, employment, and in the use of all federal funds. But although the 1964 Civil Rights Act continued to chip away at voting discrimination by speeding up the handling of such cases by the courts, it was the elimination of segregation in the use of public facilities in particular that created a popular image for President Johnson among Black voters.

Blacks had also been mobilizing all over the country that year to press for victories against various forms of discrimination. The Mississippi Freedom Democrats, a Black organization created by civil rights activists in that state, challenged the all-white delegation to the Democratic convention that year by forming their own delegation in a statewide referendum. The response to this challenge created an opportunity for the Democratic party to begin to open up to Black participation not only in Mississippi, but nationally. By November of 1964 Johnson was assured of massive support by those Blacks who were registered to vote. Thus the forces that motivated Black voters to participate were as much external (the death of Kennedy and the actions of Johnson) as internal (campaigns to challenge discriminatory treatment, segregation in public accommodations, and voting), and the existence of social movement mobilization in the Black community incorporated both factors as the fuel for a swelling voter turnout late that year. After the high Black turnout of 1964, the second and third highest years of Black voter turnout were 1968 (57.6 percent) and 1984 (55.8 percent).

Black voter turnout in 1968, though somewhat reduced from the previous presidential election, still fits into the era of high Black political mobilization, having taken place in a year of emotional events that included the deaths of Bobby Kennedy and Martin Luther King Jr., the passage of the Fair Housing Act, and the intensification of national feeling against the Vietnam War. What might be considered an anomaly then may actually have been an effect of high levels of political mobilization, which suggests why Black turnout in the 1984 presidential campaign of Rev. Jesse Jackson was over 55 percent.

The 1984 Jackson turnout level may also confirm a conclusion I have ventured before that the campaign was indeed a "campaign/movement" at the base of which was a populist ethos. I will provide some

31

added dimension to this movement aspect of the campaign by focusing on the fact that Black electoral politics, when combined with other features of strong political mobilization, can achieve high levels of turnout. Expanding on this aspect of campaigning, I will also discuss its populist dimension, an aspect of the mobilization process that contributed to the unique features of the Jackson campaign. This aspect has largely escaped analysis. Nevertheless, in order to provide a comprehensive analysis of a nontraditional campaign, such as one emerging from a minority racial or ethnic base, we must include the peculiarities of its constituency's political behavior.

"Run Jesse Run"

The movement feature of the initial Jackson campaign for president might be seen through the popular reception of his bid. The idea for a Black presidential candidacy by Rev. Jesse Jackson was born in his support for the candidacy of Harold Washington, who became the first Black mayor of Chicago in April of 1983, and the Black Leadership Forum met a month after Jackson's declaration of candidacy and voiced its approval of the idea. With or without this formal approval, however, the idea of a Black presidential campaign was an idea that could not be contained, as Jackson was figuratively swept up in the hopes and aspirations of Blacks and became, by a movement-like ethos, the leader of a new, bold, and exciting initiative in Black politics. The mass mobilization phase of the civil rights movement had waned, but Jackson had emerged from that era as one of its most popular figures: a connection between the older movement for civil rights and the newer Black Power movements, both of which stimulated civic participation in activities directed toward electoral politics.

While traditional mainstream Black leaders approved the idea of a presidential candidacy, many were still reticent to support Jackson; by contrast, everywhere Jackson went in 1983, he was urged to run by common people. An initial test of the attraction of his potential campaign was the annual convention of the organization Jackson headed, People United to Save Humanity (Operation PUSH) in the summer of 1983. To this gathering of movement ministers and civil rights workers from around the country Jackson had invited the other prospective Democratic presidential candidates, Vice President Walter Mondale and Senators Alan Cranston, John Glenn, and Ernest Hollings, who walked into an arena that had turned into a rally for Jackson's own run. His speech to the convention "was interrupted by chants of 'Run Jesse Run' with delegates having been fired up by Gary, Indiana Mayor, Richard Hatcher, whose luncheon speech had declared, 'If not now, when? If not Jackson, who?'"[2] There were few places Jackson could go without strangers uttering the phrase "Run Jesse Run!" and when he attended the eleventh annual Luke Easter Park picnic in Cleveland, Ohio, this refrain was heard at overwhelming levels, causing hosts former Cleveland mayor Carl Stokes and his brother Representative Louis Stokes to exclaim that "they showed Jesse a lot of love."[3] Indeed, it was said that this mammoth reception in Cleveland made the final contribution to Jackson's decision to run for president, having been witnessed by the close friends who later that day gathered at the house of Jackson's prospective campaign manager, Arnold Pinckney, a prominent Cleveland Democrat. Another such event took place on August 23, 1983, the twentieth anniversary of the March on Washington, when Jackson spoke at the Lincoln Memorial ceremonies; loud cries of "Run Jesse Run" filled the air both before and after his speech, even though some of the attendants knew that at that point both Coretta Scott King (the widow of Dr. Martin Luther King Jr.) and Andrew Young (former close associate of Dr. King, former member of Congress, and the American ambassador to the United Nations), who were also on the platform with Jackson, were not sympathetic to a Jackson candidacy. But as time went on, Jackson's presumptive campaign gained him popularity, and his endorsement was sought by politicians. On a visit to Boston, Massachusetts, in early October of 1983, Jackson endorsed Black mayoral candidate Mel King, and again encountered proof that his initiative had become nationalized, as the audience at one church rally chanted, "Win Mel, Win" and "Run Jesse Run."

So popular was this theme among people that three years later, after a credible showing in the 1984 primary elections, Jackson was greeted even more as a populist hero by audiences across the country. At a speech by Jackson in Oakland, California, in October of 1987, five thousand foot-stomping middle-class Blacks, including NAACP President Ben Hooks and actor Ben Vereen, all cheered lustily, "Run Jesse Run." What is more, Jackson emerged from that event to be told that among prospective candidates for the 1988 Democratic nomination he had outpolled Michael Dukakis 27 percent to 10 percent.

Movement Foundations: The Black Church

There were two pivotal pillars of support for the Reverend Jackson's presidential campaigns, one organized by the Black church and the other by the progressive labor community. And while there were other segments of the electorate, such as Black business and Black professionals, that entered more strongly into the 1988 campaign, the institutional base of the labor community was still more oriented toward mainstream candidates. For that reason, and because of the difficulty of tracking characteristics of that support, I will discuss the Black church and the labor movement contributions in separate sections below.

The Jackson Campaigns and the Black Church

In his book on the origins of the civil rights movement, Professor Aldon Morris describes in detail the dependence of the emerging civil rights movement on the church, which as a major institution with resources controlled by Blacks was thus independent of the white power structure. Professor Frederick Harris confirms this sense by his view that:

> Church activism . . . is a stronger predictor of voter participation for Blacks than for whites. Black church activists are more likely to be committed toward voting than white activists. In fact, the interaction of race and church activism is such a powerful predictor of regular participation in elections that the independent effect of church activism on voting activity is insignificant when taking into consideration the interaction effects of race and church activism. This . . . may be attributed to the degree of political activity in Black churches.[4]

The Jackson campaign benefited greatly from the network that Rev. Jackson had built over the years with Baptist churches. His associations, however, were not restricted to Black religious figures, but also included key individuals in Pentecostal, Jewish, Muslim, and other religions. This was important because Rev. Jackson frequently constructed ecumenical delegations of religious leaders as the spiritual authority for trips that he made abroad. Such was the case, for example, when he traveled to Libya in January of 1984 to secure the release of captured Navy pilot Lt. Robert Goodman.

Black churches have been involved in politics from the moment the opportunity became available to them. The church was the solitary Black institution that was allowed to emerge from slavery because it was often useful in convincing socialized slaves to accept the ultimate authority of whites. When Blacks entered electoral politics more strongly in the 1970s as a result of the Voting Rights Act and the continued civil rights movement, there was a definite interconnection between the church and the state. Among the close associates of Dr. Martin Luther King Jr., seminarians John Lewis, Rev. Andrew Young, and Rev. Walter Fauntroy all became members of Congress, partly on the basis of the credibility they had earned through the movement and partly through their sharing in a political as well as religious network of associates in the state of Georgia and around the nation. Other King staffers, such as Hosea Williams, served at a lower level of government in Georgia and throughout the South, and former members of the Southern Christian Leadership Conference (SCLC) and the Student Nonviolent Coordinating Committee (SNCC) found their way into one level of elected office or another. Rev. Jackson sought to follow this trend, but also wanted to effect a more powerful use of electoral politics that would have an impact upon public policy at a national level.

Confirmation that Rev. Jackson had the backing of the Black church establishment is found in a statement by Rev. T.J. Jemison, a powerful bishop of the National Baptist Convention, which is reputed to have over seven million members. He said of Jackson's entry into the 1984 election:

> The Black caucus did not endorse him in 1984, but we endorsed him. In 1988 we endorsed him first, then the Black caucus came on board, but they followed us. . . . Jesse comes to us as a brother, as a Baptist minister.[5]

Rev. Jemison's statement that he was behind Jackson "in numbers, in spirit and in sugar" was exceedingly important because it allowed Jackson to use the financial resources of thousands of ministers to raise the funds to qualify his campaign for federal matching funds. Political scientist Allen Hertzke also discusses the populist and religious bases of the Jackson campaign, using the "Run Jesse Run" motif and citing the fact that Jackson consciously acknowledged the fact that his base was "big church" just as Walter Mondale and other candidates were supported by "big labor."

Hertzke is correct in his view that "Jackson's early campaign strategy was almost entirely church-based," a fact that was important beyond politics. Jackson launched an initiative in American politics that was to achieve heights unknown to any other Black politician in American history, and his awareness of the magnitude of the challenge he had undertaken called upon him to use the spiritual as well as the material resources of his associates, individuals such as Dr. Samuel Proctor, who was his teacher and mentor at North Carolina A&T College as well as later in life, a role that also extended to former Jackson SCLC associates Rev. Wyatt T. Walker and Rev. Samuel (Billy) Kyles.

This association with spiritual leaders, and especially the many who had been at the forefront of social movements, gave a moral substance to Jackson's campaign agenda. His campaign was devoted to the locked-out, or as he put it, the "boats stuck on the bottom" of life, the poverty-stricken and excluded human elements of society that had been so much the focus of the life and teachings of the biblical Jesus Christ. Thus his view on various public issues reflected his moral tempering. Hertzke points out that conservative populism of the 1980s was preceded by the George Wallace campaign in 1968, a campaign that contained a strong Southern white anti-civil rights content. Indeed, as this conservative movement continued, and the Wallace constituency merged with the Republican party in 1972, the movement became the base constituency for Reaganism. Jackson responded to this with his 1984 campaign, which provided a way for Blacks and others to oppose what they perceived to be the anti-Black attitudes and public policies that they felt were not characteristic of the Republican party.

Rev. Jackson's campaign schedule in 1984 was based largely on appearances at Black churches, not only to present himself and his campaign to his most loyal constituency, but also to appeal for funds, voter registration, and other mobilization activities. By the 1988 campaign, even though the nature of events in Jackson's campaign schedule included far more nonreligious venues such as labor union gatherings and the national conventions of large organizations, Black churches remained his primary base.

On March 26, 1988, Rev. Jackson won 2–1 over Michael Dukakis (113,832 to 61,750) in the Michigan primary, dramatically upsetting the calculations of many in the country and many especially in the Democratic party. Developing the concept of "church as precinct," Hertzke describes what occurred in Michigan as a result of Jackson's strong support in the church:

> In 1988, volunteers were solicited, supporters were organized, and money was raised through these churches. When Jackson visited Detroit he would speak in one of the churches, and the ministers from all of the other churches would generate the crowd. On the Sunday before the Saturday caucuses, the individual churches, corresponding to the citywide neighborhood precincts, sponsored Jesse Jackson Day. In one church they might have a young person read a Jackson speech; in another some other activity would remind parishioners of the caucuses. Because Jackson was "one of us" the response was overwhelming. Through these networks Jackson supporters were barraged with information telling them where they should go to vote and how the procedure would work, and they were asked whether they needed a ride. This effort culminated in a massive get-out-the-vote drive.[6]

This was the style of organization that the church community delivered to the Jackson campaign in each city where there was a large Black community, and also in the rural areas of the South where the Baptist church was dominant and served as a networking institution. In fact, the techniques utilized by the churches were little changed from those used in the civil rights decades during which churches were challenged to move hundreds of thousands of people in a given direction for a just cause.

Empirical Studies on Politics and the Black Church

The classic study cited above by professors C. Eric Lincoln and Lawrence Mamiya of the role of the Black church in American politics strongly reaffirmed the role of the church in the Jackson campaign. As such they sought to establish the capacity of the Black church for militant action in refutation of the charges of Professor Adolph Reed who wrote, from a Marxist perspective, that the Black church was "intrinsically anti-political." Reed and others such as Gary Marx argued that the Black church's strong involvement in political movement created a moderating tendency, an argument refuted not only by the church's role in the civil rights movement, but also by the later Black liberation theology movement, as described by Dr. Gayraud Wilmore. Reed and Marx's assessment, however, emerged from a narrow concept of "politics," since the roots of Black church activism were vested in its expansive role in service and community building, and in the many activities that were associated with elections.

Some support for the militancy characteristic to the history of Black church activism is found in a survey by Lincoln and Mamiya of 1,894 urban and rural Black clergy among which a question of support for civil rights militancy elicited a 91 percent affirmative response. A similarly high response of 91.6 percent affirmative was elicited by a question asking whether churches should express their views on daily social and political matters. The authors note that the survey was completed in 1983, the year of the emergence of the Jackson campaign/ movement and that:

> The widespread support that Jesse won from the Black churches and clergy, even an endorsement from the previously conservative National Baptist Convention, U.S.A., Inc., has probably led to a greater politicization of the religious sector of the Black community and one could expect even higher levels of support for political involvement and civil rights militancy.[7]

The survey results indicate that the militant sentiments that undergirded so much of the civil rights movement of the 1960s had not waned by the early 1980s, and that many of the civil rights era institutions and individuals would still be available to and useful in the populist movement that fueled the Jackson campaigns.

The question of the role of the Black church in politics became the subject of a wide-ranging study initiated by scholars at the Morehouse College Leadership Institute in Atlanta, Georgia. This study was directed by Professor E. Drew Smith and surveyed 1,956 church leaders nationally in census tracts that had a 70 percent Black population, yielding a 93.4 percent Black response rate in 1999–2001.[8] With respect to the question of whether or not Black churches should be involved in politics, 37.7 percent of respondents "strongly agreed" and 41.8 percent "agreed," for a combined affirmation of nearly 80 percent. The fact that this result was about 10 percent less than a similarly worded question referenced earlier may be significant in light of a number of factors that may have had the effect of depressing the political activity of the Black church.

Some of the depressive factors cited by Professor Smith in his report on this study were contextual, such as the growing distance of Americans from the policy formation process, a "large-scale reassessment of political responsibility and social support for guarantees of citizenship participation in the nation's economic, educational, and electoral life [by African Americans]," and "increasing governmental interest in matters related to personal morality" such as reproductive rights, gay marriage, and government funding of the social service role of faith-based institutions.

Smith's very significant report contains data that support the continuing role of the Black church in electoral activity. For example, when the clergy were asked what political activities they had engaged in during the past ten years, the dominant responses may be seen in table 2.1 below. These responses by clergy represent a description of the public/political influence of the Black church because of the use of the church as the basis for such activities. The results show that Black churches focused on voter registration and turnout more than on disseminating campaign materials and advocating ballot issues. The Black church role highlights an interest in candidates, and supports the observation of scholars that the institution of the church is critical in providing the volunteers who can have an important impact on electoral mobilization.

The Morehouse study also revealed clergy attitudes toward the government funding of social programs run by churches that could moderate political activity, such as by the role they played in the Jackson campaigns. The question was asked whether it was "helpful that the government is now encouraging churches to apply for and use govern-

Table 2.1   Role of Black Churches in Political Activity

Role	Percentage[a]
Helped in voter registration drive	67.7
Gave rides to the election polls	51.7
Handed out campaign materials	24.9
Advocated on behalf of a ballot issue, proposition or referendum	22.0

Source: The percentage is from a sample of 1,956 churches surveyed by the Public Influences of African-American Churches Project in 1998–2000. The project produced a report, "The Public Influences of African-American Churches: Contexts and Capacities," submitted to the Pew Charitable Trusts by the Public Influences of African-American Churches Project, the Leadership Center, Morehouse College, Atlanta, GA, 2002, 3.

[a] Percentage of churches from survey sample that had participated in identified activity within the past year.

ment funds to provide social services." Black ministers were largely split on this question, with most disagreeing ("disagree"—19.1 percent; "strongly disagree"—33.3 percent), for a combined level of disagreement of 52.4 percent, with a lower percentage agreeing ("strongly agree"—8.9 percent; "agree"—37.3 percent) for a combined level of 46.2 percent.

Movement Foundations: Black Labor

Black Labor in Civil Rights

Black voters are distinctly part of the American working class, and as such they have become an important aspect of organized labor's attempt to improve pay, working conditions, and other opportunities in a range of industries. The American Federation of Labor, Congress of Industrial Organizations (AFL-CIO) in the first half of the twentieth century sought to organize Black workers who came up from the South to work in the automotive, steel, and service industries, as well as in the government and other sectors where Blacks were disproportionately represented. It was also in the interest of organized labor to focus on a labor force that had benefited when the modern civil rights movement came along and struck a blow at segregation, thereby increasing the social mobility of Blacks, and enabling them to seek better access to education and employment.

A. Philip Randolph, a venerable American labor leader in the pre–World War II period and founder of the Brotherhood of Sleeping Car Porters, helped in the 1960s to join the civil rights cause to the labor movement through his influence on the Central Labor Council of the AFL-CIO, bringing substantial financial and human assistance to the civil rights movement's campaigns. Randolph's closest associate in the 1960s was Bayard Rustin, a strategist and adviser to Martin Luther King Jr. and a theorist on the direction of the movement.

In the late 1960s Rustin described the progress in the participation of Blacks in organized labor by pointing out that labor experts estimated that there were between 2.5 million and 2.75 million Black trade unionists in America by that time. In a growing economy, Blacks were joining unions in large numbers because they understood that union membership was one of the keys to higher wages. Rustin suggested that it was in the vital interests of the civil rights movement to protect the gains Blacks had made in employment through organized labor, since

> seventy-nine outreach programs now operate in as many cities and have placed over 8,000 minority-group youngsters in building-trades apprenticeship training programs. Sixty percent have been placed in the highest paying trades—the plumbers, electricians, sheet-metal workers, carpenters, pipe fitters, and iron workers . . . These programs have expanded by over 400 percent and continue to grow.[9]

This progress was being made at a time when a backlash to the civil rights movement had begun, and as George Wallace's American Independent party contributed to Richard Nixon's victory in the 1968 presidential election. Then in 1971, Nixon announced his infamous "Southern Strategy" by which he would attempt to induce the Wallace bloc to join him in a winning coalition in the 1972 election, a move that attracted some support from American labor leaders, but alarmed the Black members of some of those unions. In the midst of a withering attack upon labor by white liberals and even Blacks of the New Left, Bayard Rustin mounted a spirited defense of labor, suggesting that "the trade union movement remains today the greatest obstacle to the success of Nixon's strategy."[10]

The Labor Role in the Jackson Campaigns

In the 1984 elections organized labor was attracted to Rev. Jackson, a powerful organizer, to some extent because it was suffering from both a decline in membership and a disorganization in its tactics of mobilizing for jobs and votes. In addition, many white blue-collar workers moved into the Republican party in the 1980–1983 period, largely as a result of the loss of industrial jobs and because of the success of the Republican party and the media in characterizing the Democratic party as a party comprised of minorities, women, liberals, and labor. Of all these groups, white blue-collar workers felt that the loss of their jobs was due most especially to the advantages experienced by Blacks because of support given to affirmative action by the Democratic party. These former Democrats now turned Republican, blue-collar white males especially, constituted the base of what came to be known as "Reagan Democrats," and contributed substantially to the Reagan landslide in 1984. Democratic presidential candidate Walter Mondale, previously a strong supporter of organized labor, was endorsed by the AFL-CIO in 1983, but barely carried the labor vote in the 1984 election. By contrast, in the 1984 election Ronald Reagan increased his labor support by 5 percent over his labor support in 1980.

The endorsement of Jackson by some elements of organized labor, as well as the financial and human resources that labor put at Jackson's disposal, were important because they brought much needed political might to an underfinanced campaign. These endorsements and commitments provided such necessities as: telephone bank operators, envelope stuffers, mailing lists preparers, workers to canvass for registration, and other campaign-related personnel.

What made Jackson's labor support possible, in part, was the changing social identity of many working-class Americans. Gaining entry into the middle and upper classes of a new service-oriented economy was their primary goal, but one that was thwarted in many instances by a declining industrial employment base and a new sense of disadvantage, some of which they attributed to the advancement of Blacks. Yet when these workers attempted to fight back by striking and organizing, they were vilified as the cause of the declining job situation. Thus, national champions of the working class were few, and Jackson was able to step into a considerable void. One observer noted that "a picket line gets real attention only if Jesse Jackson visits it."[11]

Even so, in the 1984 primaries Jackson was able to attract only 19 percent of the labor vote, compared to Gary Hart's 31 percent and Walter Mondale's 45 percent. Between 1984 and 1988, however, Rev. Jesse Jackson worked tirelessly for labor causes, appearing at rallies and strikes at plant gates all over the country, an effort that would bring him significant labor support in his 1988 campaign. Nevertheless, the decision by the AFL-CIO not to make an early endorsement for president in the 1988 primary elections was made not only in light of an assessment that the early endorsement in 1984 was an error, but also because that decision may have alienated Jackson's labor base, which was growing substantially. This decision worked to allow the dispersion of labor support, but it also recognized the changing face of the labor movement.

Increased support by organized labor for Jackson was made possible, in part, by the growth of Blacks as a proportion of the labor movement. Nowhere was the change in the character of organized labor more evident than in New York where Sonny Hall, president of Local 101 of the Transport Workers Union, who endorsed Jackson, said,

> We have a heavy majority of workers who are young, Black, Hispanic and female. It's a change from our union 25 years ago, when it was predominantly Irish. It would be naive not to believe that as a labor leader, I would not be sensitive to what my members want me to do.[12]

Such changes to the racial, gender, and ethnic make-up of labor were particularly felt in the Northeastern United States regional service-sector unions, such as those serving hospital, restaurant, and transit and janitorial workers. Confirming this fact, an impressive array of union support became available to Rev. Jackson in New York, including the municipal employees' union, the teachers' unions, the state Public Employees Federation, the Teamsters, transport workers, longshoremen, communications workers, food and commercial workers, and garment workers. Dennis Rivera, executive vice president of Local 1199, of the Drug, Hospital and Health Care Employees Union, an eighty-five thousand member organization, said that they constituted an army of an estimated six thousand volunteers. This strong support caused a split in some unions, as the AFSCME (American Federation of State, County and Municipal Employees Union) with its one hundred and twenty thousand members, endorsed both Jackson and Dukakis. Norman Adler, who fashioned union support for Governor Cuomo's 1982 gubernatorial campaign, said that the Jackson campaign could not have functioned in New York without labor support.

The effects of Jackson's campaign were also felt in places like New Jersey, as evidenced by a split in Local 731 of the United Automobile Workers, where one leader was working for Michael Dukakis and another leader, who happened to be Black, was working for Rev. Jackson. Labor backing for Jackson substantially transcended race and constituted an important base of his white support. For example, John Kelly, a vice president of the Communications Workers Local 1033 in Trenton, New Jersey, said, "If it weren't for Jesse Jackson, issues of concern to the American worker wouldn't have been raised the way they were. He has helped make workers and organized labor become a respectable entity."[13]

Much of the power of Jackson's labor support came into play in his victory in the Michigan primary election, which featured a caucus form of politics, an arena in which the organizing support of any cohesive force like labor was especially effective. Detroit and other cities were strongly influenced by the auto industry and its labor unions, and Jackson won there in a landslide of 55 percent of the vote to 28 percent for Dukakis and 13 percent for Richard Gephardt, who had long been supportive of labor's agenda in the House of Representatives.

The performance of organized labor in response to Rev. Jackson's championing of their cause is a classic case of political accountability. As Jackson excited his racial community, which included a large proportion of the American workforce, he was able to use this cultural resource to extend his influence to the white union colleagues of that workforce, and eventually to the leadership of certain unions serving the same workers. In this way, organized labor became an important part of Jackson's campaigns.

The Jackson Paradigm of Leverage Politics Revisited

The Uniqueness of the Jackson Campaigns

Aside from the political payoff of the Jackson campaigns that many have written about, there is the factor of the uniqueness of the Jackson campaigns that has not been characterized either in popular descriptions of the campaigns or in the academic literature on presidential politics. While it is not within the scope of this work to fully describe this uniqueness, it is important to note that it was related to Jackson's success as a candidate in reaching out to his special constituency. Some of the largely overlooked factors in the success were:

- the low-budget style of campaigning—staying with constituents, for example
- Jackson's creation of media attention by extra campaign events and initiatives
- a massive voter registration component that registered hundreds of thousands of new voters
- the presence of over two dozen issue desks within the campaign structure, staffed by representatives of organizations such as the National Organization for Women, the American Family Farm Bureau, Nuclear Freeze, the Arab American Institute, and Latino and Asian activists

- the social movement character of the campaign, including feeding hungry people and pursuing civil rights causes, and focusing the media on these issues
- race and ideological representation, rather than merely self-representation within the Democratic party organization

While some of these features have been found in other campaigns, taken together they mark the Jackson campaigns as distinctively unique in American politics. What is more, they help to explain the workings of the Jackson paradigm.

As I revisit the goals and methods of the Jackson campaign, it is necessary to restate the theoretical basis of the paradigm, which was that the broad goal of the campaign, by leveraging the power to propose and enact measures that would improve the lives of the downtrodden, would be achieved by the mobilization of political resources through a presidential candidacy.[14]

Base of Support

The Jackson paradigm focused on the development of a political constituency that was germane to his campaign by cultivating both religious and labor organizations. These organizations contain large and accessible populations that are organized into institutions and have access to mobilizing resources such as money, manpower, and national networks of influence.

The question for a Black presidential candidate who does not base a campaign on such institutions is: What other segments of the population have comparable access to such power? One possibility is the Black middle class, a growing and affluent sector of the Black community, which does not currently contribute as much to financing Black politics as it could. The substantial cadres of Black entertainers, athletes, and high-level business executives are other obvious communities to cultivate. Youths in the 18–35-year-old cohort constitute another potential population to target, since they comprise 40 percent of eligible voters, but have a voting rate that is 20 percent less than their elders. In recent times, however, this cohort has begun to direct considerable energy toward the political process and thus may emerge as a force to be reckoned with and courted.

Demonstrated Electoral Support

Primary elections are a natural arena in which Black presidential candidates can demonstrate that they have an electoral base, especially when there is not an incumbent running, or when there are multiple candidacies. In such races, a cohesive Black vote can often make electoral victories by plurality possible, as demonstrated by the influence of Rev. Jackson's campaign in the "Super Tuesday" regional primary of 1988. Super Tuesday victories in several Southern states where the Black population is a substantial portion of the Democratic vote can be a launching pad to victories in other states, or at least to the collection of additional convention delegates.

What has not yet been attempted is a serious Black campaign in a general election, a campaign similar to those waged by John Anderson, Ross Perot, and George Wallace. Indeed, the Democratic party is fortunate that the Black community has remained a loyal constituency and has not attempted an exit strategy, as with other third-party candidates. Tensions within the Democratic party, however, could motivate a candidate to attempt such a project in the future.

Campaigns and Social Justice Mobilizing

The Black presidential candidate's campaign has to be dedicated to the interests of constituencies such as the Black church and organized labor, constituencies that are overwhelmingly working class and share the same set of social circumstances. A social justice agenda that calls upon the resources of the government to fulfill its responsibilities toward the less fortunate is the direction this campaign must take because of the disproportionate number of members in such a constituency who suffer from the disadvantages of poverty, racial discrimination, gender discrimination, and poor health-care access. Another direction a Black campaign might take is to advocate those issues that call upon the government to facilitate access to resources and other kinds of opportunities by those who are prepared to take advantage of them, either by virtue of their possession of higher education, greater funds, or position in the middle class. This facilitation might include affirmative action in higher education and employment, minority business development that emphasizes Black empowerment, greater assistance to historically Black colleges and universities, and special training programs that lead to employment in the high-tech and service industries.

One problem with the Black agenda is that its range of issues is such that it encompasses those of a small nation; indeed, Blacks have been and are still considered today a "nation within a nation." Thus, more attention should be given to an agenda that has strategic elements that impact on more than one sector of Black life, such as those that focus on economic strategies at both the lower and higher ends of the social structure.

Public Policy Acumen

The future of Black presidential candidacies will undoubtedly resemble the future of candidacies in the larger society, in which individuals with experience in legislative bodies or high governmental administrative appointments stand for office. Some indication of this is seen not only in the 1972 candidacy of Representative Shirley Chisholm from New York, but in the more recent candidacy of Ambassador Carol Moseley Braun, and in speculation that the 2004 Senate victory of State Senator Barack Obama from Illinois may eventually lead to a presidential candidacy.

The assumption here is that such recruitment from the ranks of legislators would equip a candidate to successfully address the problems faced by his or her constituency in the normal legislative discourse that is the staple of political campaigns and debates.

Claiming Victory/Winning

The nature of a Black presidential candidacy cannot be understood using the same terms as those used to understand the candidacy of someone who represents a majority constituency. The Jackson campaign had to define its presence in the election for itself—on its own terms. Those terms included the role of the candidate not merely as another candidate, but as someone who had earned the right to represent the interests of an entire community in the electorate. The ability to claim such a role is predicated on the demonstrated electoral support of a substantial magnitude. In this the two Jackson campaigns have become a benchmark for measuring the viability of a Black presidential candidacy. Anything less than Jackson's 1984 achievement will be used to question the Black candidate's viability, and a performance beyond the 1988 Jackson result will therefore be regarded as very significant.

In the course of the Jackson campaign, it became necessary for this unique venture to establish what it meant by winning, since it was exceedingly doubtful that any Black candidate for president would win election. In early 1984, before the "Super Tuesday" Southern primaries, Jackson said,

> Victory on one level is watching our community come together. Part of our mission was to broaden the base of our leadership and bring about a new level of unity in our own community. If we have unity at home, then we can reach out and have the kind of magnetism to draw the people unto us and to be with us. Victory is people registering to vote for the first time. Victory is a new sense of inner security. When we step on the stage for the debates, victory is knowing that we can hang in there. Victory says we may or may not win, but we are qualified. Victory is when they are talking about foreign policy or old-fashioned policy and we can talk about it. Victory is telling our children, "Yes you can. You can do what you want to do, be what you want to be, let nothing hold you, let nobody turn you around."[15]

In these lines, one hears the cadences of Martin Luther King Jr. crying, "Give Us the Ballot," and spelling out its power for the Black community. Jackson elaborates the meaning of the role of the ballot at the level of a presidential campaign that offers the electorate a Black candidate for which to vote.

Bargaining and Negotiations

The viability of the candidate's performance is related not only to the fact that he or she might potentially represent a constituency; it will also be the most powerful ingredient in the act of bargaining to demand the accountability of the winning nominee to the interests of the Black community. Neither claimed representation of a constituency nor the mere act of accumulating resources by winning votes is sufficient to engage in bargaining: it ultimately depends upon the courage of the viable candidate to place the demands of his or her constituency before the party and its nominee. Courage is required because of the strong possibility that this demand that the party and its nominee bargain in the interests of the Black community will be rejected by the media, the winning candidate, or even by those Blacks who support the nominee's campaign. For this reason courage, together with the credibility gained by success in winning votes and states, can place a Black presidential candidate who loses his party's primary election in the best position to bargain with that primary's winning nominee.

Supporting the Party

The presumptive conclusion to successful negotiations is that the Black candidate will remain within the party. In fact, pledges to do so are the Black candidate's opening act of bona fides, the fulfillment of which works to achieve party unity and ultimately increase the chances of the party nominee's winning the presidential election. The ability of the Black candidate to work for the ticket requires both the approval of the nominee and the provision of resources to enable the Black candidate to do so. The party nominee's assent is an act that itself is partial validation of the result of the Black candidate's bargaining and negotiation, as well as a good-faith gesture promising that the rest of the Black candidate's bargaining agenda will be met by the winning nominee if he or she should happen to win the presidency.

The Black candidate will have the responsibility to rally his constituency to the support of the party nominee, not only in the exact terms of the party nominee's campaign, but also under the aspects of a campaign that appeals to the cultural style of mobilization within the Black community and conveys that appeal to the constituency interests of the community as well.

Influencing a Democratic Administration

If the party nominee should lose, the loss creates two situations. The first is that the Black candidate is able to claim to be and should become a leader of the party. The second is that the policy items negotiated with the nominee are carried forth by the losing party's organization and become embedded within the framework of the party's congressional agenda. Rev. Jackson worked so closely with members of the Congressional Black Caucus in the aftermath of his 1988 campaign that he was often considered a symbolic member of Congress, a membership that was buttressed by his role as the elected "shadow senator" from the District of Columbia, although the post was not seen as a legitimate electoral office.

The Congressional Black Caucus is the repository of much of the

Black legislative agenda in the Congress of the United States. The set of issues that becomes the normal work responsibility of the Black caucus on behalf of their individual constituents and the national Black community becomes "the Black agenda." The problem with the pursuit of such an agenda by Black members of Congress who are mostly Democrats is that their ability to deliver depends upon whether their party controls the political institutions. When a party that is sensitive to Black interests controls the White House, even though the opposite party controls the Congress, there is still an opportunity for the agenda to be pursued. Such was the case when Bill Clinton was president and Republicans controlled the Congress in the late 1990s.

The ability of the Black presidential candidate to influence any subsequent Democratic administration will rest not only on his or her ability to secure the Black agenda through the Congressional Black Caucus. It will also be a function of the migration of former campaign operatives into responsible posts in the administration. One of the products of the Jackson campaigns was the opportunity to train Black policy and political operatives at a high level of American politics, individuals who were then available for recruitment as cabinet or subcabinet officials.

Exploiting the Balance of Power

Twenty years after the 1984 campaign of the Reverend Jesse Jackson, made possible by the voting power unleashed by the Voting Rights Act and as a response to the politics of the emerging conservative movement, the political strategy of the 1984 and 1988 campaigns remains unfulfilled. As a result, Black political leaders have been unable to counter the rightward drift of the Democratic party as it has responded to this conservative shift in the political culture. The question is whether this indicates a failure of Black politicians to understand or apply independent leverage politics, or whether in fact the current context of political conservatism is too formidable to yield sufficient opportunities of doing so. And if leverage politics is not the correct strategy, what then is an acceptable use of Black voting power in presidential elections that will have concrete outcomes favorable to the Black agenda? In the absence of a more powerful theory, I believe that the application of the balance of power concept in the context of leverage politics, as elaborated by the Jackson paradigm, is an important method of utilizing the voting power of the Black community. What connects the collective exercise of the voting power of Blacks to the delivery of public policies and opportunities is the way in which the leverage of that voting power is managed; but it is most powerful when driven by a social movement.

Professor Charles Henry suggests that the attractiveness of the Jackson campaign to many of the electorate had its populist roots in a jeremiad based on the common suffering of Blacks:

> The African American jeremiad evolved out of the Anglo American jeremiad as an explanation for the collective suffering of Black people. In its most common form the rhetoric holds that Blacks are a chosen people within a chosen people. That is, the redemptive suffering of Blacks is a necessary precondition for American democracy to fulfill its mission to the world. As such, the Black jeremiad both explains Black suffering and provides a culturally acceptable protest against the Black condition.[16]

The historical corrective for this condition, therefore, is for Blacks to engage in the contest for national power and to demand that authoritative leaders respond; in this, they must select the most daring strategies to engage the political system.

3

Black Mobilization in the Presidential Elections of 1992, 1996, and 1998

The 1992 Election

The candidacy of William Jefferson Clinton for the Democratic nomination for president in 1992 did not begin with the full support of Blacks. First, he was another Southern governor who was not well-known nationally to Blacks. Second was the fact that Rev. Jesse Jackson had decided not to run for president again, but to run for shadow senator of the District of Columbia. Shadow senator was an elected role that would legitimize Jackson as a lobbyist for the District of Columbia's statehood, a statehood which, if granted, would award the District at least one senator and members of the House of Representatives commensurate with its population. Nevertheless, Jackson wanted to continue to exercise the politics of leverage with whoever became the Democratic nominee; in fact, he wanted to help select the nominee of the party.

The actions necessary to influence the selection of the party nominee would make Jackson's relations with Bill Clinton onerous. When Clinton was still governor of Arkansas he became the founding chair of the Democratic Leadership Council (DLC), a group that Jackson referred to as the "Democratic Leisure Class."[1] Following what Roger Morris has called a "bubba strategy," at the first DLC Convention in May of 1991 Clinton welcomed Black leaders such as Congressman William Gray of Philadelphia (chair of the House Budget Committee), Doug Wilder (governor of Virginia), and Rep. Michael Espy from Mississippi, but he excluded liberals such as Andrew Cuomo and Jesse Jackson. Since its founding Rev. Jackson had spoken at meetings of the DLC in his role as a presumptive presidential candidate. Al From, DLC executive director, said at the time that Jackson was not invited to the national convention of the organization in 1991 because he represented "old-styled politics."[2]

On June 13, 1992, Bill Clinton was invited to speak at the annual policy conference of the National Rainbow Coalition, an organization founded and headed by Jackson as a result of his two presidential campaigns. Clinton appeared at the conference one day after he had executed Ricky Ray Rector, a Black prisoner who had been on death row for murder, and who had also been considered mentally handicapped. In his speech Clinton rebuked Sister Souljah, a popular Black female rap singer. Sister Souljah had stated a month earlier, after the Rodney King beating by the Los Angeles police had provoked street riots, that the riots were revenge. She went on to say, "I mean, if Black people kill Black people every day, why not have a week and kill white people? This government and the mayor were well aware of the fact that Black people were dying every day in Los Angeles under gang violence. So if you're a gang member and you normally would be killing somebody, why not kill a white person?"[3] Near the end of his speech, Clinton said, "If you took the words 'white' and 'Black' and reversed them, you might think David Duke was giving that speech . . . We have an obligation, all of us, to call attention to prejudice whenever we see it."[4] The Clinton rebuke of Sister Souljah, which was covered widely in the media, had been a deliberate strategy designed by campaign operative Paul Begala to help Clinton's appeal with the white Reagan Democrats.[5] It was also meant to demonstrate that Clinton, by being willing to publicly criticize a well-known figure in the Black community, was not beholden to Jackson or the Black community.

Clinton's subsequent perception was that during the South Carolina phase of the primary election campaign, South Carolina being the state where Jackson had been born and would presumably have had some influence, Jackson retaliated for this speech. Clinton heard, erroneously as it turned out, that Jackson had endorsed another candidate, Tom Harkin, and that Jackson was attempting "to derail" him (Clinton).[6] During an interview at a radio station in Little Rock, Arkansas, Clinton said, speaking into a microphone that had been accidentally left on, "I came to his house at midnight, I have called him, I have done everything I could for him . . . To hear this on a television program is an absolute dishonor."[7] Instead of campaigning with Jackson, Clinton campaigned with former governor Richard Riley, who subsequently became Clinton's secretary of education. Despite the tension between Jackson and Clinton, however, Clinton received a majority of the Black vote in the South Carolina primary election.

Bill Clinton had begun to emerge from among a cast of presidential candidates that included Paul Tsongas of Massachusetts, Jerry Brown of California, and Senator Tom Harkin of Iowa. When Super Tuesday came on March 10, 1992, it performed the function that had been intended by its planners and gave Clinton a substantial boost in the race as the now undisputed front-runner. This largely Southern regional primary, previously won by Rev. Jackson, was laced with Black Democratic voters, and that fact greatly influenced its outcome. By the Nevada primary on March 8, Clinton had won 208 convention delegates; after the March 10 Super Tuesday primaries, he had amassed 707 delegates, with Blacks contributing 70 percent of their vote to Clinton, 15 percent to Brown, and 8 percent to Tsongas.

Clinton, however, faced a serious problem with the Black vote in that, with Jackson out of the race, the Black vote had fallen as much as 75 percent in some states from 1988 levels, and even total Democratic turnout was down 16 percent.[8] In this context, Clinton would eventually need Jackson to solidify the Black base of his campaign, but at the same time his campaign felt that he faced just as urgent a problem in attracting "Reagan Democrats," Democrats defined by political scientist Gerald Pomper as "an overwhelmingly white group of voters, who saw many of their own interests at odds with those of Blacks."[9] And although Bill Clinton proceeded to embrace younger Black leaders such as Mike Espy, and civil rights icons such as John Lewis, it was clear that Jackson's support in mobilizing the base of the Black community was more important.

Despite the difficult relations fostered by the Sister Souljah incident, Rev. Jackson and Bill Clinton eventually developed a working relationship out of the mutual necessity of a Democratic politician (Jackson) who was the leader of a significant constituency in the Democratic party, and of the presidential nominee of the party (Clinton) who required the support of that constituency to be elected. Jackson made campaign visits across the nation to mobilize his Rainbow Coalition, despite the fact that there was not yet a perfect fit between the agenda of Clinton who had been, after all, a founding member of the DLC, and that of Jackson, whose roots were firmly planted in the liberal to progressive wing of the party. Jackson's view was that for the Democratic party to win, "it takes two wings to fly."

The Brief Doug Wilder Bid

Doug Wilder, governor of the state of Virginia, began an exploratory committee for a campaign for the Democratic nomination in March of 1991, but this met with a mixed reception from Democratic leaders because of a potential conflict with Rev. Jackson. Wilder, who considered himself a fiscal conservative, had local problems with his colleagues in the Virginia legislature. He had presented eighty-six amendments proposing a $26 billion state budget that had been passed narrowly by the House but roundly defeated by 4 to 3 in a Senate where Democrats held a 3 to 1 majority. This struggle over who would set state spending priorities provoked former attorney general J. Marshall Coleman, Wilder's gubernatorial opponent, to remark, "Wilder was present at the conception of the current budget mess during the Baliles administration and has been the hapless midwife of this fiscal calamity since then."[10]

During the year Wilder also opposed the nomination of Clarence Thomas to the Supreme Court and called upon President George H. W. Bush to disavow the senate candidacy of David Duke in Louisiana. Wilder's staff considered Rev. Jackson to be a hindrance to Wilder's campaign because a Gallup poll in September of that year had showed that while Wilder polled at 4 percent, Jackson was preferred by 14 percent of respondents, second only to Mario Cuomo with 31 percent.[11] This perhaps drove Wilder to emphasize racial issues in his exploratory presidential bid, while explaining that he did not do so in his gubernatorial campaign because "it wasn't necessary. Virginia had made so much progress in overcoming the vestiges of its segregationist past."[12] Yet he was the only presidential candidate in 1991 without a prominent supporter and without a national campaign manager.

In January of 1992, however, Wilder had secured a campaign manager and he made an advertising buy related to the New Hampshire primary, an election that he planned to enter to signal that his campaign was not addressed strictly to Blacks. The Wilder presidential bid was not popular in his state, a potential political base for a serious campaign, and his approval ratings reached a low of 20 percent in some state polls in 1991. Wilder ended his campaign on January 8 of 1992, more than a month before the February 18 New Hampshire primary, and with that his rating improved to 40 percent in a February *Richmond Times-Dispatch* poll, with 63 percent of respondents approving of his leaving the race.[13] Jackson and Wilder would later team up to register voters at Virginia Union University in Richmond in September. With Wilder out of the race, Black voters were free to watch the competition among the remaining challengers.

Bill Clinton won the presidential election of 1992 by a plurality of 43 percent against 37 percent for President George H. W. Bush. The deciding factor in the contest, it was generally agreed, was the populist movement of Ross Perot, bearing what was referred to by Pomper as an "unfocused discontent" that was probably created by the disaffection of Republicans over the broken pledge of President Bush not to raise taxes, and by the lack of a popular Democratic alternative candidate. Blacks were equally indifferent to the choices, their registration and voting dropping by 4 percent and 3 percent, respectively, between 1988 and 1992, and giving Bill Clinton support in the low 80 percent range.

The Spoils of Leverage Politics

In the previous discussion of leverage politics, I noted that not all of its possible benefits were achieved in 1984 or 1988; indeed, some of the influence Jackson won in those races would carry over into the Clinton era. In this respect, the Democratic party's political director, Ann Lewis, was accurate when she said in 1984, "It is wrong to look at now, or a year from now even, to measure this impact [of the Jackson campaign]."[14] She added that it could be as many as five years into the future before the full impact of Jesse Jackson's campaign would be clear.

Ann Lewis was correct. Many individuals who had been political operatives in the Jackson campaigns of 1984 and 1988 found roles in the Clinton administration. These included Ron Brown, secretary of commerce, Alexis Herman, secretary of labor, and Minyon Moore, White House political adviser.

As opposed to the political benefits of leverage politics, such as the placement of key personnel from the Jackson campaigns in the Clinton administration, some of the policies pursued in the Jackson campaigns would also carry over into the Clinton administration. For example, in Clinton's second administration Jackson was named special emissary for peace and development in Africa, a role which functionally made him an adviser to Clinton on African affairs. This role enabled him to pursue objectives in Africa that were important to Blacks, such as securing peace in the West African civil wars and obtaining pledges from Nigeria to become a regional partner with the United States in peacemaking. Jackson was also influential in the administration's debate over whether or not to keep affirmative action, with the resulting policy of "mend it, but don't end it" being the Clinton formulation. What is more, in the last year of Clinton's term, the "New Markets" initiative, a joint effort with the only Black Republican in the House of Representatives, J.C. Watts (R-OK), was offered as an attempt to provide a tax-rebate approach to inner-city development. Jackson had formulated this idea from the model of the Overseas Development Council, an independent agency whose role was to provide seed funding for American businesses establishing operations in foreign countries. His view was that such an approach would work in deprived communities of the United States as well.

The 1996 Election: The Clinton Continuance

The fact that the Black vote dropped significantly between 1988 and 1996 was due largely to the absence of a stimulus, such as Rev. Jackson, but the general lack of turnout was also limited by the presumption of a Clinton victory in the wake of the enactment of the Personal Responsibility and Work Opportunity Reconciliation Act, a version of welfare reform that instituted the popular feature of a work requirement. Having settled one of the most nettling issues of the conservative movement left something of a void of purpose in the election, causing Professor Pomper to say, "The voters never became excited about the election of 1996."[15] If the issues did not promote excitement in the election, Bill Clinton as a leader was also not wildly popular among Blacks in 1996 since the intensity of impeachment politics had not yet risen to the fever pitch that it would reach shortly after his reelection.

Colin Powell: Black Republican Candidate?

At one point Bill Clinton had considered offering the vice presidential slot on the ticket to Colin Powell, former chairman of the Joint Chiefs of Staff. Powell was the highest-ranking military officer in the United

States, and an African American who since 1992 had been preferred by most Republicans as a possible candidate for president. Powell was regarded highly, and "surveys routinely showed him as probably the most admired figure in American public life."[16] Furthermore, in a head-to-head poll between Powell and Clinton, Powell defeated Clinton overwhelmingly; even as late as September of 1996, among Republican identifiers, Powell remained popular enough as a preference for the presidential nomination to register even (at 31 percent each) with the actual Republican presidential nominee, Bob Dole, even though Powell had formally stated his rejection of a candidacy in December of 1995.

Part of Colin Powell's attraction to white voters was that he did not consider himself a Black candidate, and they did not consider him as such either, valuing rather his service to the nation as the military leader of Operation Desert Storm during the first Bush administration. He reminded many of Dwight D. Eisenhower, a nonpolitical figure who had earned great stature in a successful military operation and who, because of this, was thereupon regarded as a credible presidential candidate. Another important consideration was that Powell appeared to be above politics, and this in an exceedingly political age when the country was becoming ever more divided ideologically between liberalism and conservatism. Powell, however, continued to reject the role of presidential candidate.

The Black Vote Responds to Clinton

The key to Clinton's initial failure to excite the Black community was his right-of-center campaign. By June of 1992, a Joint Center for Political and Economic Studies survey found his support at only 43 percent in a trial heat with Bush and Perot, but with a 57 percent favorable rating.[17] But as the campaign progressed, Clinton became exceedingly popular in the Black community. Reasons for his growing popularity included his roots as a Southerner who shared aspects of Black culture; his association with an important group of Blacks from the state of Arkansas who were key operatives in his campaign; his intelligence and espousal of issues that were important to Blacks, issues such as civil rights and social justice; and the background of his wife, Hillary Clinton, who had been a civil rights attorney in her youth.

Despite his tribulations with the conservative movement, Bill Clinton also continued to have the support of the American people, who were able to separate the indiscretion (involving a young intern), which eventually brought him into impeachment proceedings in Congress, from his national public policy responsibilities as president of the United States. Thus, when the conflict over the intern, Monica Lewinsky, arose, and the cry for impeachment rang out, the Black community supported Clinton more than ever. In fact, during a session at Martha's Vineyard in Massachusetts, members of the nation's Black leadership put their collective arms around Clinton in order to show the country that they also were able to distinguish between private and public morality.

The Million Man March

An unexpected factor in the 1996 election was the contribution made by the Million Man March. This event held on October 16, 1995 at the Capitol Mall in Washington, DC, drew the largest gathering in the history of the country. The march focused on the personal redemption of Black males and offered a protest at their projected image in the country. Participants in the march were encouraged by its organizer and main speaker, Muslim Minister Louis Farrakhan, to exercise increased responsibility for their families and to reflect on that in their political participation. Dr. David Bositis, senior analyst at the Joint Center for Political and Economic Studies, found that as a result of the Million Man March, Black voter turnout was slightly more Republican than usual, and that Black male voter turnout exceeded Black female turnout by 500,000.[18] One exit-poll organization, Voter News Service, found that Black male voting increased from 3 percent in 1992 to 5 percent in 1996, an increase of 1.5 million more Black male voters between 1992 and 1996.

The 1996 election ended with a victory by Bill Clinton over Bob Dole (50.1 percent to 41.4 percent) with Ross Perot at 8.5 percent. Were the combined vote for Dole and Perot both in the Republican column, Dole still would not have defeated Clinton. This was a different result from 1992 when the Perot vote at 19 percent could have helped defeat Clinton, who drew only 43 percent of the electorate against President George Herbert Walker Bush's 37 percent.

Besides the Perot vote, the Black vote was only moderately strong for Clinton in 1996 at 84 percent (Bush, 12 percent; Perot, 4 percent), a slight increase of 1 percent from 1992. While Blacks registered at about the same rate in 1996 as they did in 1992 (63.9 percent in 1992; 63.5

percent in 1996), they voted at a rate substantially less than in 1996 (54 percent in 1992; 50 percent in 1996). But even at a lower level of turnout, should Clinton have lost the Black vote, he would not have won the election. Given the moderate turnout levels in both 1992 and 1996 for Clinton by Blacks, it should be noted that while Clinton has been widely viewed as wildly popular in the Black community, in no election did he reach the 90 percent level of support that Al Gore would eventually attract.

Prelude to 2000: The Reemergence of Black Infrastructure

There was a general decline in total voter turnout in midterm elections from 45 percent in 1994 to 41 percent in 1998.[19] Black voter turnout, however, was approximately 40 percent in 1990, dropping to 37 percent in 1994 and returning to the 40 percent level in 1998. One reason for the reemergence of relatively strong Black voting in the midterm elections in 1988 was the fact that Blacks felt the country was generally headed on the right track and that the president was doing a creditable job, but that this was threatened by Republicans who were attempting to bring impeachment charges against Clinton. A profile of these attitudes can be seen in table 3.1.

Clinton's Democratic vote remained strong in 1998 since only 13 percent of Democrats wanted him to be impeached and 18 percent wanted him to resign, while 41 percent of those surveyed supported censure. Thus, impeachment politics appeared to be a strong motivation for Democrats to turn out to vote in 1998.[20]

Another view has been suggested by Curtis Gans who character-

Table 3.1 Black Electoral Opinions, 1998

	% Voted Democrat[a]	% Voted Republican[a]
Those who:		
believed the country was on the "right track"	63	35
approved of Congress	63	35
approved of Clinton	76	22

Source: New York Times, "The Elections," November 4, 1998, B1.
[a] Percentage of respondents who voted in the 1998 midterm elections.

ized the 1998 election as a "Seinfeld election" about nothing, essentially because Democrats were challenged by the traumatizing effect of the massive Republican victories in the 1994 congressional elections. He arrived at the conclusion that the "Republican Revolution" of 1994 had promoted a set of issues that had not been successfully countered by Democrats and that in fact, "the Democrats had offered little or nothing. They tried to make the economy an issue, but offered no program on it or largely anything else, except issues which appealed to seniors."[21]

Black Voter Impact

Black voters, on the other hand, felt that the 1998 elections were crucial in the wake of the Republican Contract with America, a set of Republican policies used to nationalize the midterm elections, and which had devalued Black interests. The contract proposed such conservative measures as constraining federal budget expenditures (which would most surely have had an impact on domestic spending); being tougher on crime (a sentiment that created the pressure to pass the Omnibus Crime Bill of 1994); and being tough on welfare by denying additional aid to mothers on AFDC (Aid to Families with Dependent Children) who had additional children.

In the 1998 elections Blacks constituted 10 percent of the total electorate and voted 88 percent for Democrats, while increasing their vote for Republican candidates by 3 percent over 1994. In general the Black vote as a total of the electorate moved from 9 percent of the total in 1994 to 11 percent of the total in 1998.[22] The Black vote for Democrats also increased from 81 percent in 1994 to 88 percent in 1998.[23] The impact of the Black vote was described in an analysis by cable television station MSNBC which said the following:

> Black voters helped lead Democratic Southern candidates and a New York Senate candidate to victory in Tuesday's elections. African Americans in Alabama, North Carolina, and South Carolina supported winning Democratic candidates.[24]

A summary of the impact of the Black vote is presented below.

Alabama: In Alabama, Don Siegelman, the Democrat lieutenant governor, defeated incumbent Fob James for governor in one of the most Republican states in the country. In this election the white vote broke nearly even with 48 percent for Siegelman and 51 percent for James but the Black vote, which constituted 19 percent of the total, gave 95 percent of its vote to Siegelman.[25]

California: California Democrat Gray Davis won the gubernatorial election over Republican Lieutenant Governor Dan Lundgren in an upset for Republicans who had held this post for the past eight years. Davis was supported by 76 percent of Blacks, 71 percent of Latinos, and 65 percent of Asians, all of whom voted in record numbers, appearing to repudiate the politics of those in California who had supported the elimination of affirmative action and bilingual education.[26] Blacks and Hispanics accounted for 26 percent of the total vote in the state of California, with the Hispanic vote moving from 8 percent of the total in 1994 to 13 percent in 1998. But Blacks had the largest increase, moving from 5 percent of the total vote in 1994 to 13 percent in 1998.[27] The strong Black and Hispanic turnout also made possible the slim victory of incumbent Democratic Senator Barbara Boxer over Republican challenger Matt Fong who won a majority of the Asian vote.[28] Los Angeles county, officials indicated, turned out to vote at an estimated rate of 47.5 percent, which, although lower than either 1994 or 1996, was still 10 points higher than the average national turnout.[29]

Georgia: In Georgia, another Southern state which had undergone a serious Republican realignment, a Democrat, Roy Barnes, defeated Republican opponent Guy Millner for state governor. In this state the Black vote was 16 percent of the total in 1994, and 29 percent of the total in 1998.[30]

Maryland: The reelection of Governor Parris Glendening was in doubt, partly because the Black Democratic leadership was split over his candidacy. With the return of both Baltimore Mayor Schmoke and Prince George's County Executive Wayne Curry to the Glendening camp in the general election, however, Glendening won handily over conservative Republican Ellen Sauerbrey with big margins in Baltimore and Prince George's County, led by a big Black voter turnout.[31] The Black vote was 12 percent of the total of all of those who voted in the state in 1994 but 19 percent in 1998.[32] In Maryland, as in other places, exit polls illustrated that about half of all Black voters said that one of the strongest reasons initiating their turnout was a show of support for Clinton in his struggle against efforts by Republicans to impeach him.[33]

Mississippi: For an open seat in the Mississippi Fourth Congressional District, which was 41 percent Black, Ronnie Shows, a Democrat and state transportation commissioner, won over Republican Mike Parker.[34] Black turnout was credited as a major source of this victory over Parker, who had switched his party affiliation from Democrat to Republican in 1995 and was reelected as a Republican in 1996.[35]

New York: Black and Hispanic turnout was also high in a heated contest for the senate seat held by Republican Senator Alphonse D'Amato, who eventually lost to Democrat Charles Schumer, a member of the House. Former Congressman Floyd Flake, a formidable Black minister from Queens, had endorsed D'Amato, but his constituents, like those in other districts who often voted for a different candidate than that of their representative, a Black member of Congress in several instances, supported Charles Schumer.[36]

North Carolina: In North Carolina Lauch Faircloth, the vaunted Republican head of the Senate District Committee, lost to moderate Democrat John Edwards. In this race the Black turnout overall was the same as in 1994, but 90 percent of Blacks voted for Democrats rather than 84 percent in 1994, and there was an exceedingly high turnout registered in some places, such as Charlotte-Mecklenburg, where it was a hefty 58 percent.[37]

South Carolina: In the election for governor, Democrat Jim Hodge defeated incumbent Republican Governor David Beasley, and in the Senate elections, Senator Ernest "Fritz" Hollings, a Democrat, won over Rep. Bob Inglis, a young Republican allied with the Christian Right, who was part of a party realignment that had seen a formerly Democratic voting majority in that state become a Republican majority. Blacks made up 25 percent of the voters in this election and gave Hodge 92 percent of their vote.[38]

Texas: In Texas incumbent Governor George W. Bush received over 40 percent of the Hispanic vote in 1998, increasing his margin among Hispanics from 30 percent in 1994 and at the same time increasing his vote among Blacks to 27 percent in 1998 from 14 percent in 1994.[39]

Illinois: One major loss occurred in the Illinois Senate race, with the victory of conservative Republican Peter Fitzgerald over Black Democrat Carol Moseley Braun (52 percent to 46 percent), even though the turnout in Cook County was a substantial 56 percent and the Black vote was particularly strong.[40] Braun's loss was expected. In an expansive post-election interview, she indicated that there were "strategic mistakes that were made in terms of how I handled some of the issues and challenges of making history."[41] She admitted two particularly damaging mistakes. They concerned questionable financial dealing with her fiancé, South African Kgosie Matthews, and his role in her trip to Nigeria to meet Sani Abacha, widely considered a brutal dictator.

As a result of these victories the Democrats, who had been expected to lose a substantial number of seats to Republicans, won 34 seats, reducing the margin between Republicans and Democrats in the U.S. House of Representatives from 11 to 5. Republicans, who had been within 180 seats of taking a majority in state legislatures for the first time since 1952, found instead that Democrats garnered a net gain.[42]

The Democratic Leadership Council claimed that its influence had been responsible for the Democratic victories since Democratic candidates campaigned from the center in order to put together a coalition of suburban, Southern, middle- and upper-class voters.[43] This point was also emphasized by Tom Edsall, who said that Democrats in the Ohio River valley won by "leaning right on 'centrist issues.'"[44] Since the major motivating issue in the campaign had to do with the plight of the president and an attempt to preserve his position and policy, it is highly uncertain that centrist policy proposals were the motivating force for voter turnout in most places. The political result of the 1998 election, which found so many Democrats winning in areas where the recent trend was toward Republican voting, could not have been caused by traditional issue voting, and must be explained by the involvement of issues that were far more emotional.

Black Political Infrastructure: A Contributive Factor

Little attention has been focused on the ingredients of leverage politics beyond the formalities of Black participation in a presidential campaign. However, there has been and continues to be a substantial political infrastructure that has been responsible for contributing to the registration and turnout of Black voters. This is one of the ways in which a cohesive cultural community deploys its organizations and institutions to participate in elections in an effort to assist in achieving the policy goals of the community. A few of the participants in this infrastructure are briefly discussed below.

The National Black Leadership Roundtable

The National Black Leadership Roundtable was rejuvenated in the summer of 1998 by a former delegate for the District of Columbia, Walter Fauntroy, for the purpose of mobilizing support organizations to participate in the fall elections. This effort eventually focused on mobilizing the eight largest Black religious denominations through the involvement of their leaders. Black churches had been pivotal in the most successful drives to register voters and get them to the polls. Fauntroy, like Jackson, belonged to the Southern Christian Leadership Conference and was therefore associated with the same network of Baptist ministers as Jackson. As a member of Congress representing the District of Columbia since March 31, 1971, Fauntroy had been heavily involved, since the presidential campaign of George McGovern in 1972, in helping to mobilize Black churches to engage in political participation.

The Black Leadership Forum

The Black Leadership Forum consists of the heads of twenty-five national Black organizations or groups, including the Pan-Hellenic Council, civil rights leaders, Black mayors, and Black business, religious, and professional organizations. This group originally supported the idea of a Black presidential candidacy in 1983 and legitimized the candidacy of Rev. Jesse Jackson. It established a task force for the 1996 presidential election that developed a set of issues and key cities with large urban Black populations in which to mobilize a nonpartisan get-out-the-vote drive.

The National Coalition on Black Voter Participation

This get-out-the-vote drive was managed by the National Coalition on Black Voter Participation (NCBVP), a nonpartisan organization that began in 1976 as an outgrowth of concern about the impact of white backlash as represented by the Southern Strategy of the Nixon administration, and out of a growing focus within the Black community on electoral mobilization at every level. The coalition met in Washington, DC, on August 24, 1976, in response to an invitation from Eddie Williams, head of the Joint Center for Political and Economic Studies, and named its strategy "Operation Big Vote" (OBV).[45] With its own executive director and staff, the project was deployed and implemented in thirty-six cities in thirteen of the states with the highest Black populations.

The NCBVP began with one of the largest coalitions in the history of the Black community, each of the partners vowing to encourage their membership to become involved in the "Big Vote" campaign in their localities.

A. Philip Randolph Institute
The African Methodist Episcopal Church
Alpha Kappa Alpha Sorority
Coalition of Black Trade Unionists
Committee on Political Education of the AFL-CIO
Council of 100
Delta Sigma Theta, Inc.
Federation of Masons of the World
Frontiers International
Improved Benevolent Protective Order of Elks of the World
Joint Center for Political and Economic Studies
Judicial Council of the National Bar Association
National Black Republican Council
National Caucus of Black School Board Members
National Caucus and Center on Black Aged
National Council of Negro Women
National Hook-up of Black Women
National Newspaper Publishers Association
National Office for Black Catholics
National Student Coalition Against Racism
National Urban Coalition
National Urban League
National Women's Political Caucus
Omega Psi Phi Fraternity, Inc.
Opportunities Industrialization Center, Clergy Council
People United to Save Humanity (Operation PUSH)
Phi Beta Sigma Fraternity, Inc.
Sigma Gamma Rho Sorority
Southern Christian Leadership Conference
Southern Conference of Black Mayors
United Automobile Workers
United Negro College Fund
Voter Education Project

Women's Auxiliary of the National Medical Association
Zeta Phi Beta Sorority, Inc.

The NCBVP's objective was to contact possible voters in the major target cities in order to get out the vote during the last week of the campaign.[46] The program of the coalition was as follows:

- To raise the political consciousness of Blacks and other minorities through a series of dramatic events that emphasized the importance of massive voter registration and voter turnout
- To use the programs and facilities (newsletters, conventions, special projects) of coalition members to supplement the voter education and registration campaigns being conducted by such groups as the Voter Education Project, the A. Philip Randolph Institute, and the NAACP
- To develop an on-going national voter mobilization program that would conduct educational activities throughout the year
- To work through a coordinating committee, consisting of persons from the staff of coalition members, that would draft strategies and carry out the decisions of the coalition[47]

The Operation Big Vote project prepared how-to guides for coordinators in its thirty-six cities to assist the coordinators in conducting get-out-the-vote drives; in the first several months of its existence, a preliminary survey of OBV field operations yielded the fact that the project had probably registered over two hundred thousand voters in its first year. With major funding emanating from organized labor and the Democratic National Committee, leaders of the mobilization criss-crossed the country, speaking at churches and union halls, and broadcasting their message on Black radio, motivated by the clear and present danger that George Wallace's Southern constituency would win the White House as a part of the Republican party. With themes such as "Wake up Black America," well-known figures including popular Texas Representative Barbara Jordan, Coretta Scott King, Rev. Jesse Jackson, Julian Bond, and John Lewis (director of the Voter Education Project in Atlanta) were the main draw for voter registration rallies that resulted in the following voter registration increases:

Brooklyn, New York—100,000
Baltimore, Maryland—44,000

Newark, New Jersey—20,000
Memphis, Tennessee—21,000
Houston, Texas—40,000

Source: Paul Delaney, "Blacks Are Pleased by Election Effort," *New York Times,* October 31, 1976, 38.

By the early 1990s the NCBVP had grown to over eighty-five national Black organizations, and the leadership had adopted a theme for disseminating messages to the media with respect to its voter registration and turnout activities. This theme was "Voices of the Electorate." The coalition's staff had also outgrown its incubation within the Joint Center for Political and Economic Studies and had become a separate organization. The coalition's major activity was and continues to be the provision of information, resources, and technical assistance in helping to mobilize Black voters through coalition member organizations working in various Black communities.

In 1996 the NCBVP developed another project, Black Youth Vote (BYV), in order to focus on the 18–35-year-old cohort more effectively, as the organization had originally intended. It developed election-skill workshops and conferences, and developed messages for dissemination that spoke to the cultural sensitivities of young people. In 2002 BYV held a conference in Atlanta that attracted hundreds of youths.[48] The coalition also developed programs to represent the interests of Black women in a Black Women's Roundtable, and then changed its name (and intentions) to the National Coalition on Black Civic Participation.[49] Discussions about the potential political role of hip-hop artists, a group of musicians that had attracted the attention of millions of youths of all races and countries, resulted in the involvement of Russell Simmons, a key producer of several artists. Simmons began to experiment in 1996 with a fusion between hip-hop and politics at the encouragement of Congresswoman Maxine Waters, who sponsored a regular forum on this subject at the annual September symposia of the Congressional Black Caucus.

In 1998 the coalition developed the "Unity Campaign" (which became the "Unity 2000" and "Unity 2004" campaigns, respectively) under the theme, "Lift Every Voice and Vote," a theme that captured the spirit of the national Black anthem, "Lift Every Voice and Sing." The Unity 2004 campaign of the coalition also began to follow a strategic plan to focus on a select set of cities with large Black populations as a means to develop stable turnout through local coalitions based on non-partisan, nonprofit organizations. These voter mobilization activities continue to occur each year, changing their emphasis with the various election cycles, but always promoting increased voter turnout.

Black Media Outlets

In the 1998 off-year election cycle, Black Entertainment Television's chief executive Bob Johnson sponsored a press conference for the Black Leadership Forum and the NCBCP, the substance of which was fed into his regular public affairs programming. The program messages featured key speakers at the press conference and their rationale for voting, and promoted the theme of both the forum and the coalition by urging Blacks to "Lift Every Voice and Vote." Johnson also sponsored a full-page nonpartisan ad in *USA TODAY* encouraging everyone to vote, and the week before the election, he dedicated all of his programming to encouraging Blacks to vote.[50]

Beginning in the 1996 campaign and continuing with every election since, popular Black media personality Tom Joyner has used his "Morning Show," syndicated in many major media markets around the country, as a communication vehicle to its estimated eight million strong, largely Black audience. In 1996 President Clinton, Vice President Al Gore, and Rev. Jesse Jackson all appeared on Joyner's Morning Show and encouraged voters to go to the polls.[51] Shortly before the election two years later in 1998, President Clinton, with a sense of the strength of the coming Black voter turnout, noted during an appearance on the Tom Joyner Show that "almost everyone can see—even the Republicans—that we're going to outperform the historical average [for voter turnout in a midterm election]."[52] In addition the Clinton administration, with Tom Joyner and other Black entertainment figures, utilized mass conference calls in order to rally various sectors of the voting public such as ministers and labor leaders.

Black Labor

Black labor unions were another significant part of Operation Big Vote. Two of the most important groups, in addition to the Committee on Political Education of the AFL-CIO, were the A. Philip Randolph Institute

(APRI) and the Coalition of Black Trade Unionists (CBTU). The A. Philip Randolph Institute was founded in 1965 as a senior constituency group of the AFL-CIO serving Black Americans. Its primary role was to build Black labor alliances, and by 1998 it had 150 chapters in thirty-six states. As a tribute to the labor legacy of A. Philip Randolph, a leader in the civil rights movement, it was seen as a complementary part of the effort to help the Voting Rights Act achieve the expectations of its promoters. Early in its history the APRI engaged in voter registration and get-out-the-vote drives directed toward its members around the country. The APRI was especially active in the 1996 campaign, mounting thirty-five grassroots get-out-the-vote operations, with its most intense activity in North Carolina, Michigan, Pennsylvania, and the state of Washington.[53]

The Coalition of Black Trade Unionists is the labor movement's most powerful Black organization and was formed in 1972 in response to the fact that the AFL-CIO seemed to be taking a neutral position on the 1972 presidential election. Black unionists at the time believed that union head George Meany had ignored the interests of Black labor, and they feared that such a position would contribute to the reelection of President Richard Nixon, whose Southern Strategy had brought a strong Southern and anti-Black bloc into the Republican party.

Venerable Black labor leader William Lucy was one of the five founding members of the coalition and became its first president. As the international secretary treasurer of the American Federation of State, County and Municipal Employees (AFSCME), Lucy already occupied a key role in the labor movement and had been important in furthering labor's participation in the civil rights movement in the 1960s. William Lucy took this view of AFSCME's role:

> At the present time, we occupy a very important and critical position in the politics of this nation, both in terms of the trade union movement as well as the political parties of this country. We are in nobody's pocket, do not intend to get in anybody's pocket, and we are going to assume a position of full partners. You see, we don't want anybody to be making decisions for us any longer, because we are quite capable of making decisions ourselves. We don't want to be a thorn in anybody's side, but we don't want to be a pivot for anybody's heel.[54]

The CBTU played an important role in the election of many officials at the local level, officials such as Harold Washington, who was elected mayor of Chicago in 1983, while units of the CBTU through their unions also supported the presidential bid of Rev. Jesse Jackson in 1984, and the CBTU itself endorsed Jackson in 1988.

By 1992 the CBTU had become a major supporter of the NCBVP, and in subsequent elections it played a vital role in the NCBVP's Unity campaigns. Several years later it also developed a Political Empowerment Network (PEN) in order to form a more systematic, long-range approach to political activism.

> The long range goal of CBTU's political action program is to increase minority representation in Congress, among statewide officeholders, the elected judiciary, and on county commissions, in city halls and on local school boards. With increased political representation and sustained activism, we can leverage real control over political, economic and judicial decisions that directly impact African American and other minority communities.[55]

The CBTU formulated a leverage model based on its local units, and although it appeared to be focused on politics at the state level and lower, the successful organization of mobilization activities at these levels, during election years, supported the programs of other institutions in the Black community and helped contribute to overall turnout.

Southern Regional Organizations

Because the long struggle for civil rights has focused on the South as the region most violently resistant to change, much of the history of voting rights has its center in Atlanta, Georgia, the home of Dr. Martin Luther King Jr., and the place where so many other prominent organizations, activists, and elected officials made and still make their home. One early organization was the Southern Regional Council (SRC), founded in 1944 as an outgrowth of violence in the Mobile, Alabama, shipyards. The SRC called Blacks and whites together to consider how they might work cooperatively to create a true interracial society in the South, and in 1962 it created the Voter Education Project (VEP). From its founding the Voter Education Project played a substantial role in creating the skill base and organizational development that have supported the growth of strong registration and voter turnout among Blacks in the eleven states that the VEP monitors. During the 1980s and 1990s the VEP served as a statistical repository and training organization for Black voting, and therefore was a substantial resource for many legal cases that attempted to alleviate barriers to, or defend against attacks on, Black voting rights.[56]

Another of these Atlanta-based organizations, the Georgia Coalition for the Peoples' Agenda, was founded by the Reverend Joseph Lowery, confidant to Dr. Martin Luther King Jr. and indefatigable voting rights advocate and activist. A human rights organization, the Georgia Coalition has played a role in mobilizing voters both in the state of Georgia and in the southern region. The Georgia Coalition played a strong role in mobilizing voters for the 2000 election, and it set a goal of one hundred thousand new registrants by the time of the 2002 elections to assist in the deployment of nineteen thousand new voting machines purchased by the state for the 2004 elections.[57] This strategy was justified in view of the fact that the number of uncounted votes (ninety-four thousand) was higher in the state of Georgia than in Florida in the 2000 election, even though the latter received a disproportionate amount of national attention.[58] Lowery and the Georgia Coalition's ardor with respect to political participation is illustrated by a comment Lowery made in Atlanta during a speech to launch the 2004 voter turnout campaign for the primary elections in Georgia: "If I was God, I'd send every Negro who didn't vote straight to hell!"[59]

Enhancing the Role of Infrastructure

The transfer of electoral power to political outcomes through effective bargaining depends upon leveraging political resources.[60] The beginning of this process depends upon the control of the Black vote and the ability to enhance its turnout effect. We have seen that since the passage of the Voting Rights Act in 1965, dependence on the raw effect of Black turnout has not been sufficient either to promote the act of voting and enhance turnout or to utilize the Black vote as a resource for political bargaining. Hence, meta-structures such as the National Coalition on Black Civic Participation and its Operation Big Vote have intervened in the process of voting as an attempt to enhance the turnout effect, just as the two presidential campaigns of Rev. Jesse Jackson intervened to enhance the bargaining role of the Black vote in presidential primary elections and in general elections.

The growing turnout effect of the Black vote has been accomplished in part by a growing political infrastructure, an important factor in the absence of a popular Black presidential candidacy and also as a complement to one. This alliance of organizations, arranged in a large-scale coalition, should become an institutional force that is able to construct formidable political operations that are essentially funded by and therefore controlled by Blacks. Such an infrastructure has figured in campaigns since 1976. Only since 1992, however, has it increasingly shown that it can improve voter turnout with massive volunteer efforts in those targeted areas where organizational resources designed to enhance turnout are used to disseminate political-education messages, operate phone banks, develop transportation systems, create radio messages, and perform other essential campaign operations.

Considerable attention has been paid to voter registration and turnout, but as the fundamental basis for these activities, the get-out-the-vote infrastructure must have the ability to engage in civic information dissemination related to public policy and politics in non-electoral cycles. This infrastructure must operate on a cycle of timing and events determined by Blacks rather than by nonpartisan funding organizations or national party organizations. It must be autonomous in its ability to follow the interests of the Black community.

The Republican Black Presidential Strategy

The Black vote has averaged less than 10 percent for Republican candidates in the past forty years. For a community that contains a substantial segment that needs governmental assistance, Republican public policy has not been supportive; Republicans have consistently worked to curtail community access to the resources of governmental assistance, in part by adopting a "small government" attitude, and in part by passing legislation that has shifted funding away from the social budget.

Blacks have followed their natural interests in supporting the Democratic party as the better of the two. The Black vote has contributed 20 to 25 percent of the total vote for presidential candidates of the national Democratic party, and because of this the Black vote has become an attractive political resource for African American political leaders to use in bargaining with Democratic candidates for the acceptance of the Black agenda of survival and development issues.

Although Republican strategists have at times suggested that they have made a wide appeal for the Black vote, in actuality they have only sought a marginal share of the Black vote as a means of reducing the power of the Democratic party coalition. In the 1996 election cycle, Republican operatives planned to attract at least 15 percent of the Black vote, 5 percent more than their usual share. Bob Dole subsequently received 12 percent of the Black vote in 1996, nearly achieving that 15 percent goal, but still losing to President Clinton. Although the average vote for Republican presidential candidates has never exceeded 12 percent, with the right tactics such an objective could be achieved in some key states. And if in the future Republicans were able to achieve this level of Black voting in key states, that would establish a competitive dilemma for Democrats, who would then have to decide whether to enhance their appeal to Black voters, or rather to campaign more strongly toward the center of the electorate. In chapter 8 I will review more thoroughly, with respect to a discussion of the 2004 presidential election, this matter of Republican tactics used to attract the Black vote.

Conclusion

The Voting Rights Act has been an important and necessary force in the empowerment of African American voters, and therefore it has helped increase the attention given to African American issues by leaders in the political system. Although one cannot argue that vast social change has occurred merely because of the role of Blacks in the electorate, the Voting Rights Act has proved itself nevertheless a most effective institutional weapon, in the arena of civic participation, for all citizens who would support the continued movement of American society toward social justice and well-being.

Maintaining and enhancing the Black political infrastructure is the most urgent political task before us, because this infrastructure is the vehicle that becomes the currency of bargaining. A critical flaw in the politics of the Black community has been the assumption that in exchange for Blacks' political influence at the polls, Democratic party leaders would reward Blacks with substantive policy. But what is the link between the influence of Black voter turnout and the reward of substantive policy? It is the ability of the Black community to control its vote through the ownership and effective deployment of the campaign resources that stimulate voter turnout. If the resources for voter turnout are controlled by the Democratic party, then the bargaining resource is in the hands of party officials rather than in the hands of Blacks themselves. But if this is so, then Blacks cannot use their political resources to extract those policy gains that depend upon the need for their vote. Because the Black vote is currently a function of the resources provided by others, rather than by Blacks themselves, the Black vote has been diluted in its impact. Increasing the impact of the Black vote by preventing its dilution is one condition that the Voting Rights Act was designed to fulfill. But to achieve the fullness of that objective, Blacks must exercise greater control over the process of voter mobilization.

4

Diluting Black Voting Power: The Supreme Court in the 1990s and the 2000 Presidential Election in Florida

Structural Discrimination in Voting

The tremendous growth of the Black vote and its impact on presidential politics has been endangered by a weakening of the Voting Rights Act (VRA), both in the act's underlying constitutional foundation and in its actual implementation. In this chapter, I will present a brief discussion of the three factors that are chiefly responsible for this weakening of the Voting Rights Act and the Black vote: Supreme Court decisions in the 1990s, the consolidation of white voting within the Southern Republican party, and the events in Florida during the 2000 presidential election wherein Blacks and other groups alleged that their voting rights had been abused, a result that was legitimized by the Supreme Court in its decision *Bush v. Gore.*

My discussion of structural discrimination will address the prevailing view of the Supreme Court in *Shaw v. Reno,* but it will orient the implications of that decision toward presidential politics rather than toward redistricting. Although the Voting Rights Act is one of the factors that have influenced the districting by which Blacks have increasingly elected their own representatives, the power of the Black vote at the national level is most evident in presidential election years when both congressional and presidential candidates stand for office.

Similar to national voter turnout trends, Black voter turnout is stronger in presidential election years than in off-year congressional or odd-year local races. The obviously greater turnout for presidential elections, as shown in table 4.1 below, places a premium on the intensity of political mobilization in years when both the presidential and congressional offices are at stake. But the table also shows that Black turnout was relatively stable from 1980 to 2000, ranging between 50 and 55 percent, except for a surge of Jackson voters in 1984 and 1988. This immediately raises the question of what the level of Black turnout would have been in those years if the barriers to the Black vote that dramatically came to light in the 2000 and 2004 presidential elections had not existed.

Exploiting Political Opportunity

The 1965 Voting Rights Act

The Voting Rights Act of 1965 was intended to promote the act of voting as defined in Section 14(c)(1) of the act:

> The terms "vote" or "voting" shall include all action necessary to make a vote effective in any primary, special, or general election, including, but not limited to, registration, listing pursuant to this Act, or other action required by law prerequisite to voting, casting a ballot, and having such ballot counted properly and included in the appropriate totals of votes cast with respect to candidates for public or party office and propositions for which votes are received in an election.

Thus, the law was meant to apply not only to the narrow act of casting a ballot, but also to the enforcement of that act's registration in and influence of the political system, as well as to the requirement that the resultant vote be counted properly and included in the total of all votes

Table 4.1   Black Turnout for Presidential and Congressional Elections, 1980–2000

1980	1982	1984	1986	1988	1990	1992	1994	1996	1998	2000
50.5	43.0	55.8	43.2	51.5	39.2	54.1	37.1	50.6	39.6	53.5

Source: U.S. Bureau of the Census, "Reported Voting and Registration by Race, Hispanic Origin, Sex, and Age Groups, November 1964–2000," Department of Commerce, February 27, 2002, revised June 3, 2002.

cast in any specific election, whether that election is for the election of public officials, the selection of political party candidates, or the ratification of public policy issues.

Section 2 of the Voting Rights Act struck down onerous residency requirements that had formerly been used in a discriminatory fashion against Blacks. As a result, no citizen who was found to be otherwise qualified to vote, either on-site at a polling station or by absentee ballot, could be denied that opportunity by virtue of the application of a residency requirement.

As I indicated in chapter 1, this limitation on the power of the states was necessary because state law as constituted in the South often offered structural impediments to participation in American democracy by a large segment of the population. The acts specified in the Voting Rights Act were significant, but they were by no means an exhaustive enumeration of the barriers that had been erected to prevent Black participation in elections. In fact, even as some barriers were outlawed by constitutional amendment, others, such as the poll tax (subsequently outlawed by the Twenty-fourth Amendment), were established to take their place. And even though some of the barriers were blatantly obvious, those that took their place were often more subtle, but just as effective. A list of barriers related to voting, compiled by the American Civil Liberties Union as a result of a 1968 report by the U.S. Commission on Civil Rights, found that Blacks experienced the following:

- ballots wrongly disqualified
- inadequate or wrong instructions at the polls
- discrimination in the location of polling stations
- failure to provide sufficient voting facilities or to operate them effectively
- racially segregated voter lists
- exclusion and interference with African American poll workers
- voter fraud by election officials
- discrimination in the selection of poll managers, inspectors, judges, and clerical workers.[1]

Such structural impediments affected the right of Blacks to vote and to have their vote legitimized by proper handling.

The focus of lawmakers and activists on implementing Section 2 of the Voting Rights Act resulted in an emphasis on developing single-member districts for Black candidates and representatives. This emphasis, however, came to be concerned only with the existence of fair conditions under which Black candidates might be elected, and so it sought to define what was meant in Section 2 by "political opportunity." In comparison, not as much attention was paid to the residual fetters that prevented a vote even from being cast and, especially, counted fairly under circumstances where it was clear that Blacks would not be the beneficiaries of that vote.

I agree with Professor of Law Kathryn Abrams who argued,

> The opportunity to elect candidates, while important, is not the sole or even the most crucial element of political efficacy. Important political goals, such as expression of preferences and alteration of substantive policies, are accomplished not simply by pulling a lever, but by engaging in activities such as discussion, lobbying, and coalition-building with others. Minority voters can be barred from these kinds of interaction by the present effects of past discrimination . . . that perpetuate these effects.[2]

In broadening the discussion to include forms of sociopolitical interaction, Professor Abrams also provides the basis for a more enriching discussion of the nature of Black political participation.

One of the reasons why I believe that the Jackson campaigns are seminal to thinking about the use of the political system by Blacks is that in developing a presidential campaign, there was the necessity for Jackson to exploit political opportunity to the utmost degree. Jackson did this by marshaling a comprehensive set of resources and by exploiting various sociopolitical relationships as he sought to effectively master the various aspects of the nominating system. A general election can be an even more intense experience in this regard, but the arena of the Democratic party primaries and caucuses is even so a formidable place in which to begin the search for the Black community's enhanced political viability. This set of conditions substantially expands the meaning of the concept of political opportunity.

Beyond a Black presidential candidacy, there is the necessity to consider how the presidential election process might facilitate the agenda of the Black community in ways that are still guided by the principle of comprehensively exploiting political opportunity. Abrams states that the act of voting is one of "interest aggregation," especially for cohesive minorities. She believes that such aggregated preferences may be established in other ways, and not only by using a mechanical device such as a voting machine.

> Much of the process works in a different way. Individuals deliberate together in groups to determine what they want. Groups engage in bargains or exchanges with other groups to increase their chances of obtaining what they want. The action is associative or collective; the means of attaining goals are collaborative or cooperative.[3]

Abrams has described the inner workings of the infrastructure central to the process of Black political mobilization, a process that occurs within the Black community, in coalition-building among and between Black organizations, as well as with allies that remain outside the Black cultural community. Her view is that political participation, thus elaborated, is important in maintaining and developing the coherence and effectiveness of a community as it seeks to interject its common interests into the political system.

Professor of Law Steven Lapidus has stated that when considering the 1982 amendments to the Voting Rights Act, both the House and Senate Judiciary Committees sought specifically to eliminate measures that inhibited voter registration by Blacks, regarding such measures as tactics that would amount to dilution of the Black vote.[4] The 1982 amendments were general in their specification of those barriers, citing any tactic contained in the election plan of the covered states that had a racially discriminatory effect, rather than a racially discriminatory intent. Since there is substantial evidence that such practices have historically depressed Black registration rates, Professor Lapidus proposes as a remedy that members of Black organizations become more actively involved in the electoral process by serving as deputy registrars, thereby reducing voter intimidation and promoting fairness in registration and voting procedures. This recommendation, made at the time of the passage of the 1982 amendments to the Voting Rights Act, appears somewhat optimistic because decisions of the courts in the late 1980s and into the 1990s created a more pessimistic atmosphere. That atmosphere influenced the conditions under which Blacks attempted to utilize their voting power in the 1990s and more recently, and therefore weakened the political opportunity of Blacks to achieve their goals.

Weakening Voting Rights in the 1990s: The Courts

The Voting Rights Act has had a positive impact on the ability of Black Southerners to vote. There has been a growth in that region's participation in national politics, both by white and Black voters, and at the same time Blacks have become a proportionately larger part of the Democratic base vote because of white defections to the Republican party. Race has divided the once solid political structure of the South into a racial/party region.

Shaw v. Reno (1993)

There is much concern among Blacks that the Voting Rights Act has been weakened by several actions of the Supreme Court. The first such action was the 1993 decision in *Shaw v. Reno* that limited the use of race in the drawing of political district boundaries. Many legal scholars have adopted a view consistent with the supposition that "*Shaw* and the Voting Rights Act are contradictory—one says you must consider race when drawing district lines, while the other says that you should not make decisions on the basis of race."[5] It is now the case that the use of race must be "narrowly tailored" to achieve the Section 2 goals of the Voting Rights Act, but it must also survive "strict scrutiny" in its use, to the extent that it is permissible to be aware of race, but race must not be the predominant factor in drawing district boundaries. This decision, while ignoring previous precedent in cases that supported the use of race as a primary factor in drawing political boundaries, has served as a new precedent for a number of similar cases and is consistent with the narrowing of the use of race overall in affirmative action policy.

Although there has been no measurable reduction of Black elected officials in light of the *Shaw v. Reno* decision, it is a fact that if the boundaries of future districts should be drawn so as to create Black majority districts, that redistricting could be challenged by those who object to the outcome as having been determined by racial considerations. This makes the potential creation of additional Black majority districts somewhat questionable and shifts the emphasis to the use of political incumbency, rather than race, as the major factor in redistricting.

The *Shaw v. Reno* decision strongly suggested that it is a negative for Blacks to have racial interests and to have those interests protected in order that they might be asserted in the political system both as a functional value and as a manifestation of a pluralistic representative democracy. I will address the issue of whether or not Blacks have binding group interests which might be projected into the political system, and will then address the system itself, focusing upon whether or not Black majority districts have been an impediment or an adequate vehicle for the projection of those interests through the representation of Black communities.

No Binding Interest

Justice O'Connor's view was that racial redistricting that proceeded on the assumption that Blacks had a unified cultural interest was highly questionable. She suggested,

> By perpetuating stereotypical notions about members of the same racial group—that they think alike, share the same political interests, and prefer the same candidates—a racial gerrymander may exacerbate the very pattern of racial bloc voting that majority-minority districting is sometimes said to counteract.[6]

By questioning the fact that Blacks share similar interests, O'Connor attempts to neutralize what has been a positive characteristic of Blacks, whites, or any other culturally coherent group: the positive benefits of their unity as the primary context through which they are able to exercise their political opportunity. O'Connor takes direct aim at the issue of the psychological and political coherence of Blacks with the clear suggestion that it would be a negative outcome of redistricting, when such coherence has long existed traditionally as a source of the positive outcome of enhanced social power.[7] This can be easily demonstrated by reference to any criterion of political behavior. How, for example, would Justice O'Connor explain the fact that the majority of Blacks cast their ballots for the same candidates at local, state, and national elections, or that 89 percent of Blacks voted for Democrats in the election of 1998, while 90 percent of Blacks voted for the Democratic presidential candidate (Gore) in the 2000 election?[8] This pattern of political coherence, as reflected in the 1998 and 2000 elections, has been traditional in both local and national elections over time and is illustrated in table 4.2.

If there is little community of interest among Blacks, then how is it that Blacks, representing their communities, elect the members of the Congressional Black Caucus (CBC) who cast similar votes for similar issues and consistently have the highest liberal rating in Congress as a group? According to one study, the CBC exhibited a "unity threshold of 90 percent in an analysis of roll call votes during the 1980s," which was sustained regardless of the degree of prior consultation.[9] Dr. David Bositis has also found in his analysis of the 103rd Congress that CBC members maintained "great cohesion" and a "remarkable degree of agreement." In an analysis of forty-five votes, he found that on nine (20 percent) of these votes the CBC was unanimous, but that "CBC members voted, on average, 83.9 percent of the time [together]."[10]

By considering Justice O'Connor's position, we are driven to the absurdity of having to avoid racial stereotyping by denying the existence of a Black community of interest and adopting a wholly unsophisticated sociological perspective on the issue of Black goal construction. For example, whites may consider Black actions through the prism of all sorts of stereotypes, a phenomenon that is not controlled by Blacks. The fact that Blacks behave coherently has enabled them to defeat these stereotypes by achieving their social goals.

Justice O'Connor is correct in stating that not all Blacks share the same interests, but inasmuch as there is a preponderant view among Blacks with respect to many issues, providing the basis for a dominant pattern of political behavior, the result of her position is to empower a minority within a minority. This has the effect of making law based on the marginal interests of Blacks who may not agree with the mainstream opinions of their community, or on the marginal interests, say, of whites who may constitute a minority within a largely Black community, and who therefore feel unrepresented.

Justice O'Connor and others impute that the need to refocus on race with respect to representation, identity, and other aspects of cultural unity is an impediment to political "color blindness," and is therefore a barrier to the achievement of a society that reflects this political value. Yet O'Connor's view that America is color-blind is wholly subjective and without evidence, since racial representation is often powerful in itself as a symbolic referent for society with which to measure the progress of color blindness. One cynical observer says of Justice O'Connor's perspective on this issue,

> The Court's decision is truly a color-blind one. It has a vision of what politics must be. A person who "happens to be African Ameri-

can" can be elected to office, but no African American person can be elected to office for the purpose of representing African American people. African American people as such can have no representation. They do not exist but such districts might cause them to exist. To recognize race is immoral and racist.[11]

The Court's decision and its resulting reinterpretation of the Voting Rights Act runs counter to the original intent of the act's framers. This change in the meaning of the Voting Rights Act, because it limits the creation of majority-minority districts while using race as a dominant criterion, may result in fundamental damage to the primary political interests of Blacks, such that there may eventually be a reduction of Black majority congressional districts.

Nevertheless, the impact of the decisions of the Supreme Court upon presidential elections is not clear. If the change in the law results in fewer Black districts, and if that in turn depresses the political opportunity of Blacks to vote (by dampening their motivation to mobilize or to successfully challenge the remaining barriers to ballot access), then the change in law will have had a negative effect on Black turnout in presidential elections. That is to say, if it becomes less a matter of government interest to protect the right of Blacks to organize their community to participate in the electoral process and to vote, since not to do so would have the effect of diluting the Black vote, then such decisions will have a grave impact indeed.

Since congressional districts have become a vital base of Black political mobilization due to the prominence of the Congressional Black Caucus, what may be in the most immediate danger is the culture of political mobilization presented earlier by Abrams. This includes not only the culture that has been elaborated through the formation of political coalitions involving Blacks and other kinds of organizations but also, as the infrastructure has developed, the interaction within that culture of groups and individuals using networks to facilitate such work. The point of view as outlined above therefore challenges the concept of broadness inherent in the view of Abrams and others by reducing the necessity to continue to sponsor the many kinds of civic activity that support such a culture. These civic activities include fund-raising and meetings and conferences among youths and other cultural stakeholders; extension of the culture through chapter and organizing model development at other sites; skill development in specific areas of message development for the media; polling, turnout activities, and registration processes; interaction with election leadership in various states; and contact with national agencies and private organizations involved in electoral work.

Nevertheless, the view of Justice O'Connor that using race to create Black majority districts results in "political apartheid" suggests that Blacks must again bear the burden of the historical segregation of their communities. This view coincides with the position of the Democratic party that Blacks should be spread among districts so that there is an opportunity to create biracial political coalitions and by so doing to elect moderate (Democratic) representation. This formula, however, would eliminate Black political representation altogether. Furthermore, the charge is misplaced, since there already exists a level of national political polarization based on race that has nothing to do with districting, as can be seen in table 4.2 below (compare also table 4.3). Between 1964 and 2000, the average Black vote for a Democrat for president has been 85 percent while the average white vote for Republican presidents has been 55 percent—a substantial difference. And since whites have become predominantly Republican, this increasing difference in voting behavior marks a distinctly racial pattern.

The more important question here is whether the chance to exercise their political opportunity in Black majority districts enhances Blacks' political participation. Since the history of Black social and political mobilization has most often been based on the ability of Blacks to affect the various elements of their culture and institutions, it would appear that to disperse Blacks among various districts dominated by whites would have a dampening effect on that influence. However, there is little research to substantiate this position one way or another.

A further question here is that if whites are then allowed, by the creation of Black majority districts, to create white majority districts, what is the danger to Blacks or to the political system? One might argue

Table 4.2   Black Democratic Vote for President, 1972–2000

	1972	1976	1980	1984	1988	1992	1996	2000	Avg.
Black Democratic vote	82	83	85*	90	86	83*	84*	90	85

Source: New York Times, "Portrait of the Electorate," November 10, 1996, 28; Voter News Service, November 1996 and November 2000.

*Significant third-party candidate—1980: John Anderson, 7%; 1992: Ross Perot, 20%; 1996: Ross Perot, 9%.

that biracial districts in such places as the South might have a leavening effect on the strength of the racial animus of the conservative movement, and that it might provide for representation that would take Black interests into account. At the same time, it is also important to note that in many white majority districts in the South the interests of Blacks are ignored. For proof of this, we need only take note of the strongly conservative legislative ratings of white representatives from districts with significant Black populations. For example, Mississippi CD-4 had a Black population of 36.5 percent in 1992, but a rating from the liberal organization Americans for Democratic Action (ADA) of only 30 percent in 1992 and a 40 percent NAACP rating in 1994. Similarly, Mississippi CD-3 had a 27.9 percent Black population and the same ADA and NAACP ratings. Even Virginia CD-4, which had a Black population of 30.7 percent, had an ADA rating of 55 percent in 1992 and an NAACP rating of 50 percent in 1994.[12]

It is also the case that the creation of largely white, Republican districts has provided greater opportunities for the creation of Black majority districts, as well as for the election of a greater number of Blacks to the U.S. House of Representatives. The case of Texas is well known. Here members of the Republican-controlled legislature, supported by a powerful Texas member of the U.S. House of Representatives, Tom DeLay, carried out a redistricting midway through the ten-year cycle so as to adjust the state's districts to correspond with the state's Republican majority. This resulted in an increase in the number of Republican seats in the state legislature and in the House of Representatives, and created an additional seat for a Black member of Congress.

Due to this, the Congressional Black Caucus grew from forty to forty-three members, its three additional members having come from Texas, Wisconsin, and Missouri. This result allowed a reinterpretation of the nature of redistricting because, as one journalist observed, "the three new African American members of the House all won in districts that were not drawn to have a Black majority under the Voting Rights Act to empower minorities to select a representative of their choice."[13] The clear inference here was that a racial result in the race-neutral process of redistricting was the preferred state of affairs.

It is therefore important for Blacks to be elected to office, to be allowed to compete through the resources provided by their cultural unity, and to engage the political system in a manner that creates influence at the national level in politics and public policy. To support this view, let us briefly address the emergence of the conservative movement in the South.

The Realignment of Southern Politics

Next to the Supreme Court decisions, the second greatest force for weakening the impact of the Voting Rights Act has been the realignment of Southern politics. Many have suggested that the creation of single-member Black majority congressional districts has been responsible for the political realignment.[14] The following recommendations are typical of this school of thought:

> Outside the South, substantive minority representation is best served by distributing black voters equally among all districts. In the South, the key is to maximize the number of districts with slightly less than a majority of black voters.[15]

But it is specious to suggest that a viable Black agenda will be furthered by the distribution of the Black population among white majority districts, since elected white moderates consistently vote more conservatively than do Black representatives.[16] This distribution would also result in the absence of Black representation in legislative bodies and, by devaluing the importance of descriptive representation for the Black community at large in American legislative bodies, would undermine the principle of the Voting Rights Act as a means of promoting democracy. The powerful role of the rise of conservative ideology as a motivating force in the changing politics of the South has largely been ignored out of a narrow concern with the impact of the Voting Rights Act on racial redistricting.

Professor Charles Bullock asserts, "The most remarkable change in American politics in recent generations has been the emergence of partisan competition that has transformed the once solidly Democratic South."[17] The extent to which whites in the South have largely shifted to the Republican party has created not just a competitive region politically but a "racialized" party system. As seen in table 4.3, whites in America shifted their presidential votes to Republican candidates in the 1996 and 2000 elections, with Southerners accounting for 31.8 percent and 32.3 percent, respectively, or one-third of the Bush vote in each election.[18]

Table 4.3   White Republican Vote for President, 1972–2000

	1972	1976	1980	1984	1988	1992	1996	2000	Avg.
White Republican vote	67	52	56*	64	59	40*	46*	54	55

Source: New York Times, "Portrait of the Electorate," November 10, 1996, 28; Voter News Service, November 1996 and November 2000.

*Significant third-party candidate—1980: John Anderson, 7%; 1992: Ross Perot, 20%; 1996: Ross Perot, 9%.

One of the reasons the Southern vote has become so important is not only its cohesiveness, but the fact that voter turnout in the South has improved markedly since the early 1960s. Data show that the difference between the turnout in the South and the rest of the nation was 12.6 percent in 1964 but closed to 1.2 percent in the 2000 election. Thus, the South as a region now turns out essentially as the rest of the nation. And whereas the national Black turnout in 1964 compared to the Southern Black turnout was 14.5 percent higher, by 2000 Southern Blacks voted at a 0.4 percent greater rate than Blacks nationally. Finally, the difference in white Southern turnout in 1964 and Black Southern turnout was 15.5 percent, which had closed to 0.3 percent by 2000. Blacks in the South, therefore, are voting at a somewhat greater rate than Blacks in the rest of the nation and at about the same rate as whites in the South. It is the increased turnout capability of Blacks in the South, together with their role as representatives of a disproportionate share of the Democratic party base, that continue to make the region competitive.

A majority of the South has voted for Republican candidates in four of five elections from 1972 to 1988. The one exception was the election of 1976 where, as it was explained to Professors Earl Black and Merle Black by a Southern businessman, "I voted for him [Carter] because he was a good ol' Southern boy, but he just didn't have it."[19] This motivation was also visible in Southern support for Bill Clinton who, as a "New Democrat," promised an agenda closer to the values of the region. Professors Black and Black suggest that the initial receptiveness of Southern voters to the Republican party, a receptiveness created by Richard Nixon in 1972, was temporarily destroyed by the Watergate scandal. They go on to cite Dunn and Woodard who argue that the grounding of Southern conservatives in the Republican party came through Ronald Reagan who "promised a new era of national renewal emphasizing traditional values—the dignity of work, love for family and neighborhood, faith in God, belief in peace through strength and a commitment to protect freedom as a legacy unique to America."[20] The Democratic party, on the other hand, appeared to stand for values with a contrary perspective.

Nevertheless, it is odd that race has not been regarded as a central polarizing factor in the shift of partisan allegiance on the part of many white Southerners. In rejecting the idea that Southern politics is polarized solely along racial lines, Professors Black and Black cite other factors emerging from the 1996 election exit polls, factors supporting an individualistic culture of personal responsibility, a diminished role for government in providing a secure standard of living, and a reduction in taxes. The new coded language of race has been reinterpreted in terms of public policy positions that are highly race-valued. For instance, the argument for the adoption of more personal responsibility by the individual has been utilized as an explanation for the failure of Blacks to achieve equality in American society. Similarly, since government has historically been perceived as a major force in promoting the economics of the welfare state and of a social policy of rights (such as affirmative action) that has valued Blacks at the expense of whites, a reduction in the role of government has become a major aspect of conservative policy.[21]

It should not be forgotten that the legal cases that have challenged the Voting Rights Act have come predominantly from the South, including the landmark case in North Carolina of *Shaw v. Reno,* and the Georgia redistricting case *Miller v. Johnson* (1995). Analysts of Southern politics who have taken the "New South" as an article of faith, and who see it as a more racially moderate region because of its progressively more liberal responses to surveys, should be more attentive to the subtleties discovered by Professors James Kuklinski, Michael Cobb, and Martin Gilens.[22] These authors agree with Bullock on the importance of the shift in Southern Republican allegiance, but also discover the persistence of negative racial attitudes supporting that change. Whereas some researchers have supported the theory of a regional convergence in racial attitudes over the last thirty years, what Kuklinski and his colleagues found was evidence that Southerners have not changed their racial attitudes as much as they have changed the ease with which they admit their real attitudes toward Blacks. This finding led Kuklinski and his colleagues to conclude,

Historically, the South has been the stronghold of racial prejudice; it apparently continues to be so today. Some of the prejudice is blatant, as manifested in the anger [some whites] expressed at the very thought of a Black family moving in next door. Some might be latent, with affirmative action serving as the target. We must not forget that racial prejudice exists outside the South; nonetheless, it is the South, the region that tried to secede from the union nearly 150 years ago as to maintain Black slavery, that stands out today.[23]

I agree with Professors Black and Black, who observe that another important factor fueling the shift in partisan alignment has been the degree to which many public issues came to be interpreted as moral questions, with the result that ministries such as Rev. Jerry Falwell's Moral Majority have had a substantial role in bringing this Southern conservative constituency into the Republican fold. In this context, the mobilization of white Southern Evangelicals becomes a distinct counterpart to the support that Black religious leaders contribute to the Democratic party. Indeed, the combination of white and Black Christians has made the South the most Christian region in the country, with 87 percent of Southerners identifying themselves as Christians according to exit polls in 1996. It may be noted here as well that the highest rate of church attendance nationally is in the South.

Returning to our discussion of the impact of the Voting Rights Act on this issue, Bullock argues that the attack on racial redistricting by the courts, and the development of a greater number of white majority and Black majority districts in the South, reduced the number of biracial voting coalitions. If this is true, then Blacks must come to depend increasingly on political resources developed within their own social networks.

Professors Alan Zuckerman, Nicholas Valentino, and Ezra Zuckerman found in their study of British and American political behavior that political networks form the structure that influences the political choices of their members.

The effect of social context on vote choice is conditioned by social and political networks. (a) By itself, membership in a social category does not much influence vote choice. (b) The greater the number of reinforcing social and political interactions, the more likely someone is to vote persistently in support of one party and in opposition to other parties. (c) Multiple and reinforcing interactions with others who have the same political preferences have a greater impact on voting decisions than do connections to people of the same social class or ethnic group.[24]

The most important point here for Blacks is the inference that their cultural networks are important in helping them create the opportunity for "reinforcing [the] social and political interactions" of those people involved in the political process who have interests similar to theirs. And although the researchers find the intensity of social interactions to be more important than mere membership in an ethnic or racial group, this is a logical conclusion in a racial context where such a group has exhibited a high degree of coherence in political behavior on various issues.

It is possible to conclude then that the effect of such a highly partisan, racialized system at the state level works in a way similar to smaller at-large districts to thwart the purpose of Section 2 of the Voting Rights Act and to promote the dilution of the Black vote in statewide and presidential elections. Effectively, white majorities that have shifted their voting allegiance to the Republican party constitute large monolithic voting blocs, or effective voting majorities, that cancel out the impact that the Black vote might have on the Electoral College vote. Because of the American winner-take-all voting system, the effect of a group on the Electoral College magnifies the impact of that group. This was nowhere more evident than in the presidential election of 2000, in which a contributing factor in the defeat of Al Gore, the Democratic candidate, was his inability to win a single state in the South. The Southern region, then, has become a "balance of power" in presidential politics because it depends on the united vote of whites in each state, and this results in a strongly racialized vote that does not exist to the same extent in any other region of the country.

The Strength of Black Voting in the 2000 Presidential Election

Registration and Turnout

Contrary to popular belief, Black voters have made great progress in political participation, virtually erasing the gap between themselves and white voters in the percentage turnout of eligible voters. In the 2000 election cycle, the difference between white and Black registration was 2.0 percent, a significant decline from 9.8 percent in 1976. The difference in actual voting also declined from a high point of 12.2 percent in 1972, to 2.9 percent in 2000. This is confirmed by the fact that voting was so strong in 2000 that in eight states (Alabama, California, Florida, Illinois, Louisiana, Missouri, Tennessee, and Texas) the Black percentage of the total vote either matched or exceeded the proportion of the Black voting age population (see table 4.4 below). These eight states were understandably important in the electoral outcome because their strong voter turnout influenced the popular vote and thereby influenced contests that depended upon the popular vote, including the presidential, senatorial, and gubernatorial contests.

Another way to assess the strong Black voter turnout in 2000 would be to say that the increase in the Black vote, in comparison to the increase in the white vote, was much larger. While the white voter turnout grew to 51 percent in 2000 from 49 percent in 1996, Black voter turnout at the same time grew from 37 percent to 50 percent, an increase of 13 percentage points.

The strength of their voting has made Blacks an indispensable part of the coalition of the national Democratic party in both presidential and local elections. In fact, in states such as Louisiana, South Carolina, and Mississippi, because of the withdrawal of whites into the Republican party, Blacks now constitute nearly half of the total constituency of the party, making Black turnout critical to the fortunes of any Democratic candidate for statewide office.

The general tendency of the Black vote to influence the margin of victory of the Democratic party more than that of the Republican party

Table 4.4 States Where the Black Share of the Total Vote in 2000 Approximately Matched or Exceeded the Black Voting Age Population (BVAP)

State	BVAP	% Total Vote
Alabama	23.9	25
California	7.1	7
Florida	13.4	15
Illinois	13.9	14
Louisiana	29.6	29
Missouri	10.1	12
Tennessee	15.0	13
Texas	11.8	15

Source: David A. Bositis, "The 2000 Black Vote," Joint Center for Political and Economic Studies, November 2000.

also held true in 2000, since Black turnout constituted 19 percent of the margin for Al Gore, while the general election margin was the closest in history at less than one-tenth of 1 percent.

In the eighteen states with a more than 8 percent Black voting age population in 1996, only four had turnout rates over 50 percent. In 2000, according to data provided by Voter News Service, there were nine such states with a turnout rate of 50 percent or above: Alabama (50.3), Florida (50.7), Illinois (52.5), Louisiana (54.2), Missouri (57.5), Michigan (57.2), Ohio (54.3), Pennsylvania (53.3), and Virginia (51.8).[25] It is therefore reasonable to conclude that the Black vote influenced the shape of the U.S. Senate by promoting the victory of Mel Carnahan in Missouri over John Ashcroft, Debbie Stabenow in Michigan over Spencer Abrahams, Dianne Feinstein in California over Tom Campbell, and Bill Nelson in Florida over Bill McCullum.

The Black Infrastructure

The size of the Black vote for Al Gore was also interesting, since the vaunted popularity of Bill Clinton in the Black community had produced a Black vote of 82 percent in 1992 and 84 percent in 1996, but the Black vote for Al Gore in 2000 was 90 percent nationally. This result was to some extent due to two factors, the first of which was get-out-the-vote targeting of the Black population in the so-called battleground states, and the second being an ad campaign of messages that were decidedly anti-Bush. Missouri, Illinois, Michigan, and Pennsylvania, which were the battleground states, were targeted for concentrated visits by candidates and their surrogates, substantial spending on political advertisements, and ground-war get-out-the-vote operations that were mounted by thousands of volunteers who had been brought into the states by the campaigns and their political parties.

In this context, the Black political infrastructure also targeted these states. That infrastructure consisted of, first, Rev. Jesse Jackson who made trips into many states to rally the Black vote; Tom Joyner, host of the *Tom Joyner Morning Show,* a syndicated radio talk show, who together with Tavis Smiley used the *Morning Show* to educate and motivate Black voters; the NAACP National Voter Fund campaign that energized their more than two thousand branches and placed television ads in critical markets; the National Coalition on Black Civic Participation that managed get-out-the-vote operations in several states; and the partisan program of the Congressional Black Caucus, directed by Charles Rangel (D-NY), that mounted a bus tour through ten states. These activities were supplemented by various organizations made up of locally elected officials such as the Congressional Black Caucus, Black mayors, and Black state legislators in various jurisdictions, as well as Black churches, whose venues also served as polling stations in many cities.

The Motivation Factor

The issue framework of the 2000 presidential campaign, while persuasive, was not decisive. The campaign wavered between whether the personality of the candidates would be the most important factor, or the issues that each candidate espoused. In the end, both factors were integrated to the extent that Black voters may have decided that, based on the issues, they would vote against George Bush, since Gore's stand on the issues was more favorable to their interests. This anti-Bush rather than strong pro-Gore posture is suggested by the fact that in October of 2000 a survey by the Joint Center for Political and Economic Studies found that when Black voters were asked whether they would vote for Gore or Bush, Gore was favored by 74 percent of the poll respondents, with 14 percent undecided.[26] Comparable surveys in past elections had generally found Black intent to vote for the Democratic presidential nominee at least 10 points higher one month before the election. This is an indication that although Gore was not a strongly attractive candidate, Black voters found Bush's position on the issues threatening to their interests, and it explains why, according to exit polls, Blacks made a meteoric leap to 90 percent support for Gore on November 7.

Early in the primary election season, George Bush established a negative issue set in the minds of Black voters by his appearance at Bob Jones University, an institution in South Carolina that prohibited interracial dating. In addition to this, Bush was opposed to affirmative action and instead championed what he termed "affirmative access"; he did not support a federal hate crimes law, and had not been visibly supportive of the family of James Byrd of Texas, a man who had been brutally dragged to death from the back of a pick-up truck by two white men; he had been governor of Texas, the state with the most vigorous use of the death penalty in the country, with a high proportion of those death-penalty cases involving Blacks; and finally, he was more supportive of school vouchers and not as supportive of public schools as Al Gore. In addition,

Bush did not consider Africa as a place where the U.S. should concentrate its interests in peacekeeping, peacemaking, and development.

Al Gore, on the other hand, through his Senate career, his eight years of activities as vice president in the Clinton administration, and his support for critical aspects of the Black agenda was fairly well-known to the Black leadership. In addition, Gore had announced that one of his first acts as president would be to formulate a policy against racial profiling. He also favored affirmative action, supported hate crimes legislation, and opposed vouchers. In stark contrast to Bush, he had been a strong supporter of Africa, evidenced by his position on the Mbeki-Gore Commission on South Africa and by his stewardship of the National Summit on Africa in 1997. The latter focus on Africa, and especially South Africa, was important at a time when South Africa had just emerged as a Black majority–ruled state with an exceedingly popular president, Nelson Mandela, who depended upon support from the United States for the initial stability of his government.

The Gore campaign suffered initially from the indecision of Blacks about Gore's choice of vice presidential running mate, Senator Joseph Lieberman (D-CT) because of Lieberman's previously centrist positions on issues such as affirmative action and school vouchers. Lieberman, however, at the Democratic National Convention was questioned vigorously about his views by the Congressional Black Caucus, and he promised fidelity to the Black agenda if elected. Subsequently, there were no indications in the final voting that Black voters found Lieberman a hindrance to the Democratic ticket. The result was that the issues of the Gore-Lieberman Democratic team were a motivation for Black voters to support the Democratic ticket, when those issues were compared to the issues proposed by the Bush-Cheney team, all of which were considered threatening to Black interests.

In this context, the political infrastructure that was active in encouraging voter registration and turnout in the Black community worked harder—and depended upon the enforcement of the Voting Rights Act—for Black voting strength maximization.

Disenfranchisement in the 2000 Presidential Election

The Florida Impasse

In Florida the drama of the 2000 election season was focused on the razor-thin margin between the two presidential candidates as the balloting on election day, November 7, closed with a statewide difference of 1,800 votes between the candidates. This margin automatically triggered a recount and eventually a hand count of ballots in four contested counties: Miami-Dade, Broward, Volusia, and Palm Beach. In 1996 the Black vote in Florida had been 527,000, but it grew to 925,000 votes in 2000, with Blacks contributing 93 percent of their vote to Al Gore, 6 percent to George Bush, and 1 percent to Ralph Nader. The additional 398,000 Black votes in 2000, nearly 40 percent greater than in 1996, boosted Gore's share of the Black vote from 9 percent in 1996 to 14 percent in 2000, in a state where the margin between Gore and Bush was less than 1 percent.

During the recount George Bush's margin closed to 327 votes, and the Gore campaign asked Secretary of State Katherine Harris to delay certification of the result until the recount was completed. The Bush campaign, however, filed suit to prohibit a manual recount. As the margin narrowed to 288 votes, the Bush campaign lost its suit, and the Florida Supreme Court decided that the recount could continue, at the same time extending the deadline for certification to November 14. Bush's subsequent opposition to this decision failed in the Federal District Court in Atlanta and eventually failed with the Florida Supreme Court. However, the Bush campaign appealed to the U.S. Supreme Court, and on December 1, 2000, the U.S. Supreme Court decided to hear arguments by the Bush campaign that the Florida Supreme Court had exceeded its authority by changing state law as to which votes could be certified.[27]

Black Disenfranchisement

On midday of election day Kweisi Mfume, president of the NAACP, had been informed of complaints of voter irregularities that were being received (and would continue to be received until late evening) at the NAACP's national headquarters. While these complaints originated from around the country, most of them came from the state of Florida.[28] Mfume immediately contacted the Justice Department, which sent an officer to NAACP headquarters to monitor the nature of the complaints.

Thereafter the Florida state branch of the NAACP, and legal organizations such as the Lawyers' Committee for Civil Rights Under Law and the NAACP Legal Defense Fund, began to receive numerous complaints alleging the denial of the right of Blacks to vote.

The NAACP subsequently held hearings to give voice to these complaints and to document them, and sent a record to the Justice Department, suggesting that the Civil Rights Division of the Justice Department would find blatant violations of Section 2 of the Voting Rights Act, and recommending that on those grounds the Justice Department should intervene.

The cumulative nature of these complaints was reflected in public hearings held by the NAACP on Saturday, November 11, 2000, during which individuals testified that,

- the head of the state NAACP, Ms. Adora Nweze, was initially not allowed to vote because a poll worker said that she had been sent an absentee ballot, a ballot that Ms. Nweze said she never received
- many members of Miami's Haitian community were not given language assistance when they came to vote
- three ballot boxes found at different locations in Black areas were secured and had serial numbers that indicated they contained ballots that were not included in the initial count
- voters who registered online through various services were told that the information they had provided conflicted with election information regarding their addresses
- elderly voters and others who arrived at their regular polling stations were told that they had arrived at the wrong polling station, or they discovered that their voting location had been changed without notification
- a disproportionate number of ballots in Black neighborhoods were invalidated because they contained either an over-vote or an under-vote for president
- Black voters were disproportionately purged from voter lists so that many who had duly registered through the normal process were told their names were not on the rolls
- an election official in Hillsborough County gave a list of fifteen hundred voters to a talk show host and cited irregularities with the list, since it contained registered voters who had filed absentee voter applications that were rejected by voting officials
- many individuals were denied the right to vote because they did not possess two forms of identification
- Black students from Bethune-Cookman College who had regis-

tered were sent from one polling station to another, eventually being denied the right to vote

- police stopped people on their way to the polls in Daytona Beach; and police stopped people in the district of Woodville outside of Tallahassee, as indicated by the London *Guardian*
- people who spoiled their initial ballot were not given additional ballots as the law requires
- Black students at Florida A&M University were unable to vote because their voting machines did not operate on election day and were not repaired in time for them to cast a vote

As a result of the NAACP hearings, the U.S. Commission on Civil Rights investigated the complaints and found a similar pattern of allegations including substantial statistical evidence that ballots from Black majority counties had been invalidated at a rate greater than those from either white or Hispanic majority counties.

In addition, there was ample evidence that Black votes had been thrown out disproportionately. Professor Allan Lichtman, a voting expert, testified at hearings conducted by the U.S. Commission on Civil Rights on these and other voting irregularities in Florida:

> An analysis of the entire state using county-level data and at Miami-Dade, Duval, and Palm Beach counties using precinct-level data, demonstrates that blacks were far more likely than non-blacks to have their ballots rejected in the 2000 Florida presidential election. [This was based on] a strong positive correlation between the percentage of black registrants in a county and the percentage of rejected ballots, [and a] correlation . . . between the percent of ballots rejected in the presidential election and the percentage of blacks among voters.[29]

Professor Lichtman confirmed that about one hundred eighty thousand or 2.9 percent of all ballots cast in Florida in 2000 were "spoiled ballots" which constituted either over-votes or under-votes. The over-votes (ballots that show more than one recognized vote) outnumbered the under-votes (ballots that do not show a recognized vote) by two to one.[30] In their rationale for contesting the vote in heavily Democratic selected counties, the Al Gore campaign complained that many over-votes were created by the use of a complex "butterfly ballot," which resulted in the elimination of many votes intended for Gore. Many of the eliminated votes originated in areas such as Duval County, where twenty-two thousand votes were thrown out, ten thousand of them from voters in Black neighborhoods. Indeed, the pattern that Lichtman referred to is illustrated in table 4.5 below that captures ballot spoilage in the nine Florida counties with the highest Black populations. Duval County shows the highest number of spoiled ballots, accounting for a 9.2 percent spoilage rate, but all nine of these high Black population counties reported a high spoilage rate, regardless of the method of voting. This outcome raises questions that concern the lack of voting assistance at polling stations, faulty voter education, and poor ballot machine condition—factors beyond the butterfly ballot itself.

A study by the *Washington Post* soon after the election found that the punch-card voting system caused Black votes to be eliminated on a greatly disproportionate basis in such states as Florida and Georgia, while the highest disparity was in Cook County, Illinois, where Blacks represent nearly 30 percent of the population, and where more than one hundred twenty thousand votes, or 5 percent of the total, were thrown out. The *Washington Post* cited an Ohio State University political scientist who said, "Poor people are more likely to invalidate ballots because of their unfamiliarity with punch-card systems," and who noted that voters in affluent areas spoil their ballots 2 percent of the time, while those in poor areas do so 20 percent of the time.[31] This suggests

Table 4.5   Spoiled Ballots in the 2000 Presidential Election by County, Race, and Ethnicity

County	Voting System	Spoiled Ballots	% Spoiled	% Black	% White	% Hispanic
Gadsden	optical	2,085	12.4	63.0	36.3	3.3
Jefferson	punch card	571	9.2	48.8	50.7	2.7
Madison	punch card	480	7.2	46.6	53.0	2.1
Hamilton	optical	389	8.9	44.2	55.1	4.3
Jackson	optical	1,170	6.7	30.3	68.8	4.2
Duval	punch card	26,909	9.2	28.5	67.9	3.9
Leon	optical	181	.2	28.3	69.2	3.4
Union	paper/hand	258	6.3	27.8	70.9	6.2
Gulf	optical	421	6.4	26.2	72.8	1.4

Source: "Population and Voting Characteristics of Florida Counties (Ranked by Percent of Votes Spoiled)," hearings, U.S. Commission on Civil Rights, June 2001, Appendix I.

that the mechanics of voting, with regard to the misuse or malfunction of voting systems, may have a disproportionate impact upon Black voters, since a much higher proportion of them vote less consistently than whites.

Florida Felon Voting Rights

In addition to ballot irregularities, there were problems with registered voter lists. Florida was one of seven states in 2000 that imposed a lifetime voting ban on those convicted of a felony, a situation that affected over 600,000 people, 58 percent of them Black. This comprised 31 percent of Florida's total Black male population (204,600), all of whom under law were ineligible to vote due to felony convictions.[32] In preparation for the 2000 election, Florida Secretary of State Katherine Harris, the highest authority for election administration in the state, had 173,000 names removed from the voter list. She contracted with a firm, ChoicePoint, which had offices in Atlanta, Georgia, and Austin, Texas, to clean the voter rolls and to perform such activities as removing the names of felons from the rolls. Nevertheless, after the election Florida refused to count 179,855 votes, 97,000 of which had been cast by Blacks considered to be felons, when in many of those cases the supposed felons had not been convicted of any crime.[33]

The impact of the felon voting rights issue on the 2000 election is evident when one considers that the contest was decided by 537 votes in Florida. Greg Palast, journalist for the British newspaper *The Observer,* says that based on estimates provided by David Bositis of the Joint Center for Political and Economic Studies, the national felony conviction rate for African Americans is 45 percent, a figure that Palast says is confirmed by the fact that in Hillsborough County, Florida, 54 percent of the voters who were eliminated due to their presumptive felon status were African Americans.[34] Thus, the thousands of Blacks eliminated from the final voter rolls might have made a difference in the race in 2000.

Professor Guy Stuart says that Florida's felon voting law dates to 1838 and was used to limit the number of freed slaves who were eligible to vote. As a part of its attempt to reinstate white control over state power after the Civil War, Florida, like other Southern states, amended its constitution to limit Black access to the ballot, and the loss of voting rights for the commission of a felony was, accordingly, one of the mechanisms used to criminalize large portions of the Black male population.[35]

At the turn of the century Florida also passed a literacy test, as well as a "grandfather clause" that gave voting rights only to those voters whose grandfathers had voted, a requirement that few Blacks met. But while many of these prohibitions to voting, along with the white-dominated primaries that they governed, had been rendered illegal, the prohibition of felon voting remained legally permissible.

Professor Stuart points out that Article 1, Section 2 of the Constitution authorizes states to determine who is eligible to vote in federal elections and, thus, has allowed the states to utilize felon disenfranchisement as a criterion of eligibility. He also cites the irony that the Fourteenth Amendment to the U.S. Constitution reduces the representation of states in the Congress as their population is disenfranchised, "except for participation in rebellion or other crime." The other side of the coin is that voting rights organizations have often, by utilizing Section 1 of the Fourteenth Amendment, brought suit against the practice of disenfranchisement of convicted felons.[36]

This issue eventually came to be involved with the Voting Rights Act in the run-up to the 2004 election, due to the fact that fifty-four thousand felons had been either released from incarceration or had concluded their parole and were therefore eligible to apply to have their voting rights restored. The only way that a felon can have his or her voting rights restored in Florida is for the felon to apply for and receive executive clemency.[37] By March 15, 2004, there was a backlog of 35,585 applications for executive clemency, five times more than in July of 2001.[38] Then, in May of 2004 Governor Jeb Bush ordered a purge of the voter rolls, as must be done six months before a presidential election, a move that would purge as many as forty thousand supposed felons from the rolls.[39] And in July of 2004 Governor Jeb Bush decided that rather than filing a one-page clemency application form, all felons had to apply to the Office of Executive Clemency, a move that he justified on grounds that it would reduce paperwork, even though it involved hearings.

However, in December of 2003 a decision of the Eleventh Circuit Court, based on a class action suit by the American Civil Liberties Union and the Florida Justice Institute, found that the permanent disenfranchisement of felons in Florida was designed to prevent African Americans from voting.[40] As such, the suit alleged racial discrimination as a violation of equal protection under the Fourteenth Amendment. While the original suit was dismissed by the Fourth District Court, the Eleventh Circuit Court reversed and remanded the suit because of the failure of the defendant (the state of Florida) to show that the originally racially discriminatory purpose for which the felon voting prohibition was established in 1868 was not a motivation when the law was reenacted in 1968. The equal protection claim was sustained.[41]

Meanwhile, two other cases directly raised the question as to whether the Voting Rights Act might apply to felon disenfranchisement by the states. In July of 2003 in Washington State the Ninth Circuit Court of Appeals issued a ruling that the Voting Rights Act could, in fact, be applied to felon disenfranchisement maintained by the state of Washington, finding that the law interacted with racial bias such as to deny minorities an equal opportunity to participate in the electoral process, considering that the disproportionate impact of such a disenfranchisement on Blacks for this reason could place that law in the category of a voter qualification test or prerequisite that is denied by the Voting Rights Act.[42]

A subsequent case that sought to take advantage of this finding, however, *Locke v. Farrakhan,* filed by four Black males, was remanded to the district court by the Ninth Circuit judges, and in the subsequent en banc hearing that preceded this action, it became clear that there was a substantial difference of opinion with respect to the intent of Congress as regards the proper use of the Voting Rights Act. This case and a New York case, *Muntaqim v. Coombe,* which argued for the restoration of the voting rights of current felons in that state, were sent up to the Supreme Court. In November of 2004 the Court refused to hear the case, no doubt on the grounds that it was premature, since similar cases were in the federal court system and the issues had not been sufficiently explicated by the lower courts.[43]

This is an important problem since 1.4 million Black males (13 percent of all Black males), who constitute 40 percent of the 3.9 million felons nationwide, are disqualified from voting for this reason.[44] The disenfranchisement of convicted felons thwarts the intent and effectiveness of the Voting Rights Act, which was passed in order to eliminate such barriers. It is a serious problem that should be corrected, since in the 2000 election as many as two million votes were thrown out for this reason.

Bush v. Gore

On December 11 both campaigns argued before the U.S. Supreme Court and on the next day a decision was rendered that stayed the Florida Supreme Court's allowance of the recount. This decision gave Bush the presidency. Justice Antonin Scalia, writing for the Court, held that the recount violated the Fourteenth Amendment equal protection rights of George Bush. Although recounts continued in Leon, Miami-Dade, and Palm Beach Counties, Florida could not guarantee uniform procedures in each of the several counties where the recount was occurring.[45] Scalia went on to invoke the startling assumption that "the individual citizen has no federal constitutional right to vote for electors for the President of the United States unless and until the state legislature chooses a state-wide election as the means to implement its power to appoint members of the Electoral College."[46] Furthermore, employing Voting Rights Act case law (*Harper v. Virginia Board of Elections*, 383 U.S. 663 [1966]), he held that the state, once having granted its citizens the right to vote as its method of selecting electors, had then to provide such a method under the context of equal protection that afforded each person's right to vote equal value to another's. As such, invoking another Voting Rights Act case (*Reynolds v. Sims*, 377 U.S. 533 [1964]) to erect a standard prohibiting voter dilution, he held that "the right to vote is protected in more than the initial allocation of the franchise [by the state]."[47]

By reversing the decision of the Florida Supreme Court and prohibiting the recount, the U.S. Supreme Court legitimized the resulting vote count authorized by Florida Secretary of State Katherine Harris, which gave to George Bush a winning vote margin of 527 votes, ceding to him Florida's twenty-five electoral votes and the presidential election. And although the Supreme Court legitimized this result by utilizing the Voting Rights Act, and by ignoring the ancillary acts of voter suppression that contributed to the result, *it also legitimized that aspect of the manner in which the vote was accumulated.* That is to say, by inference, the high court legitimized the violation of due process argument of George Bush's campaign, but ignored many of the irregularities in the process of voting that appeared to weaken the force of the Voting Rights Act, and in so doing, the Court violated the act's spirit and letter.

Conclusion

One way to understand the attempt to curtail the impact of the Voting Rights Act in the areas discussed above is with regard to the force of social movements. In the first instance, the *Shaw v. Reno* decision was the result of a surge in Black political representation in Southern congressional districts after the census of 1990. The attempt by the states to continue to draw Black majority districts and to empower Black voters had begun to test the limits of the countermovement of the Republican realignment in the South. This movement of Republican realignment was first and foremost an ideological movement of substantial proportions through which Southern social conservatives utilized the Republican party's economically conservative base to create a political alliance that resulted in electoral dominance at the national level. The involvement of the court once again, in the case that resolved the 2000 presidential election, *Bush v. Gore,* also surfaced as a result of the substantial movement of Blacks to vote in the state's election for president. That movement overran many of the traditional aspects of structural discrimination that had suppressed the Black vote in the past and subjected them to the public scrutiny of hearings, research, and ameliorative legislation.

In our continuing attempt to understand the dynamics of electoral participation by Blacks and other minorities, it is instructive to note the interplay between social forces and the electoral system. Many studies have attempted to understand the outcome of elections by analyzing voting patterns and exit polls. However, this work takes the position that the outcomes of elections are most often a result of what happens in society, as reflected in the electoral system, both in the outcome of the voting and in the attitudes expressed by voters.

In the following chapter I will examine the continuing barriers to the right to vote and the issue of election reform that emerged as an outgrowth of problems with the 2000 election. In considering this problem, I will also attempt to recommend changes that argue for continued implementation of the Voting Rights Act and for strengthening of the National Voter Registration and Help America Vote acts.

Election Reform:
Revisiting the Right to Vote

Confronting Modern Barriers to Voting Rights

The Long Shadow of Jim Crow

Black voters have long been a subject of interest to both Democrats and Republicans, even though Blacks have been fiercely loyal to the Democratic party, since Republican victories are often in competitive districts and are often dependent upon the lackluster turnout of an otherwise significant Black electorate. Historically, first Democrats then Republicans suppressed the Black vote. And though intentional Black voter disenfranchisement is a form of racial discrimination in the electoral process, it is a well-known fact that intense partisan competition heightens both the practice and the perception of Black vote suppression, even though in relatively noncompetitive elections Blacks have also been denied the right to vote. Nevertheless, the suppression of the Black vote is a phenomenon that has survived the implementation of the Voting Rights Act, the National Voter Registration Act, and other laws designed to protect the rights of Blacks and other American citizens to vote.

In case there are doubts about the fact of Black voter disenfranchisement, consider the evidence presented in a report issued by the NAACP and People for the American Way in September of 2004, which stated a reality facing Black voters: "In every national American election since Reconstruction, every election since the Voting Rights Act passed in 1965, voters—particularly African American voters and other minorities—have faced calculated and determined efforts at intimidation and suppression."[1] The report begins with a statement boldly confirming such practices by a Republican state legislator representing Troy, Michigan, who noted shortly before the 2004 primary elections, "If we do not suppress the Detroit vote, we're going to have a tough time in this election,"[2] a comment directed at a city that is 83 percent Black. The NAACP report goes on to document incidents of suppression:

- plainclothes officers of the Florida Department of Law Enforcement questioned elderly Black voters in their homes about suspected incidents of voter fraud in connection with voting irregularities in the March 23, 2004, mayoral election
- in 2004, college students at Prairie View A&M were told that they would not be able to vote locally in the presidential election, a view upheld by a local judge
- Republicans in Jefferson County, Kentucky, on election day in 2003 stationed vote challengers in the Black precincts of Louisville and did the same in the fall 2004 presidential election
- in the 2003 elections in Philadelphia, Blacks attempting to vote were systematically challenged by white males carrying clipboards and driving vehicles with insignia designed to resemble law enforcement insignia
- in the 2003 elections, Republican poll watchers in Pine Bluff, Arkansas, challenged Black voters, saying, "Before you vote, I want to see your identification"
- in the 2002 elections in Maryland, flyers distributed in African American communities listed the wrong day for elections and stated that parking tickets, overdue rent, etc., had to be paid before persons would be eligible to vote
- a similar incident occurred in the 2002 Senate elections in Louisiana when flyers distributed in Black communities gave the wrong date for the election

The report lists many other incidents of voter intimidation, and describes tactics for suppressing the vote that date back to the civil rights movement era. It also cites a particularly illuminating 1981 study of Black voter intimidation and suppression in Georgia by researcher Brian Sherman, who found that Blacks experienced various forms of discrimination by poll watchers and in the administration of polling stations. Sherman observed that "because the Voting Rights Act has outlawed the most blatant measures, those who have wanted to limit Black participation in politics have had to resort to more subtle and subterranean tactics."[3]

Clearly such patterns did and do still exist today, formerly perpetrated in large part by the Democratic party when it was the dominant party in the South, but today primarily by the Republican party in both the North and the South. The Republican party has traditionally mounted what it has called "ballot security" or "voter integrity" programs to prevent voter fraud, programs that have largely targeted Black voters and are now increasingly being used against Hispanics and Native Americans. The result is that the Republican party has been the recipient of three consent decrees by the Department of Justice instructing it to refrain from such practices. The first such case was in New Jersey in 1981 where armed guards were used to challenge Hispanic and African American voters. In 1987 similar vote suppression programs were implemented in Louisiana, Georgia, Missouri, Pennsylvania, Michigan, and Indiana. The Louisiana program alone found its sponsors claiming to have eliminated "60–80,000 folks from the rolls." More recently, in the 2004 election cycle the Republican party mounted an extensive attempt to examine voter rolls for ineligible voters, and it enlisted thousands of poll station challengers in fourteen states widely regarded as the battleground states that could determine the election.[4]

Black Voters and the 2000 Presidential Election

The election of November 7, 2000, was a milestone in African American politics because of the strength of the turnout of Black voters, *achieving relative parity with the white vote for the first time in history*. The rate of Black registration was only 2.1 percent (65.7–63.6) less than the white rate, and voter turnout was only 2.8 percent (56.4–53.6) less than the white rate, virtually eliminating the substantial gap in relative voter participation that had existed prior to and following the passage of the Voting Rights Act.

As we now know, this election was also historic because of the closeness of the vote between the candidates Al Gore and George Bush. The aftermath of the election also revealed that in many places, most significantly in Florida, Blacks experienced a massive denial of their right to vote. Immediately after the vote on November 7, 2000, there was a shower of complaints from African Americans, Haitians, whites, Hispanics, and the elderly who said that their ballots had been counted wrongly or not at all. Various sources of the problem surfaced: the confused construction of the butterfly ballot, the intimidating effect of police checkpoints, felony status monitoring of potential voters which thereby disqualified them from voting, summary poll closures with people in line both inside and outside polling stations, and the mailing of absentee ballots to people who did not request them, with the consequence that those people were stricken from the voting rolls and were not allowed to vote when they appeared at polling stations.

The strength of political competition in 2000 and the resulting high Black turnout led to investigations that uncovered the existence of many practices that the Voting Rights Act of 1965 had been designed to abolish. Indeed, many of the barriers experienced by Blacks in their attempt to vote in the 2000 elections dated back to the period of the rampant Jim Crow practices that had been the original target of the Voting Rights Act.

Mass Demonstrations

In response to the questionable conduct of the election in 2000, a veritable storm of protests arose at various points in the process, attesting to the anger of Blacks and others at having been denied the right to vote and to have their votes counted. Ironically, Jesse Jackson had warned of such an outcome in a speech to the Democratic Convention on August 12, 2000, at a meeting of the rules committee, during which he suggested that, rather than practicing the diversity they portrayed at their convention, Republicans were "masters of deceit and diversion," and that they were "wolves in sheep's clothing who could neutralize voters who normally voted Democratic."[5] Three months later, Jackson would be the first to call for a rally in Miami to protest the outcome of the vote, saying, "People whose votes have not been counted need to have their votes counted and their voices heard."[6] Then, demanding new elections in Palm Beach County, on November 9 he joined one thousand demonstrators outside the county courthouse, where some nineteen thousand ballots had been thrown out, explaining, "It's not about Black or white, it's about wrong or right."[7]

As the scene shifted in late November to Supreme Court arguments on the first of the Florida Supreme Court decisions challenged by the Bush campaign, Jackson mounted protest demonstrations in Washington, DC, along with other civil rights and labor leaders. And when the

Supreme Court rendered its decision in mid-December, demonstrations again erupted, this time in Tallahassee, led by a coalition of Florida politicians, activists, and national civil rights leaders. This same coalition took advantage of the January Martin Luther King Jr. commemorations and the inauguration of George Bush to mount massive "national day of moral outrage" demonstrations at the Florida state capitol building in Tallahassee. The event was led by Rev. Joseph Lowery, former Atlanta mayor Maynard Jackson, and NAACP President Kweisi Mfume, the latter of whom framed the purpose of the demonstrations when he said, "As the eyes of the nation are on Washington, and on this inauguration, we come back to Florida to say that we remember and we must not ever forget. We come back to say, never again."[8] The strong emotions undergirding the attitude of Blacks toward what had occurred were captured by comments of U.S. Rep. Corrine Brown who said, "What happened in Florida will go down in history as a coup d'état. We're not talking about guns . . . We're talking about [Secretary of State] Katherine Harris, we're talking about [Florida Governor] Jeb Bush."[9]

Through public protest over what had occurred in Florida, activist and legal mobilization would help to transfer the energy and emotion of the electoral process into a pressure for election reform. This would coincide with a national feeling of embarrassment at the difficulties experienced by the most self-professedly democratic nation in the world appearing to have selected its president by court decision rather than through an election process that was perceived to be fair by its citizens.

Electoral Reform 2001–2003

Much of the response to voting irregularities came at the state level, where the National Association of Secretaries of State played a leading role in advising members of state legislatures about both the problems of and potential solutions to electoral reform. By mid-February of 2001 more than three hundred pieces of legislation had been filed, as determined in a survey by the *Wall Street Journal*.[10] One example of this was a piece of legislation offered by a state senator who chaired a committee with jurisdiction over electoral matters and who referred to his bill as "the 2000 Presidential Election Debacle Reform Bill of 2001."[11]

In the U.S. House of Representatives and in the Senate, approximately twenty pieces of legislation were presented, five of which were proposed before the new Congress began in January, and fifteen of which would be offered by June of that year. In the same period an estimated fifteen hundred bills were introduced in state legislatures. Broadly speaking, there were two types of bills, one type that had an omnibus flavor and sought to establish a commission to address a wide variety of perceived problems, and another type that meant to address the specific problems associated with elections. Lawmakers were also concerned about the scope of reform legislation, and whether such legislation should tackle a wide variety of structural problems (such as whether or not there should be a voting holiday, or whether a relatively narrow standard should be constructed that would not infringe on the constitutional right of the states to administer elections). Finally, there was the question of whether or not election reform should deal with problems essentially related to race and the question of voter suppression, problems that included changed voting stations, missing ballot boxes, voter intimidation tactics by police, and technical issues such as the fact that older and often malfunctioning voting machines were frequently placed in predominantly Black districts.

By mid-October of 2002 Congress had passed the Help America Vote Act (HAVA), a law mandating federal standards in federal elections to be administered by state and local election officials. Passed in the House 357–48 and in the Senate 92–2, it provided $3.9 billion in federal funds that would be used by the states to upgrade their elections systems, replace punch-card balloting and lever voting machines with newer electronic equipment, provide training for poll workers (including college students), develop accurate voter rolls, provide fair access to polling stations for the disabled, and establish a commission to monitor election standards.

Regarded as "the first Civil Rights Act of the twenty-first century" by its chief Senate sponsor, Christopher Dodd (D-CT), it contained identification requirements that were objected to by the two New York Senators, Charles Schumer and Hilary Clinton, who voted against the bill on the grounds that it would prove onerous to the poor and to immigrants. Despite opposition, the bill was signed into law two weeks later by President Bush amid differing interpretations of the impact of its identification provisions. The minority community was split in its support of the bill. The Congressional Black Caucus (CBC) and the NAACP supported it, with Rep. Eddie Bernice Johnson (D-TX) saying, in effect, that the bill was a good initial effort, while other organizations such as the National

Council of La Raza, a major Hispanic organization, and the American Civil Liberties Union, along with half of the House Latino delegation (seven for, six against), opposed the bill.

Election Reform Proposals

The Initial Concern: Florida Reform

The manner in which the presidential election of 2000 was decided and, specifically, the role of Florida in that process, including the role of Florida's Governor Jeb Bush, the brother of presidential candidate George Bush, created considerable sensitivity in Florida with respect to its election processes. Governor Jeb Bush thus moved quickly to establish a bipartisan twenty-one-member task force to consider changes to the election process, including its voting procedures, standards, and technology.

Another important pressure on Florida was the fact that the CBC in the U.S. House of Representatives spoke out forcefully on the issue. In a hearing sponsored by the House Democratic Caucus, Rep. Carrie Meek from Miami referred in her remarks to the "Florida election debacle." She said that "African American voters in Florida feel cheated. They want to express their outrage and exasperation over the flaws in the system."[12] Her approach was to offer a bill to address the fact that so many eligible voters had arrived at the polls only to find their names had been inadvertently stricken from the rolls by a private firm that had been contracted by the state to purge only the names of felons and dead persons from the rolls. Other members of the CBC, however, according to the *Miami Herald,* lamented that these election abuses, although receiving widespread attention in Florida, "had not penetrated the top rung of issues in Washington."[13]

The Florida legislature did address election reform, and in two months of deliberations its committees developed a report containing seventy-eight pages of recommendations that were then taken up. The legislation proceeding from this report, known as the Election Reform Act, passed in the Florida House 120–0 and in the Senate 39–1. The act was quickly signed into law by Governor Bush and presented to the nation as a model for other states.

There was some reluctance on the part of the Florida Conference of Black State Legislators to wholeheartedly adopt the legislation because of the act's narrow focus on the voting process. The group decided, however, to "give a little, get a little," in a spirit that suggested they would continue to perfect the law. Chair of the conference, Rep. Frederica Wilson from Miami, said that the legislation was good "in some ways," such as in requiring poll locations across the state to use the same kind of equipment and in promoting voter education among youths.

Another important initiative was the restoration to felons of their right to vote, and in December of 2000 the Brennan Center for Justice in New York City initiated a suit to do this. Then in March, under the auspices of the Florida Equal Voting Rights Project, which encompassed a broad coalition of groups, a suit was filed with the lesser objective of invoking the responsibility of the state to assist individuals in completing the administrative process of applying for clemency from the Florida Governor's office. Filed in Leon County Circuit Court, this suit claimed that the Florida Department of Corrections had a responsibility to assist offenders in filing the necessary paperwork for seeking clemency, and that the department should meet this responsibility by issuing accurate forms, assisting with the completion of those forms, and then processing them for the governor's office.

In June of 2001, one week after recommendations were issued by the U.S. Commission on Civil Rights requesting that Florida consider automatic restoration of the voting rights of convicted felons, Governor Jeb Bush announced new administrative guidelines that would help felons obtain their voting rights more quickly. These reforms reduced the clemency application form from twelve to four pages, allowed some felons convicted of nonviolent charges to forgo lengthy hearings altogether, eliminated the requirement that felons with $1,000 or more in unpaid court fines or at least three felony convictions go before a hearing board, and made other minor administrative changes. Simultaneously, state officials admitted that 66,204 ex-offenders from 1998 to 2000 should have been considered for the restoration of their voting rights, but that 14,208 were not sent to the officials processing clemency requests, and that a backlog existed on 12,296 others.

U.S. Commission on Civil Rights Recommendations

Previously I referred to the hearings by the U.S. Commission on Civil Rights with respect to conditions in Florida that led ostensibly to the disenfranchisement of many people. The recommendations of the commission, reached after several such meetings in 2001, may provide a tool with which to measure whether election reform has resolved many of the problems that occurred during or subsequent to the 2000 election. It is clear from the hearings that inasmuch as the majority of the proposals for election reform concerned the process of voting, those issues that related to poll administration on election day, such as the process of voting and of counting the vote, were central. In contrast, despite hearings by the NAACP and the U.S. Civil Rights Commission, few such proposals were directed to the issue, in the words of the commission, of "no count." This concept was included in a statement of the commission released between February and June of 2001 that summarized a status report of the investigation it had initiated of Florida voting practices. The statement said,

> Voter disenfranchisement appears to be at the heart of the issue. It is not a question of a recount or even an accurate count, but more pointedly the issue is those whose exclusion from the right to vote amounted to a "No count."

The status report pointed to what it called "an array" of problems that were responsible for the no count of Black ballots:

- Key officials anticipated before election day that there would be an increase in levels of voter turnout, based on new voter registration figures, but did not ensure that the precincts in all communities received adequate resources to meet their needs
- At least one unauthorized law enforcement checkpoint was set up on election day, resulting in complaints that were investigated by the Florida Highway Patrol and the Florida Attorney General's Office
- Non-felons were removed from voter registration rolls because of unreliable information collected in connection with sweeping, state-sponsored felon purge policies
- College students and others submitted voter registration applications in a timely manner to the persons and agencies responsible for transmitting those applications to the proper officials, but in many instances the applications were not processed as provided for under the National Voter Registration Act ("motor voter law")

- Many Jewish and elderly voters received defective and compli-
  cated ballots that may have produced over-votes and under-
  votes
- Some polling places were closed early and some polling places
  were moved without notice
- Old and defective election equipment was found in poor precincts
- Many Haitian Americans and Puerto Rican voters were not provided language assistance when it was required and requested
- Persons with disabilities faced accessibility difficulties at certain
  polling sites
- Too few poll workers were adequately trained and too few funds
  were committed to voter education activities

The issue raised here is whether or not the final legislative solution to
election reform in response to the problems in Florida and elsewhere in
2000 took into consideration these "no count" issues, many of which
uniquely affected Blacks and resulted in suppressing the right of Blacks
to vote. Since either the intentional or unintentional result of suppressing
the right of Blacks to vote is a violation of the Voting Rights Act,
whether or not the act came into play in the amelioration of this problem
is an important question.

The Help America Vote Act (HAVA)

High Points of the Act

A summary of the Help America Vote Act by the Department of Justice
defines the law as having provided for three central functions.

Creating a new federal agency to serve as a clearinghouse for
election administration information

Providing funds to states to improve election administration and
replace outdated voting systems

Creating minimum standards for states to follow in several key
areas of election administration

Title II, Subtitle A of the law sets up a new Election Assistance
Commission, a body that administers a Standards Board to determine

election system standards and provide certification for state systems; a Board of Advisors to advise which standards might be useful and to correct significant problems; and a Technical Guidelines Development Committee. The composition of the Standards Board consists of 110 individuals, half of whom are state officials with chief responsibility for election administration, with local election officials to make up the other half of the board, whereas the Board of Advisors consists of 37 appointees. The latter advises the Standards Board on relevant issues in the process of voting that require the establishment of uniform procedures. The Technical Guidelines Development Committee is charged with reducing the advice of the Board of Advisors to a useful form for the implementation of such changes in the state voter systems.

Title II, Subtitle B, in many ways, is the heart of a new bureaucracy in that it authorizes assistance to states for the voluntary testing, certification, decertification, and recertification of voting system hardware and software provided by accredited laboratories. The National Institute of Standards and Technology, a preexisting government agency, is responsible for the ongoing monitoring of the laboratories that provide the hardware and software.

Title II, Subtitle C makes provision for public studies on various aspects of election administration. This includes

- election technology
- ballot design
- methods of conducting voter registration
- methods of conducting provisional voting
- accessibility to polling places by various groups challenged by disabilities
- voter fraud and deterring voter intimidation
- methods of recruiting and training poll workers
- voter education
- voting times, dates, and locations

These and other matters, such as the processing of absentee ballots, will be addressed later in this section. It is important to realize that the commission was not fully active in time for the election of 2004, and that thirty-one states applied for waivers of the implementation of the law until the 2006 election cycle. Moreover, the original schedule of funding was set to disseminate $1.4 million for FY02–03, $1 million for FY03–

04, and $600,000 for FY04–05, but funding was not approved until 2003, delaying full implementation of the law.

It is relatively obvious that the heavy emphasis in this legislation on the technical matters involved in balloting and poll management for voters does relatively little to deter other aspects of the intentional suppression of votes. Indeed, the administration of the National Voter Registration Act was transferred to the Election Assistance Commission, a move which suggests that the establishment of HAVA was not intended to venture far into the prerogatives of states and, therefore, to touch upon constitutional questions of the relative authority of states versus the federal government, or to make new laws and rights as such.

The latter issue is important because of the litigious environment created by the 2000 election which led to hopes that HAVA would, in fact, establish new rights for voters, implicit in the availability of provisional ballots (contained in the language of the act that addresses how to handle such issues as absentee ballots), the posting of information for voters, and the handling of computerized registration lists. The language in the act concerning provisional ballots is as follows:

> If an individual declares that such individual is a registered voter in the jurisdiction in which the individual desires to vote and that the individual is eligible to vote in an election for Federal office, but the name of the individual does not appear on the official list of eligible voters for the polling place or an election official asserts that the individual is not eligible to vote, such individual shall be permitted to cast a provisional ballot.[14]

Although there are further refinements to the provision, it nevertheless appears to establish a new right for voters.

Interpreting HAVA

In the interpretation of HAVA, there have been several conflicting decisions with respect to its authority and impact. For example, in Michigan the Democratic party and the NAACP challenged Republican Secretary of State Terri Lynn Land and Bureau of Elections Director Chris Thomas to permit individuals to execute provisional ballots in voting precincts other than those to which they had been assigned, if those individuals were duly registered to vote. Five days later, a federal judge ruled that

Michigan citizens who voted in the wrong district, as long as that district was located in the right city or township, must have their votes, although cast by provisional ballot, counted. The Michigan attorney general appealed this decision to the Sixth Circuit Court of Appeals, which decided that, according to Michigan law, HAVA required voters to vote only in their right political jurisdiction. The court then issued a stay of the previous order, an action that was precisely the same as an Ohio court's issuance of the previous day.

More importantly, the original Michigan decision (*Bay County Democratic Party and Michigan Democratic Party v. Terri Lynn Land, Michigan Secretary of State, and Christopher M. Thomas*) found that HAVA created privately enforceable rights for individuals by plainly stating, when it instructed election officials to post information on elections, that "the right of an individual to cast a provisional ballot" should be included. The court concluded, "There can be little question . . . that the language quoted above was intended to benefit voters (individuals) who are turned away from the polls." It is this type of unmistakable rights-focused language that the Supreme Court has used to establish a private right of action in other contexts.

In Florida, however, state election officials limited the extent of the issuance of provisional ballots to the precinct in which the voter was eligible to vote. Democratic challengers in Florida also felt that if a voter moved from a precinct but was still a resident of the area and was otherwise eligible to vote, that the voter should have a right to a provisional ballot. On this reasoning, they sued election official Glenda Hood in *Florida Democratic Party v. Glenda Hood, Florida Secretary of State.* This case is unique in that the U.S. Department of Justice, which was charged with the enforcement of HAVA, issued an amicus curiae in support of Ms. Hood's motion to dismiss the charges.

The argument of the Justice Department was that HAVA did not federalize the process of elections, but only established minimum standards in support of the states as the ultimate authority on the implementation of their voting systems, noting that conferee Democratic Senator Christopher Dodd said, "Nothing in HAVA establishes a federal definition of when a voter is registered or how a vote is counted." The Justice Department brief argued that Title III of HAVA looked to the states to define the terms of the eligibility of voters and to administer the counting of provisional ballots.

The Justice Department further argued that HAVA does not invite private action or suits against the government by private parties for its enforcement, as does the Voting Rights Act, and neither does it create a new set of rights, as does the Voting Rights Act. The Justice Department's view was that the focus of HAVA was not on the right of an individual but on the system by which elections were to be administered in a given state. After a review of the conditional language of Title III that carefully preserved the right of a state to be the authoritative factor in the administration of the provisional ballot, the Justice Department brief concluded,

> It is clear that Section 302, like the other provisions of Title III, focuses on the duties and obligations of state and local election officials in administering federal elections. While making provisional balloting easier may benefit individual voters, that alone is insufficient to create an individual right. As a result, Section 302 simply does not unambiguously confer individual rights.[15]

This latter assertion was surprising, inasmuch as it contradicted a widespread impression that HAVA established the right of voters to have access to a provisional ballot. What this suggests is that the enforceable rights that apply to individuals are located not in HAVA, but in the Voting Rights Act and the National Voter Registration Act. I will comment upon sections of these laws in a discussion of the problem of intentional voter suppression, a form of racial discrimination prohibited by these laws.

Electoral Reform and the Black Community

The Legal Challenge to Florida Disenfranchisement

The first demands for election reform following the 2000 presidential election were made by Black groups who felt violated by the process of disenfranchisement, as reflected in the sentiment of Florida State Rep. Anthony Hill who said, "We have been disrespected as a group."[16] In response to this feeling, one of the first suits was launched on December 5, 2000, by U.S. Rep. Corrine Brown (D-FL) against the election board of Duval County, where twenty-eight thousand ballots had been invalidated by an all-white Republican canvassing board. An estimated 42 percent of these votes were assumed to have been cast for Al Gore, owing largely to Duval County's core city, Jacksonville, which is 80 percent Black. This suit was summarily thrown out on December 14 when the Supreme Court halted the count.

On January 10, 2001, another suit was filed by the NAACP Conference and five other civil rights organizations against Florida Secretary of State Katherine Harris on the behalf of the NAACP and twenty-one Black voters. The complaint alleged that the state had violated the constitutional and statutory rights of Black voters by stationing inferior voting machines in Black voting precincts, poorly managing and illegally purging voter registration lists, and placing the names of Black voters on a list of inactive voters, which prevented those Black voters from casting ballots. These practices contributed to the fact that Blacks were "denied the opportunity to vote, denied assistance they were entitled to, or were exposed to a significantly higher risk that their votes would not be counted in the official results for the presidential election."

By September of 2002 a settlement was reached in this case which found the state of Florida agreeing to engage in the following provisions of election reform, many of which were contained in the state's own legislation and in HAVA, which was then pending in the U.S. Congress.

- **The Central Voter Database:** Eligible voters who were removed from the voter rolls in error will be identified and restored to the lists. New procedures will be implemented that will [correct the misidentification of some voters as having felony records].
- **Poll-worker training:** [The preparation of] a poll-worker manual that provides examples of election administration procedures as required by the new election laws.
- **Alternative Voting Procedures:** [Counties would be encouraged to provide] provisional ballots and voting by affirmation and to [provide information to voters on why their vote was not counted].
- **Voter Registration:** The State will create a position for a National Voter Registration Act Coordinator within the Division of Elections [to assist] the Secretary of State [in administering state election laws].[17]

These measures of redress appear similar to HAVA insofar as they are also focused on the accuracy of registration and voter rolls, the voting process itself, and poll station management. The settlement did not incorporate other allegations of civil rights groups that related to denial of the right to vote. Thus, the issue here is whether the settlement addressed intentional racial discrimination through administrative procedures of the voting process, rather than or in addition to effective measures that would trigger enforcement of the Voting Rights Act, which had been intended to protect the rights of Black voters and to establish penalties for the violation of those rights.

Enforcing the Right to Vote

The question of whether or not these proposals, pursuant to the settlement of the Lawyers Committee lawsuit, and the provisions of HAVA are both adequate to address the many violations of the right to vote experienced by Blacks in Florida and around the nation, must take into consideration what occurred and the remedy proposed.

Problem Experienced	Affected Aspect of the Voter System
sent an absentee ballot but it was never received; absentee voter applications rejected	electoral system absentee voter list management by election officials
rejection of language assistance	behavior of polling station officials
ballot boxes not picked up, included in the count	behavior of polling station officials
online voter registration list not transferred to regular voter rolls	electoral system voter list management by election officials
lack of proper notice of polling stations	electoral system polling station selection by election officials
ballots from Black neighborhoods cast wrongly	voter error/election officials tabulation error/election equipment malfunction
purging of Black voters from lists	electoral system management of voter list
requirement of more than one form of voter identification	election system management of voter ID/behavior of polling station officials
police roadblocks established in Black neighborhoods	intervention of nonelectoral system department of government into election affairs

| voters not given more than one ballot | election system management/ behavior of polling station officials |
| malfunction of voting machines not corrected | election system management |

It is clear from the above that the difficulties Blacks experienced in attempting to vote were caused not by the mechanical aspects of voting but by human interference with their attempt to cast their ballot. While a considerable amount of this problem has been attributed to voter error and lack of education, most of the problems cited stemmed from maladministration of the election system by those officials responsible for purging voter lists, establishing polling stations, notifying specific communities about changes in polling stations, and providing polling station officials with proper information on voting procedures. Other problems were located at the polling stations themselves where the proper management of voting procedures on a fair and unbiased basis, and in accordance with the law, often did not occur. Here, officials who closed down polling stations with voters in line, who prevented voters from voting without first properly checking identification or voter registration status, and who did not help elderly voters or extend language assistance contributed enormously to the voting barriers faced by Blacks which may or may not have been because of race, but all the same resulted in serious civil rights violations.

My conclusion then is that the election reforms thus achieved weigh heavily on the side of the mechanical aspects of voting systems, including the nature of the ballot and the modernization of voting machines. But the reforms do not adequately deal with gross violations of the civil rights of Blacks attempting to exercise their right to vote. The issue in so many cases appears to be human error or outright racial prejudice because polling station officials have been allowed to exercise considerable discretion in the management of their stations. We do not know the extent to which such discriminatory behavior by local polling station managers and officials stems from tradition, inference, or specific instructions given to them by authorities to suppress the Black vote. *In any case, the preponderant involvement of human conduct in the administration of the right to vote and the possible link of these individuals to a system of competitive politics places a value on strongly exercising the sanctions in the Voting Rights Act and the National Voter Registration Act for wrongful actions against those who are subsequently harmed.*

Reviewing Sanctions

Since the discriminatory behavior discussed above is punishable under the Voting Rights Act or the National Voter Registration Act, a review of these two acts is in order to determine their adequacy to protect the voting rights of Blacks and others. This is especially warranted where the Justice Department is concerned, considering its critical role in removing such barriers to voting and its failure at times to act. Our review of both acts is outlined under five headings.

A. **Developing a better method of invoking the intervention of the Justice Department,** with its considerable powers, to prevent voting irregularities from being experienced by African Americans or others while the process of voting is occurring. Under the Voting Rights Act, the Justice Department has the ability to intervene. Title 42, Chapter 20, Subchapter I, Section 1971(c) states:

> Whenever any person has engaged or there are reasonable grounds to believe that any person is about to engage in any act or practice which would deprive any other person of any right or privilege secured by subsection (a) or (b) of this section, the Attorney General may institute for the United States, or in the name of the United States, a civil action or other proper proceeding for preventive relief, including an application for a permanent or temporary injunction, restraining order, or other order. If in any such proceeding literacy is a relevant fact there shall be a rebuttable presumption that any person who has not been adjudged an incompetent and who has completed the sixth grade in a public school in, or a private school accredited by, any State or territory, the District of Columbia, or the Commonwealth of Puerto Rico . . . possesses sufficient literacy, comprehension, and intelligence to vote in any election.

B. **How or whether the Voting Rights Act should be amended to provide for automatically sending federal election observers to states that are already under Section 5 monitoring.** On election day of November 7, 2000, the voting rights section of the Justice Department dispatched 314 election observers around the country to monitor the voting process. No such federal observers were sent to Florida because the procedure used by the Justice Department requires that a request for federal observers be made by the relevant state authority. Since no such request was made by Florida state officials, no observers were sent, even though Florida is and was a covered state under the Voting Rights Act. It would appear that observers should be sent to such a state to monitor voting procedures even without a request from state officials.

C. **Since so many Blacks were disenfranchised through the lack of their presence, or the reported lack of their presence on voter rolls, a strong culpability in the denial of Blacks to vote rests with state election officials and others for their maladministration of voter lists.** The question here is how might state officials be prevented from excluding qualified voters from the rolls in contravention of federal law. Part (a)(2) of the U.S. Code cited above states:

> No person acting under color of law shall—
>
> (A) in determining whether any individual is qualified under State law or laws to vote in any election, apply any standard, practice, or procedure different from the standards, practices, or procedures applied under such law or laws to other individuals within the same county, parish, or similar political subdivision who have been found by State officials to be qualified to vote;
>
> (B) deny the right of any individual to vote in any election because of an error or omission on any record or paper relating to any application, registration, or other act requisite to voting, if such error or omission is not material in determining whether such individual is qualified under State law to vote in such election.

Item (c)(2) of Section 1973gg-6 of Title 42 permits the purging of voter rolls, but item (d) also says:

> A State shall not remove the name of a registrant from the official list of eligible voters in elections for Federal office on the ground that the registrant has changed residence unless the registrant (A) confirms in writing that the registrant has changed residence to a place outside the registrar's jurisdiction in which the registrant is registered; or (B)(i) has failed to respond to a notice described in paragraph (2); and (ii) has not voted or appeared to vote (and, if necessary, correct the registrar's record of the registrant's address) in an election during the period beginning on the date of the notice and ending on the day after the date of the second general election for Federal office that occurs after the date of the notice.

The law also says in Section 1973gg-6, item (e)(2)(A):

> A registrant who has moved from an address in the area covered by
> one polling place to an address in an area covered by a second poll-
> ing place within the same registrar's jurisdiction and the same con-
> gressional district and who has failed to notify the registrar of the
> change of address prior to the date of an election, at the option of
> the registrant: (i) shall be permitted to correct the voting records and
> vote at the registrant's former polling place, upon oral or written
> affirmation by the registrant of the new address before an election
> official at that polling place.

There is ample authority in the law allowing for the right of individuals who are registered and who have recently voted in federal elections to vote at an alternate site within the jurisdiction of the district
where they live, upon oral or written confirmation of their address. It is
evident that in many cases election officials did not follow the law in the
management of polling stations in according to Blacks who were duly
registered the right to vote.

D. **One-third of Black males in the state of Florida are ineligible to
vote due to their status as having been tried and convicted of felony of-
fenses.** Florida Secretary of State Katherine Harris had one hundred sev-
enty-three thousand names purged from voter rolls in the spring of 2000
in order to eliminate the names of convicted felons from those rolls.
However, as indicated above, the information used in identifying the
names of felons on the voter rolls was often inaccurate, and thus, as
many as eight thousand names were incorrectly eliminated from the
rolls, a number far exceeding the fewer than five hundred felons who
were allowed to vote. Title 42, Section 1973gg-6, item (g), "Conviction
in Federal court," indicates that the responsibility for keeping accurate
information on felony convictions rests with the United States attorney
and the chief election officials in a given state:

> (1) On the conviction of a person of a felony in a district court of
> the United States, the United States attorney shall give written notice
> of the conviction to the chief State election official designated under
> section 1973gg-8 of this title of the State of the person's residence.

The U.S. attorney has responsibility for providing other such information as requested by the chief election official of a state, but it is the

state official who has final responsibility to pass on accurate information on the felony status of voters to local election officials as indicated by Paragraph (5) of the same item:

> The chief State election official shall notify the voter registration officials of the local jurisdiction in which an offender resides of the information received under this subsection.

There are two problems here, the first of which is that a large proportion of the Black male population of Florida and other states is unable to vote because of felony conviction status. Double punishment of individuals who have paid their debt to society is immoral, and it prevents the full impact of the Black vote in American elections. The second problem is that the inaccurate information given to local voting officials by the secretary of state in Florida invites a review of the mechanism by which such information is transmitted and suggests that a review of state electoral records should be held by federal authorities to correct any deficiencies in this respect.

E. **There does not appear to have been political equity in the purging of the Florida voter rolls because the contract for doing so was awarded to a firm that had ties to the Republican party.** It would appear that in order for an electoral system to be fair and to have the appearance of fairness, it must be administered in a way that does not give unfair advantage to one party or one sociological group. As a result of what occurred in the 2000 elections, many state election administrators are now aware of the need to operate electoral systems with nonpartisan personnel or in a bipartisan or multiparty fashion. In any case, states should take into consideration measures to depoliticize the electoral system, to include minorities in the system's administration, and to contract for the maintenance of local electoral systems in a nonpartisan way. Since many of the practices that cause the disenfranchisement of Blacks and others are of human origin, the racial integration of electoral systems may provide an important deterrent to such practices.

Campaign Finance Reform

For a considerable period, Black legislators voted with their white counterparts on the issue of limiting the role of so-called soft money in elections. According to Public Law 107-155, soft money is direct, unregulated cash contributions to a national party by corporations, unions, and wealthy individuals, while hard money is direct cash contributions to a candidate, with a limit of $1,000 per contributor per election.

The Senate passed its version of the McCain-Feingold Bill on April 2, 2001, and the House followed in January 2002. The House version of the bill was known as Shays-Meehan, and it was opposed by Rep. Bob Ney (R-OH), representing the House Republican leadership, who felt that campaign finance was a form of freedom of speech and that Shays-Meehan would be an unconstitutional fetter on the First Amendment. The McCain-Feingold/Shays-Meehan compromise was eventually passed, signed into law on March 27, 2002, by President George Bush, and found constitutional by the Supreme Court on December 10, 2003.[18]

The McCain-Feingold Bill, however, saw a different attitude emerge among some Black legislators because of their perception that a limitation on soft money could further tilt the financial imbalance between their constituents in the Black community and the constituents of wealthier districts. Several members of the CBC including Reps. Albert Wynn (D-MD), Bill Jefferson (D-LA), and Bennie Thompson (D-MS) supported the Ney bill and opposed McCain-Feingold while others, such as Rep. Harold Ford Jr. (D-TN) and Rep. Stephanie Tubbs Jones (D-OH), did not.

According to Professor of Law Spencer Overton, Federal Election Commission records show that whereas the average member of the House raises $661,000 in an election cycle, Black members of Congress raise an average of only $379,000. The implications of this are twofold. First, Black members of Congress are limited in the amount of money they can spend to help other campaigns, support their own legislation, bring lawsuits, promote policy advocacy activities, and support constituent expenditures. Second, Black members of Congress are less able to finance their own campaigns at the level often necessary to fend off challengers. A ban on soft money also limits the ability of the Black community to assist in voter registration and get-out-the-vote activities.

The CBC suffered a loss of two of its members in the election of 2002 when Reps. Earl Hilliard (D-AL) and Cynthia McKinney (D-GA) were defeated by challengers who had accepted large direct contributions from individual donors. The point made by Professor Overton is that the low-income structure of Black districts prevents their congressional representatives from raising sufficient funds to compete with well-funded challengers who can rely on hard money donations. Support for this position is found in a report by the Fannie Lou Hamer Project and the William C. Velasquez Institute, which found in a zip code analysis of political donor race and ethnicity that, not unexpectedly, individuals in wealthy white neighborhoods contribute 90 percent of the funds used by parties and their candidates in presidential primary elections. This study, while supporting public funding for federal elections, recognized that "any reform of the presidential public finance system should strive to lessen the racial and ethnic inequities inherent in private financing of campaigns."[19]

The largest problem, however, is that the Black infrastructure of organizations that engage in voter registration and turnout activities, which includes the NAACP, depends on such contributions. In fact, in the 2000 election cycle, the NAACP received a donation of $7 million to use in such activities, and with this money it established the National Voter Institute, some of whose issue ads were later opposed by the Bush campaign. Other organizations such as the National Coalition on Black Civic Participation, the Rainbow/PUSH Coalition, and Black churches across the nation draw their funding for such activities from the same source.

Thus McCain-Feingold raises the economic issue of the comparative ability of Black legislators—or various other similarly situated groups—to engage in the political process in the same way as whites when the economic structure of their community does not allow it. Whether Blacks should be subject to a law that restricts their participation in the electoral process is an open question, and a question that may fall under the jurisdiction of Section 2 of the Voting Rights Act as a matter of creating Black vote dilution, since unequal funding impinges on the ability of Blacks to vote. Here it is important to recall that in our expansive concept of the act of voting, the act involves more than merely casting a ballot. It involves equally the myriad actions and organizational participants that help to facilitate that act.

This will perhaps become even clearer when it is understood that the McCain-Feingold limit on soft money promoted the creation of a new entity, an organization based on Paragraph 527 of the code. A Paragraph 527 organization is permitted to raise and spend unlimited sums, provided that it operates as a private organization and is not directly associated with a political party or candidate. These new organizations, known as 527s, have been oriented toward the Democratic party candidates and have drawn the opprobrium of the Republican party, which would have them regulated as political organizations under the law. And although the Federal Election Commission has attempted to address the issue, at this writing it has failed to reach any decision, though the matter will most surely be revisited by either the commission or a Republican-controlled Congress in the future.

There have been widespread complaints by organizations that have traditionally been associated with the Black infrastructure, and which are engaged in voter registration and turnout, that funding for their operations has suffered because they have been by-passed by an estimated $200 million that has gone to the 527s.[20] The donors of these funds—labor unions, wealthy financiers such as George Soros, corporate interests, and well-known entertainers—have created a network of organizations, all aligned under the umbrella of America Coming Together, a 527 run by Steve Rosenthal, former political director of the AFL-CIO. The techniques employed by this and similar organizations, such as hiring canvassers to register thousands of new Black voters, have had impressive results, but have also largely devalued the prominence of the Black get-out-the-vote infrastructure, and have substantially shifted the focus of mobilizing influence within the leadership of the Black community.[21] This change could, like the legal status of the 527s, become a subject for further examination and attention.

Conclusion

Election reform, then, came to center largely on the integrity of the balloting process, with proposals to replace paper balloting with electronic voting machines. In one sense this was the result of focusing, in a politically competitive environment, on the least controversial aspects of the problem.

Perhaps this is also why the Help America Vote Act did not successfully address the issue of intentional Black voter disenfranchisement. This issue is critical because, as I indicated at the outset, one political party or another will attempt to reduce the number of Black voters in order to obtain a clear electoral advantage when an election is particularly competitive, and, thus, the racial factor is highly material in some contests as additional fuel to the partisan competition.

Addressing this issue depends upon effective enforcement of existing voting rights laws, but that enforcement is subject to the vagaries of politics, even when the U.S. Attorney General is part of an administration that is favorable to the Black community. Under these circumstances, the mere acquisition of a constitutional right to vote will help, but it will not automatically guarantee the enforcement of existing voting laws. I consider this further in chapter 8.

African American organizations now enter a new era of modern electronic political participation in which voter-verified paper ballots matter, training for the error-free processing of votes is essential, the protection of the right to vote is being overseen by legal organizations, and the Black community is generally on guard with respect to the purging of voter rolls and stands ready to demand that poll station management allows fair access to the polls.

One consequence of this concern with the mechanical aspects of the voter process is that with respect to the commitment of financial and other resources, far less than adequate attention will be paid to the reformulation of election law and rights, so as to promote the development of measures to ensure the enforcement of the law, to provide for the proper training of election officials in the fair administration of voter procedures, and to educate minority and poor voters. The following recommendations are designed to correct this deficit.

- Eliminate or greatly reduce prohibitions on voting by convicted felons
- Provide for a review of state records by federal officials to ascertain a correct list of individuals with felony convictions
- Amend Title 42 to provide a more effective trigger for action by the Justice Department
- Provide for stronger enforcement of existing provisions of the Voting Rights Act and National Voter Registration Act to protect voters against egregious violations of procedures by state and local officials that result in the denial of their right to vote. Procedural violations include:
  the intimidation of voters by police officials on election day
  the purging of voters from lists
  the refusal to allow duly registered voters to vote at places other than their assigned district stations
- Offer expanded programs to provide language training for poll-

ing station workers that will allow them to assist voters on election day

- More vigorously commit resources to contact points and media outlets in minority and poor communities in order to communicate changes in polling stations, election procedure, and voter registration status to potential voters
- Automatically deploy federal election observers in states and counties covered under Section 5 of the Voting Rights Act
- Provide for multiple forms of notice (mail, e-mail, fax, phone) to individuals with respect to problems involving their voting status
- More securely control ballot boxes, perhaps with an immediate alert system if boxes have not been picked up or counted and their status publicly posted
- Study new voting systems and their potential problems of equity for poor and minority communities
- Vigorously train election officials in polling station management, public relations, and election law
- Fund grassroots programs in communities on election law and procedure with the objective of educating minority voters on their voting rights and the procedures of voting
- Determine the impact of macro-system issues on Black voting and registration
- Establish requirements for an established matching fund that will:
  require the participation of minorities from both parties in poll station training
  give priority to communities in poor neighborhoods for new equipment
  contract with minority firms to participate in developing election processes
- See that electoral commissions contain members representing those communities where voting irregularities occur

6

Leverage Politics and the 2004 Primary Election Scenario: The Sharpton and Moseley Braun Campaigns

The Sharpton Attempt at Leverage Politics

In *Black Presidential Politics in America* I argued that the character of Black politics in general amounted to "Leverage Politics," and I sought to illustrate the manner in which this theory worked in presidential elections.[1] It is possible to assert that to the extent that Black candidates for president seek to represent the distinct interests of the Black community primarily, they must utilize leverage politics. The vehicle for leveraging the Black vote in the 1984 and 1988 elections was the campaign of the Reverend Jesse L. Jackson Sr. He was successful in using the status given a presidential candidate to present issues of importance to the Black community and to focus the media on important problems beyond the immediacy of his campaign. Most importantly, as a candidate he was successful in attracting the balance of the Black vote in the primary elections, then using the legitimacy he had won to bargain for issues, party positions, and campaign resources. This model, which I refer to as the "Jackson model," is heavily dependent upon the support given to it by the majority of Blacks.

Al Sharpton was originally from Queens, New York, and was raised in a somewhat comfortable atmosphere, quickly proving that he was an unusual child who could express himself verbally at an early age. This led him to become a child preacher and an ordained Baptist minister by the age of ten, and his novelty attracted the attention of prominent entertainers such as James Brown, one of whose backup singers is Sharpton's former wife. Sharpton attended Brooklyn College and went on to pursue his religious career and to exercise his leadership skills as a participant in the civil rights movement.

At an early point in Sharpton's life, Rev. Jesse Jackson had been a mentor to him. It was said that Sharpton sought the counsel of Rev. Jackson in regard to how he might evolve as a leader in Jackson's style. Sharpton explained the method of Rev. Jackson's mentoring in this way: "Jesse was almost brutal. He'd tell me: 'The grammar was wrong, you're being a showoff. You need more substance.' "[2] In the same vein, it was also clear that Rev. Sharpton would follow the example set by Rev. Jackson in his bid for influence within the councils of the Democratic party, and there was much speculation that Sharpton initiated his presidential campaign because of his feeling that Rev. Jackson needed to be replaced as the most visible leader of the Black community.

In the 2004 election cycle, the campaign of the Reverend Al Sharpton for the Democratic nomination for president posed a unique challenge for Black politics and for American politics in general. For the major candidates, there was the understandable expectation that Sharpton could not win the nomination and that therefore his presence in the race was the politics of a "spoiler." A definition of this concept will depend upon Sharpton's specific impact on the primary elections.

Whites in general consider Sharpton controversial in terms of his history as a civil rights leader, the issues that he has confronted, and the manner in which he has confronted them.[3] He led numerous campaigns against police brutality in high-profile cases that included the retaliation by members of the Jewish community against Blacks in Crown Heights, Brooklyn, in 1991; the brutal killing of a Black youth in Howard Beach, New York; the killing of unarmed Guinean immigrant Amadou Diallo in a hail of forty-three bullets; and the police torture of Haitian immigrant Abner Louima. Sharpton is most well-known for a 1987 incident involving a young Black woman, Tawana Brawley, who alleged that she had been raped and abused by then Dutchess County prosecutor Steven Pagones, who eventually brought a successful $65,000 defamation suit against Sharpton, who had acted as an adviser to Ms. Brawley. Journalists raised this case repeatedly as indicating a flaw in his character when Sharpton began to move toward a presidential candidacy. Editorials in the *Wall Street Journal,* for example, excoriated the ties between Rev. Sharpton and Hilary Clinton, because these ties helped to legitimize

Sharpton, and the editors of the *Journal* felt that this expressed indifference "to [Sharpton's] history of racial rabble rousing and character assassination."[4] With this strong animus toward Rev. Sharpton, it was clear that his reach into the white community would be limited, and that he would have to essentially depend upon a Black political base for his campaign.

The Black community, however, saw Rev. Sharpton not as a rabble-rouser but as a courageous leader who would take up difficult issues and treat them aggressively—once even provoking a demonstration that stopped traffic across one of the largest bridges to Manhattan from Queens—and in a manner that made those issues unavoidable. Although Sharpton was supported by many of the top political figures and community leaders in New York City and the nation, he felt that racism was at work in the rejection of his candidacy. He made his campaign appeal in saying, "[I have] represented victims all of my life (and have not become rich doing it), but still my motives to run for public office are questioned. We still have to deal with the subtlety of racism and how it's projected in America."[5]

Rev. Sharpton did have political credentials from having previously run for elected office. He ran for Senate from the state of New York in 1992 and 1994 in the Democratic primary, and in the latter he won more than 178,231 votes, or 26 percent of the total, against popular incumbent Senator Daniel Patrick Moynihan. In 1997 he ran for mayor of the city of New York against Ruth Messinger and won 34 percent of the vote (131,848), nearly forcing Messinger into a runoff. Nevertheless, the media widely regarded him as being without political experience, a fact that hampered his credibility as a presidential candidate in much the same way as an assumed lack of political experience had hampered Rev. Jackson.

Given the record of Rev. Jesse Jackson, Blacks were challenged to consider the Sharpton campaign as the best vehicle for exercising their political leverage at a time when the popular Clinton era had come to an end. Even though the media dismissed his candidacy, Sharpton defended his attempt to attract white votes in the Iowa caucuses by expressing the view that "I've run in New York and gotten more white votes in my races than [Howard Dean] has gotten Black votes in Vermont. Why aren't we talking about that?"[6] This challenge provides a glimpse into the way in which the Sharpton campaign fits the model of the Jackson campaign.

To the extent that Sharpton's message caught on, there was concern among some Democratic leaders that he would pull the party to the left, with the fear that the ensuing conflict between the mainstream of the party and its progressive base would create a serious degree of dissension during the primary election season, and that this dissension would carry over into the general election in November 2004 and reduce potential Black turnout. For this and other reasons, the Sharpton campaign was received coolly by both the media and the leadership of the Democratic party. Opposition to Sharpton also extended to the Republican party as the popular moderate, Senator John McCain, urged Democrats to distance themselves and others from Sharpton and suggested that Democrats should repudiate Rev. Sharpton as rap singer Sister Souljah had been repudiated in 1992 by then presidential candidate Clinton at the annual policy conference of Rev. Jackson's National Rainbow Coalition.

The Jackson Model

Candidate Motivation

The nature of a Black presidential candidacy cannot be understood using the same terms as those used to understand the candidacy of someone who represents a majority constituency. The Jackson campaign had to define its presence in the election for itself—on its own terms. Those terms included the role of the candidate not merely as another candidate, but as someone who had earned the right to represent the interests of an entire community in the electorate.

Rev. Al Sharpton decided that he would run for president in May of 2001 during a forty-day period of incarceration for having trespassed upon federal property at the U.S. naval station, Camp Garcia, while demonstrating with 187 others in support of Puerto Ricans who opposed the use of the Vieques military installation on Puerto Rico for U.S. military exercises. Having made the decision to run, he began a series of consultations with law professor Charles Ogletree of Harvard Law School, and eventually asked Professor Cornell West to chair his presidential exploratory committee. On August 20, 2001, Rev. Sharpton announced at the National Press Club that he would run for the Democratic nomination for president, and he then began to organize the necessary support. Throughout that year, and from 2002 to 2003, he assumed the mantle of the presumptive presidential candidate just as Rev. Jackson had assumed the same mantle in 1983.

When Rev. Sharpton initiated his exploratory committee on January 21, 2003, he was immediately faced with questions about his motivation for running, to which he answered that the major motivation for his campaign was his assessment that the Democratic party had "left its base" of Black voters and had moved precipitously to the right. He said to Thulani Davis of the *Village Voice* in February of 2003, "Many people that are running, in my judgment, are to the right of Republicans." Sharpton went on to declare that he was in a battle for the soul of the Democratic party, and that this meant running against the existing forces that had moved the party to the right. The following year, in his candidate announcement speech at the National Press Club on August 20, he said,

> We intend to challenge the drift of the Democratic party toward abandoning its base that has been loyal to it, but in some policies they have not shown a reciprocal loyalty . . . And without a challenge I don't think they will voluntarily deal with them.[7]

More recently, he reiterated this theme:

> The Democratic party has floated way from its roots. It is in many ways no longer the party of Roosevelt and Johnson and Adam Clayton Powell, a party that believes that Government ought to be there to protect people. We began mimicking the Republican party endeavors toward big business, toward trying to be right of center, and I think there needs to be a challenge to bring the party back to its roots.[8]

And in a theme that he later honed as a standard part of his stump speech:

> I think we've got to stop being imitators of the Republicans. The strategists have said, in effect, that we've got to be elephants in donkey jackets to win. I think that that is why we lost. Because people say, "If you're an imitator, I might as well go with the real thing. If you're going to be reactionary, I'm going with the real reactionary." And it makes those that want to be morally centered just stay home. I think if we stand up for workers' rights, stand up for a peace plan

worldwide, stand up for the constitutional rights of every American,
those people will come back and those people are the majority of
Americans.[9]

Then he asserted, as I mentioned above, that he was running in order to
make America a "more perfect union." This was a reference to his platform, which contained proposals to pass amendments to the U.S. Constitution dealing with the right to vote, the right to an equal high-quality
education, the right to health care, and equal rights for women.[10] The
initial expectation of Sharpton was that his campaign would be an insur-
gent vehicle for a challenge to the Democratic party and that it would
have the credibility to force the party to consider change. This suggests
that Sharpton would have had to achieve a performance that was at least
equal to the level of Jackson in 1984 or 1988 if his campaign were going
to meet his expectations.

The magnitude of the threat posed by a presumptive Sharpton
candidacy to the existing party's centrist orthodoxy was determined by
whether or not the Sharpton campaign could mobilize a substantial base
of voters, beginning with the formation of a substantial Black base in
the primary elections. However, Sharpton faced at least three formidable
impediments: a hostile reception by the media; a hostile reception by the
Democratic party, which wanted to play down intra-party conflict; and
a challenge from within the Black community by former Illinois Senator,
and most recently a U.S. ambassador, Carol Moseley Braun.

There were two main reasons why Rev. Al Sharpton mounted this
campaign, the first being to bring the Democratic party back to its traditions, and the second to mobilize the politically excluded to participate
in and therefore enhance their power inside the political system. To assess these reasons we must look briefly at the current posture of the
Democratic Leadership Council (DLC), the prospect of its message retaining its current preeminence within the party, and the challenges to
the Sharpton campaign that would keep it from effectively mobilizing
his constituency.

The DLC convention, which took place in July of 2003, featured
organizers such as Mark Penn who argued that, based on a national survey, "in order to take back the White House, Democrats must make inroads among suburban and middle-class families with children. This
growing segment of the population holds the bulk of swing voters—and
favors Republicans by an increasingly wide margin . . . The Democratic

party is at its weakest position since the dawn of the New Deal. Exciting the Democratic base alone will not bring enough voters into the Democratic fold."[11] This view is at fundamental odds with those on the left of the party who would argue that the way to be competitive is to expand the base rather than to fight for the same constituency as the Republican party's.

By highlighting the growth in number of married persons with children at home, Penn gives short shrift to the explosive increase of Blacks and especially Hispanics as a portion of the American economy as well as of the Democratic party. Blacks and Hispanics together constitute 20 percent of the American electorate and 33 to 40 percent of the base vote of the Democratic party (nearly 50 percent in some Southern states such as Louisiana, Mississippi, and South Carolina). Blacks, who have increased their voting percentage from 1996 to 2000 by 2.9 percent, constitute 12.9 million votes; Hispanics, who increased their percentage in the same period by 0.8 percent, constitute 5.9 million. Blacks have to be considered a vital part of the party's focus in any attempt to garner victory, especially in the South.[12]

The Necessary Support of a Community Base

The Jackson paradigm focused on the development of a political constituency that was germane to his campaign by cultivating both religious and labor organizations. These organizations contain large and accessible populations that are organized into institutions and have access to mobilizing resources such as money, manpower, and national networks of influence.

Sharpton had considerable problems in developing the credibility of his campaign since the Black community was divided on his candidacy for the same set of reasons that made him too controversial for prospective white voters. However, the most important complication to his campaign was the absence of a "movement" atmosphere which had been a catalyst in the Jackson campaigns. Table 6.1 shows the results of a June 2003 Gallup Poll that asked the question: "Who do you think is the most important Black leader in America today?" The precipitous drop in the perception of African American leadership in Colin Powell and Jackson to Al Sharpton clearly places Sharpton at a secondary level of leadership, evidence that Blacks, at a point previous to the primary campaign, might not support him politically as they had Jackson. In an-

Table 6.1   Most Important Black Leader in 2003 (as a percentage of 1,385 adults)

Leader	All	Non-Hispanic Whites	Blacks
Colin Powell	23	23	18
Jesse Jackson	18	19	17
Al Sharpton	3	2	4

Source: Gallup Poll, nationwide, taken June 12–15, 2003, for non-Hispanic whites and June 12–19 for Blacks. PollingReport.com, 4, www.pollingreport.com.

other poll, taken at the end of 2003 by the Joint Center for Political and Economic Studies, Blacks were asked for their preference in Black leaders, viewed either favorably or unfavorably. Rev. Jackson was viewed favorably by 83 percent (9 percent unfavorably), while only 37 percent viewed Rev. Sharpton favorably (29 percent unfavorably).

Yet Sharpton's position in the Black leadership structure did not prevent him from seeking to operationalize the Jackson model with a similar constituency. Declaring, "we got more with Jesse losing than with Clinton winning," in August of 2003 Rev. Sharpton spoke at the Progressive National Baptist Convention's annual 2.5-million-member conference in Charlotte, NC, and asked the conference of activist ministers to support his campaign. In response, Rev. T.J. Jemison, who had encouraged Rev. Jackson to run for president, did the same with Rev. Sharpton, leading a cheer of "Run, Sharpton, run." Thus, Rev. Sharpton had some of the same base support in the Black church as Rev. Jackson had had, but apparently Sharpton did not succeed in capitalizing on it as forcefully.

During his speech at the Progressive National Baptist Convention conference, Sharpton also admonished his listeners, saying, "History beckons for us to stand up at this time. There are many of us that are afraid to stand up . . . If you're scared, say you're scared—then sit down, shut up and let somebody else say it!"[13] He addressed the issues of homeland security and the war in Iraq, which were part of the legacy of the attack of September 11, 2001, and were then the context in which the election was occurring. Citing the history of the negative association of the Black community with domestic law enforcement, he alluded to the possibility that some Blacks could be intimidated to refrain from voting if they were afraid that they would be punished for siding with those who took a position against government programs such as the Patriot Act. Nevertheless, he asked for their support as a candidate who strongly opposed the war in Iraq and the Patriot Act. These positions were decidedly to the left of those espoused by Democratic party leaders, including the leading candidates in the race for the Democratic presidential nomination.

The Democratic party may have preferred the Braun candidacy, and it certainly did not want to entertain the notion of a severe conflict over its direction, either because the negative fallout of a public debate might give Republicans an advantage, or because the formula of rightward or centrist politics had been successful. Sharpton's view of why Democrats lost in the 2002 off-year elections was that authentic Democrats did not represent the party, and had not represented the interests of the party's core constituency in other elections.[14] Donna Brazile, former Al Gore campaign manager and a top African American official in the Democratic party, at the outset proposed a "favorite son" strategy in which prominent Blacks from each state would field a symbolic campaign for president. This would prevent Sharpton from carrying those states and winning convention delegates.[15]

Campaign and Social Justice Mobilizing

The Black presidential candidate's campaign has to be dedicated to the interests of constituencies such as the Black church and organized labor, constituencies that are overwhelmingly working class and share the same set of social circumstances. A social justice agenda that calls upon the resources of the government to fulfill its responsibilities toward the less fortunate is the direction this campaign must take because of the disproportionate number of members in such a constituency who suffer from the disadvantages of poverty, racial discrimination, gender discrimination, and poor health-care access.

One of Rev. Sharpton's core themes, perhaps the most important, as I've mentioned, was that the Democratic party had drifted from its base. However, he was not the only candidate in the 2004 election cycle making this charge. The 2002 election cycle ended with Republicans winning victories in Georgia, Maryland, New York, and other states where the post-election assessment was that Blacks didn't turn out strongly to vote. In fact, it was suggested that the Democratic base did not turn out as strongly as in recent elections because it was confused by the lack of a strong message and by Democratic candidates who largely supported the policies of the current Republican administration. The question arose then, who or what is a Democrat? That question was accompanied by a strong effort on the part of party activists on the left to invigorate the 2004 presidential campaign by supporting presidential candidates who would provide a clear contrast to the sitting administration on the war in Iraq, tax cuts, and health care. In this atmosphere, the Democratic party candidates for president competed to be the one candidate who represented the legitimate sentiment of the Democratic party. Howard Dean shocked viewers by stating in the early debates that he represented "the democratic wing of the Democratic party." Rep. Dennis Kucinich of Ohio campaigned on the fact that his record demonstrated that his policies were far different, as a progressive candidate, than those of George Bush and even some of the moderates in the Democratic party. The "real Democrat" competition among a wide number of candidates diminished the force of Sharpton's role as the only challenger with a progressive platform, and normalized that issue in the context of the campaign.

The National Action Network (NAN) was founded by Rev. Sharpton in 1991 and was utilized by Sharpton as a key vehicle for mobilizing Blacks in the city of New York to his various causes. The organization was therefore a convenient tool, and Sharpton used it to expand his base. He spent most of 2003 establishing a network of twenty-two chapters of the organization in various cities, and these chapters would serve as the foundation of his campaign.

Nevertheless, Al Sharpton did not use his National Action Network to engage in simultaneous social justice organizing as extensively as Rev. Jackson had with Operation PUSH, partly because Rev. Jackson's Operation PUSH had been established as an organization during the civil rights movement and boasted a group of seasoned organizers and associates with an agenda and organizing acumen that were also part of that era. Sharpton was limited to utilizing his relatively newly established National Action Network as a campaign organization and as an organizing unit for his speaking engagements, some of which were associated with the campaign, while others were a part of his civil rights activities.

Public Policy Acumen

The future of Black presidential candidacies will undoubtedly resemble the future of candidacies in larger society, in which individuals with experience in legislative bodies or high governmental administrative appointments stand for office.

The position of the DLC was a controlling factor in the selection of campaign issues in the era of Bill Clinton, as witnessed by Clinton's positions as expressed in the crime bill of 1994 and the welfare reform bill of 1996. In the 2004 election cycle the DLC fought hard to make its version of a campaign policy agenda preeminent. One of the places where it made a bid for such prominence was in the themes of a number of the presentations by speakers at the annual DLC convention that year, themes that suggested that the new Democrat agenda would address such issues as:

- neutralizing the "security gap," a result of 9-11, that was supposed to favor Republican candidates
- returning to a balanced budget and fiscal responsibility, and rejecting the "lethal stigma" of "tax and spend" Democrats
- rehabilitating the image of government
- reforming welfare by promoting opportunity and responsibility
- supporting the Earned Income Tax Credit
- expanding AmeriCorps to tap a wellspring of patriotism in the young

These issues were systematized into a DLC state and local government issues playbook for the 2004 campaign cycle. The playbook focused on such topics as: education, e-government and e-commerce, the environment, energy and transportation, health care, homeland security and crime, social and family policy, and state economic policy.[16] These issues and the themes above focus on suburban white families and the corporate community, and they are telling in what they exclude. They exclude any reference to minority rights or to supportive policies for urban areas and the disadvantaged sectors of American society, and they exclude a strong emphasis on the rights of working people. In short, the policies advocated by the DLC bear striking resemblance to those favored by the Republican party. Authors of the DLC playbook, Penn and Bruce Reed, confirm this perspective, and indicate that the survey upon which their interpretation of these issues was based revealed strong support among moderates for this agenda. This means that the DLC message strategy was consistent with the DLC's political strategy of competing for the same constituency as that of the Republican party—and in nearly the same terms.

Al From, founding executive director of the DLC, suggested that the debate over party direction should be encouraged, and that it was healthy for the Democratic party.[17] From touted the impact of DLC policies as relevant to the success of the Clinton administration and thus to the administration's role in having "saved the party." He admitted that "what is at stake is what kind of party we're going to be, the definition of our party." Believing that this issue approach contributed to the Clinton victories of 1992 and 1996, From said this approach would "save the party again" by expanding its party base into the middle class.

This relatively conservative program put forth by the DLC was supported by DLC Chair Sen. Evan Bayh (D-IN), who felt that the Democratic party was "once again under threat from those on the far ideological left and the right," and that in response the DLC should pursue the "vital center."[18] This idea that the party was threatened from the left was also put forward by 2004 presidential candidate Sen. Joseph Lieberman. Journalist Jim VandeHei observes,

> In appearances before crowds of Democrats looking for sharp attacks on President Bush's tax cuts, trade pacts and foreign policy, Lieberman is sounding a bit like a Republican as he laments the "old" and "outdated" solutions advanced by many Democrats. "It's right out of [Bush political director] Karl Rove's playbook," said [Howard] Dean spokeswoman, Patricia Enright.[19]

VandeHei goes on to suggest a corollary point, that in attacking candidates on the right who were perceived as soft on the war in Iraq, or who favored health-care proposals with a high government price tag, Lieberman was courting the alienation of the party's progressive activists who were a substantial segment of the voting base.

By contrast, the Sharpton campaign, like the Jackson campaign before it, addressed the needs of the voiceless, those in American society who felt deprived of the ability to access the resources of the country, and who therefore did not have a strong motivation for political participation. A direct link to the Jackson family was implied by Sharpton's adoption of the proposal of Rep. Jesse Jackson Jr. (D-IL) to adopt an amendment to the Constitution on a federal right to vote. Sharpton also hired long-time close associate to Rev. Jackson and former Jackson campaign official Frank Watkins. In order to accept the post with Sharpton, Watkins left his position as press secretary to Rep. Jesse Jackson Jr., a position in which he had co-authored the work *A More Perfect Union,* which presented a substantive argument for the adoption of a constitutional amendment establishing a federal right to vote. This was seen by Rep. Jackson and Watkins as a strategy to elevate the discussion of voting rights to a national level in a similar manner to that of the two Jackson campaigns, by which Jackson had been able to effectively promote legislation severing U.S. economic relations with apartheid South African government in the mid-1980s.

Additional items of the Sharpton platform that defined why he was running for president included,

> Raise issues that would otherwise be overlooked
> Increase political consciousness and awareness
> Stimulate more people to get involved in the political process
> Increase voter registration
> Strengthen our real national security by fighting for human rights, the rule of law, and economic justice at home and abroad
> Fulfill American democracy by supporting voting rights or statehood for the six hundred thousand disenfranchised citizens of the District of Columbia
> Declare the right to vote a human right
> Declare education a human right

This list reflects the fact that the Sharpton campaign, in an internal primary campaign struggle for policy prominence, intended to assert the value and policy agenda that Sharpton favored as a counterbalance to that of the DLC.

Demonstrated Electoral Support

Primary elections are a natural arena in which Black presidential candidates can demonstrate that they have an electoral base, especially when there is not an incumbent running, or when there are multiple candidacies. In such races, a cohesive Black vote can often make electoral victories by plurality possible, as demonstrated by the influence of Rev. Jackson's campaign in the "Super Tuesday" regional primary of 1988. Super Tuesday victories in several Southern states where the Black population is a substantial portion of the Democratic vote can be a launching pad to victories in other states, or at least to the collection of additional convention delegates.

At the outset Al Sharpton wanted to campaign in primary and caucus states that did not have large Black populations in order both to show that he wanted a crossover vote and to dominate in states with large Black voting constituencies, with a special focus on the Super Tuesday races.

His first such opportunity was the Iowa caucuses where he participated in the third debate in the "Black and Brown Forum" sponsored by Blacks and Latinos to present their issues. During the debate Sharpton attacked former Vermont Governor Howard Dean for Dean's poor record of installing minorities in his government and especially his cabinet. Dean responded with his endorsement by members of the Congressional Black Caucus, but Sharpton shot back, "I think you only need cosigners if your credit is bad." By that point in the campaign, Howard Dean had electrified the Democratic party, was raising a considerable amount of money, and was widely considered the front-runner. Sharpton realized that he had to compete against Dean in order to gain recognition. Sharpton won no delegates in either Iowa or New Hampshire, however, and while Dean's popularity dramatically declined, John Kerry established himself as the clear front-runner by virtue of his victories in both the Iowa caucuses and the New Hampshire primary.

After Iowa and New Hampshire, where Sharpton had given a more than adequate performance during the Democratic presidential debates, Sharpton set his sights on winning the South Carolina primary and then using that as a critical anchor to his fortunes in the other Super Tuesday states. South Carolina was a logical target, being a state where the Black vote was nearly 50 percent of the base of the Democratic vote in the 2003 elections, and where late in 2003 a poll taken for the Edwards campaign showed Edwards at 19 percent among likely Black voters, followed by Al Sharpton and Joseph Lieberman at 13 percent each. Sharpton began to make regular visits, criss-crossing the state, but focusing on Spartanburg, Orangeburg, and Santee.

Sharpton was severely challenged in South Carolina by Senator John Edwards who had been born in the state and who represented nearby North Carolina in the U.S. Senate. Sharpton's focus was on large Black churches and Black colleges and universities, but Edwards won South Carolina with 45.1 percent of the vote (132,660), leaving John Kerry second at 29 percent (87,620) and Al Sharpton at 9.7 percent (28,495). This was a blow to the Sharpton campaign because it highlighted the division among Black voters who split their votes among

Edwards, Kerry, and Sharpton. Sharpton also suffered from not having been endorsed by James Clyburn, a Black member of Congress with considerable influence among voters in the state. Clyburn endorsed Kerry and this allowed Kerry, without an organization in the state and without having campaigned there, to win second place.

The next major race was in the District of Columbia, a city that is 60 percent African American, where Sharpton was expected to win. Notwithstanding this Black majority, a higher voter turnout makes whites the effective majority here, and now Howard Dean benefited from their disproportionate support, winning with 42.7 percent of the vote, while Al Sharpton (34.3 percent) came in second.

Sharpton took his last block of delegates in his home state of New York, where he won a substantial part of the New York City vote.

Bargaining and Negotiation

The viability of the candidate's performance is directly related to his or her continued presence in the election, short of the possibility of winning. The candidate's presence reflects his or her role as a representative of the Black community and of its status as a vital constituency within the Democratic party. Such a presence is the most powerful ingredient in the act of bargaining to demand the accountability of the winning nominee of the party to the interests of the Black community.

Rev. Sharpton's bargaining expectations were also similar to Rev. Jackson's, and when Sharpton announced his presidential exploratory

Table 6.2   Number of Delegate Votes Received by Al Sharpton in the 2004 Democratic Primaries (February and March 2004)

State	Date	Delegate Votes
Delaware	February 3	1
Missouri	February 3	1
Michigan	February 7	7
District of Columbia	February 14	4
New York	March 2	11
Texas	March 9	2
Illinois	March 16	1

Source: AllPolitics, "Primary Election Results," CNN.com, www.cnn.com (accessed March 2004).

committee in January of 2003, he is said to have predicted that "he would walk into the convention with an army of delegates disenchanted with the party's move to the center," thus commanding the same influence and attention that the Rev. Jesse L. Jackson enjoyed when he ran for president based on a similar appeal in 1984 and 1988. Although Sharpton understood, as he stated in a January 2003 *New York Times* interview, that politically the accumulation of delegates would give him "tremendous leverage," he was unable to accomplish this, and his ability to exact leverage suffered accordingly.

Having won only twenty-seven convention delegates by early March, Sharpton signaled that he would leave the race officially and fold his campaign into Kerry's, and on that basis discussions with the Kerry campaign were initiated (table 6.2). The ostensible price for what was regarded as Sharpton's "conditional exit" was dependent upon a number of expectations:

- Kerry would assist in retiring Sharpton's campaign debt estimated to be about $600,000
- Kerry would advocate that the federal government aggressively combat police brutality and racial profiling
- Kerry would make a strong commitment to promote affirmative action, public education, and universal health care
- Kerry would support positive U.S. foreign policies in areas of the world such as Africa, the Caribbean, and Haiti, while opposing continued American unilateral engagement in Iraq

With respect to the campaign, Sharpton also suggested that Kerry commit to hiring more minority staffers, buying advertising and services from minority-owned firms, and purchasing ads on Black- and Latino-owned radio and television stations. In return, Sharpton said that he would "take whatever role [in the Kerry campaign] was conducive to winning" and would work to bring the Black religious community into harmony with the Kerry campaign. On March 15 the Sharpton campaign issued a statement by Sharpton endorsing John Kerry as "a good man who would make a solid nominee for president," and pledging to help strengthen Kerry's candidacy "among my constituents" in order to unify the party for the fall campaign. Kerry responded with a noncommittal statement welcoming the endorsement and saying that he shared many of Sharpton's concerns.

Sharpton had indicated that he would remain inside the Democratic party and that he would support the nominee, a pledge that had been sought from all of the previous candidates in the election. This was a pledge that had been uniquely sought from Rev. Jackson by Democratic party operatives inasmuch as Jackson would have had the capacity, if alienated, to cost the party nominee a strong Black voter turnout in the fall campaign. So the customary pledge was sought from and made by Sharpton as well.

The Carol Moseley Braun Challenge

In this campaign there was competition from a second Black candidate, Carol Moseley Braun, who had less name recognition than Al Sharpton but who had amassed a substantial set of credentials befitting any major candidate for president, by virtue of having been an Illinois county official, a state legislator for ten years, U.S. senator from Illinois, and U.S. ambassador to New Zealand. Ambassador Braun made a decision in January of 2003 not to run for her former seat in the U.S. Senate due to fierce opposition to her candidacy from the media and citizens in the state of Illinois. Much of this animus surfaced in her 1998 reelection bid loss to Republican Peter Fitzgerald. The negative reception occurred because her tenure as a senator was seen to have been deeply flawed by scandals that included a report that she had used her 1992 campaign funds to pay personal bills; a controversial trip to Nigeria that she made as a senator and that appeared to lend credibility to Sani Abacha, widely considered a brutal dictator; and complaints made by unnamed Senate staffers who alleged a harsh administrative style. However, an exhaustive investigation by federal officials found no impropriety in her campaign spending, and there were no charges filed.

Ambassador Braun had been encouraged by women's groups to enter the race. Donna Brazile, former manager for Al Gore's 2000 presidential campaign, said that Braun was "extremely well qualified," and that "I think she should run and we should have [a] woman running this year." In the same vein, Eleanor Smeal, president of the Feminist Majority Foundation, said, "All of us are itching to have a woman in this race," echoing the sentiment of Marie Wilson, president of the White House Project, who said that "this is a time when more women should be out there."

In an August 2003 event at the National Press Club in Washington,

DC, the National Organization for Women (NOW) endorsed Carol Moseley Braun, and its president Kim Gandy praised the campaign of a "strong and accomplished woman running for the highest office in the land, serving as an inspiration to women and girls of all ages." NOW and the organizations above pledged to raise funds for the Braun campaign and consequently, on September 22, Braun officially announced her candidacy for the Democratic nomination for president. At the National Press Club endorsement by NOW, Braun had expressed her motivation to run, saying, "I have the qualifications to put this country on the right track. I will create jobs, make the economy work for everyone, improve our educational system and insure that people have retirement security. I'm running because it's time for us to revive and renew this country."

Braun's potential candidacy was received enthusiastically by Democratic party leader Terry McAuliffe, largely because he thought that Braun could provide a counterpoise to Rev. Al Sharpton who was a more threatening candidate to the Democratic party. From the Black perspective, the potential threat to the Sharpton campaign by Carol Moseley Braun was taken seriously, since at issue was the extent to which the presence of two Black candidates in the race would foster intercommunity division and, as such, detract from the strategic value of a unified Black vote.

In the polling data in table 6.3, it is clear that both candidates failed to become competitive beyond the second tier of candidates, a meaningful point, since there are only two tiers indicated by the polling data and defined by media analysts. It would seem that Sharpton was clearly more competitive than Braun in July up until the Quinnipiac poll, but that Braun became more competitive with Sharpton in later polls. Nevertheless, the presence of both Sharpton and Braun in the race appeared to prevent either from achieving a higher level of competitiveness, since they both relied on essentially the same constituencies (African Americans, women, progressive whites), constituencies that were shared by the most competitive Democratic candidate, Howard Dean, and the least competitive candidate, Dennis Kucinich. The combined position of both Sharpton and Braun was a steady fifth place. This rank could have been a substantial jumping-off point into the first tier for one Black candidate, but for two Black candidates competing for the same constituency, that was much less plausible.

Carol Moseley Braun did not ignite support for her campaign

Table 6.3 The Sharpton–Braun Performance in the Summer 2003 Polls (by percent and by placement in the polls)

Poll	Sharpton[a]	Placement[b]	Braun	Placement	Combined Placement[c]
Fox News (Aug. 12–13) Reg. Dem. voters	5	5th	4	6th	5th
CNN/USA Today/Gallup (Aug. 4–6) Reg. Dem. voters	4	8th	5	5th	5th
NBC News/Wall Street Journal (July 26–28) Likely Dem. voters	3	8th	5	5th	5th
Ipsos-Reid/Cook Political Report (July 22–24) Likely Dem. voters	3	8th	3	6th	5th (tied)
Quinnipiac University (July 17–22) Dem. voters	6	5th	4	7th	4th (tied)
Time/CNN (July 16–17) Reg. Dem. voters	5	6th	4	8th	5th
Zogby America (July 6–17) Reg. Dem. voters	4	5th	2	7th	5th
Newsweek (July 10–11) Reg. Dem. voters	6	6th	3	8th	5th
ABCNews/Washington Post (July 9–10) Democrats	6	6th	4	7th	3rd (tied)

Source: "White House 2004: Democrats," PollingReport.com, August 24, 2003, www.pollingreport.com. Compiled by author, University of Maryland, College Park, August 24, 2003.

[a] Percentage of sample vote received by candidate.

[b] Rank of candidate among all candidates in race.

[c] Combined rank of both candidates among all candidates in the race.

among a broad swath of Democratic women because she had tailored her campaign toward the interests and political commitment of women across racial lines as her primary constituency. While she eschewed the party conflict that motivated Sharpton, she was critical of President George Bush on issues such as education (the "No Child Left Behind" program), the lack of a school rehabilitation program, the closing of health-care gaps between the races, and economic development concerns that included good jobs and a living wage.[20]

In the first half of 2004 Ambassador Braun's campaign did not receive much funding from the women's groups that had pledged their support, and although she had begun her campaign with the enthusiastic support of the Future Political Action Committee, an organization of two hundred fifty Black women, she was unable to remain competitive with Rev. Al Sharpton, but at the same time complicating his attempt to gain credibility by being the major Black candidate in the race.

The campaign of Ambassador Braun was devoted not to seeking independent leverage on behalf of the Black community but to promoting the concerns of women. Curiously then, in her speech to the Democratic convention she made no reference to women's issues. It is clear that although multiple campaigns by Black candidates were a unique feature of the 2004 election cycle, it was also frustrating for those Black voters who understood the benefits of unity as a requirement of effective leverage politics. To be asked to choose between a candidate with strong credentials such as Ambassador Braun and a dynamic candidate such as Rev. Sharpton made for a difficult choice. Here we return to our comparison of the Black candidacies of 2004 with the Jackson campaigns of 1984 and 1988. In June of 1983, shortly after it had been announced that Jackson would mount a bid for the presidency, a poll showed him in third place (at 8 percent) behind Walter Mondale (42 percent) and John Glenn (26 percent).[21] Although Jackson was only in third place, his appeal was potentially at a higher level in the entire electorate because of its movement character.[22] In this context, the relatively low performance of Rev. Al Sharpton in the late spring of 2003 places his appeal at half that of Jackson, and only the appeal of Sharpton and Braun together would be comparable to Jackson's.

An Assessment of the Sharpton Bid

Having failed to achieve Jackson's 1984 or 1988 appeal, Sharpton needed to find a way to ignite the Black community and the Democratic party's progressive base in order to gain credibility. Sharpton was pre-empted from achieving this task when Dean ignited the Democratic party base and John Kerry came to be perceived as the most electable of the candidates. In truth, Sharpton barely constructed the rudiments of a presidential campaign, a fact acknowledged by those who worked for the campaign and by those who observed it from a greater distance.

For instance, because the campaign suffered from lack of funding and proper management, Sharpton was often late for events, or absent altogether. And even when Sharpton focused the energy of his campaigning, as he did in South Carolina, his campaign was unable to respond to the request of a local newspaper, the *Greenville News,* for Sharpton's position on the issues. The result was that Sharpton was the only candidate whose positions were not listed in the *Greenville News* January 2004 special on the views of all the candidates.

I conclude with two points. First, if a Black presidential candidacy should be as successful as the Jackson campaign of 1988, with the effect of contributing to a positive African American view of the Democratic party and pulling the party ideologically to the left, will the party still be competitive in its ability to win general elections? Within the Democratic party, the interests of Blacks, a powerful liberal minority, and the relatively more conservative interests of the white majority are often incompatible. And the effect of this incompatibility will eventually cause such a dysfunction that leverage politics will not bear fruit. This depends, however, on whether Black leadership aggressively pursues the interests of the Black community, or accommodates the white majority by the relegation of African American interests within the party to a lower priority, in order to allow the party to win elections.

Second, in *Black Presidential Politics in America* I characterized the attempt by Blacks to leverage influence within the party system in accordance with the predetermined, subordinate role of that leverage as "dependent-leverage."[23] The Sharpton challenge illuminates the existence of conditions that contribute to intensifying the dynamics of dependent-leverage. At issue is whether the essential problem lies in a candidate who poses the same problems as Sharpton himself, or in the fact that the attitude of Blacks and their level of voting mobilization depends on factors outside the candidate's appeal within the Black community.

Independent leverage (as distinct from dependent-leverage) is founded on the proposition that a candidate's politics should reflect the interest of the constituency that the candidate represents, and should seek to mobilize those interests in the political system by utilizing methodologies that do not compromise them. It is in this sense that the campaign of Rev. Jackson was an independent thrust within the Democratic party; and the position taken here is that this thrust functioned to influence or leverage a change in the direction of the party. This works only if the politics of the Black leadership are strong enough and true to fundamental elements that reflect the socioeconomic condition of the Black community and its political interests.

A lack of sufficient national support, either within the Black community or through a biracial coalition, hampered the fund-raising of the Sharpton campaign. While the Jackson campaign was able to raise an estimated $3.2 million in 1984, the Sharpton campaign raised and spent less than $1 million. Sharpton had raised only $283,529 by December of 2003, an ignominious sum with which to begin a presidential campaign. Moreover, his 2004 contributions were not much greater, at $398,439. A listing of Sharpton campaign donors includes Earl Graves Publishing ($8,000), PepsiCo Inc. ($6,000), Rush Communications ($5,000), Don Coleman Advertising ($4,000), HealthNet Affiliates ($4,000), Goldman Sachs ($4,000), BET Holdings ($3,000), Time Warner ($2,300), the city of Newark ($2,250), and UniWorld Group ($2,250). The list indicates a heavy concentration of donors from the New York City area, rather than from a national donor base. Sharpton's largest contributor, Radio One ($15,000), was an exception.

In May of 2004 the Federal Election Commission voted to prohibit payment of federal campaign matching funds to Rev. Sharpton's campaign, an extraordinary step, because of the commission's assessment that Sharpton had overspent the $50,000 personal contribution limit on funds that a candidate could contribute to his own campaign, and because the Sharpton campaign lacked supporting documentation for its expenditures. These documents would have supported the contention of the Sharpton campaign that the commission was counting as Sharpton's personal contribution travel expenses that had been paid by NAN. Sharpton's response to the commission's action was that he never actually put cash into the campaign, but charged his credit cards to help defray campaign expenses.

So strained were Sharpton's finances at this point that he enlisted the assistance of Roger Stone, described as a "flamboyant individual," who had worked for Richard Nixon and who maintained strong Republican ties. Stone was said to have provided Sharpton with the material

Sharpton used during the Iowa debate to question Howard Dean's minority hiring record, and an investigation by the *Village Voice* revealed that Stone helped Sharpton to qualify his campaign initially for federal matching funds by preparing the application and collecting checks from friends and associates in various states, and Republican sources. Stone was said to have contributed significantly to NAN, these contributions becoming no doubt the source of Federal Election Commission inquiries into the relationship between NAN and the Sharpton campaign. Stone also stationed some of his staff inside the campaign to run critical operations for a period of time.

After his campaign had ended, Rev. Al Sharpton worked for the Kerry campaign as a senior adviser, and with the Democratic Convention in Boston approaching, he was solicited by Kerry to be one of the keynote speakers. Asked about his invitation to Sharpton in an interview on Black Entertainment Television Kerry said, "That's my call . . . If he wants to do it, he can do it . . . Let me just say to you . . . if he wants to do it, I'd like him to do it. I think he'll add something . . . there's no plea necessary. It's my invitation."[24] Asked why he made this invitation, Kerry went on, "He certainly earned the right to be part of this process, and I think he can be very, very helpful in motivating people, in helping to register people."

Sharpton made what was widely regarded among Blacks as the most important and dramatic speech of the Democratic convention. Some cable news shows featured the fact that Sharpton's speech had run over its allotted time, but the dramatic high note of the speech was reached when Sharpton pointedly directed his remarks to Kerry's opponent, President George Bush, explaining that Blacks would not support Bush because they would not betray their interests, and saying that "the Black vote is not for sale!"

Conclusion

The presidential campaign of the Reverend Al Sharpton was unable to mobilize a significant Black base of voters and had few white supporters, which hampered the candidate's attempt to utilize leverage politics. Leverage politics would have been based on a substantial number of delegates controlled by Sharpton, a fact that would pose a threat to John Kerry and would force him, in return, to seek accommodation with

Sharpton by bargaining. There is little evidence that John Kerry seriously bargained with Rev. Sharpton, despite the substantial list of items that Kerry was requested to consider, and despite Kerry's assent to a speaking role for Sharpton at the Democratic Convention. Sharpton did play a role in the Kerry campaign as a surrogate speaker and a team mobilizer of the Black religious community. However, the failure of the Kerry campaign to publicly honor the agenda promoted by Sharpton gave the agenda little visibility. The result was that Kerry had to deal with some issues on that agenda, such as staffing his campaign to achieve effective minority outreach, in a more contentious atmosphere later in his campaign.

Some analysts, notably Jonetta Rose Barras, a Washington, DC, journalist, believed that the less than spectacular results of the Sharpton presidential campaign could be accounted for by at least two factors. The first of these was the urgent feeling on the part of Black voters that opposition to George Bush was so important that they could not afford to waste their vote on a symbolic candidacy. Barras also felt that Sharpton's failure signaled the end of the politics of Black leverage, citing Ron Lester, a Black pollster, who said, "We're at a different point in the life cycle of Black empowerment and Black politics. The fact that you're Black is less important today than it was ten or fifteen years ago."[25]

I do not believe that the politics of leverage are at an end. Evidence from the 2004 campaign clearly shows an attempt by Black leaders to use the politics of leverage, a politics that does not depend exclusively on the presence of a Black presidential candidate in the primary elections, but which can be operationalized by Black leaders on the strength of the fact that the Black vote is an important contribution to the Democratic party's showing in a general election. As I explained in *Black Presidential Politics,* independent leverage may be attempted at two major points, either in the primary or in the general election. In addition, the failure of Rev. Sharpton to run an effective Black campaign does not signal that a more accomplished Black politician will not be able to do so in the future. The fact that Barack Obama, a Black politician from Illinois, won election to the U.S. Senate has already stimulated many references to his potential role as a future candidate for either the presidency or the vice presidency. If either of these roles materializes, the question of whether he will choose to initiate leverage politics on behalf of the Black community will be a major consideration.

7

Black Turnout and the 2004 Presidential Election

Opportunities for Leverage Politics

There are two opportunities for the African American vote to exist as a resource for political bargaining: the first, in the primaries and caucuses of a presidential election year, and the second, in the general election. This is what I refer to as the "two ballot scenario." The Voting Rights Act has served to enhance Black voting in presidential elections by protecting the rights of Blacks in the balloting process. It has also enhanced the possibilities of leverage strategies in both the primary and general elections. In this chapter, I examine the second ballot scenario in order to describe and analyze the extent of the leverage Blacks were able to obtain through the performance of the Black vote in the general election of 2004. Several factors were at work, including the unique context of this election, the nature of the connection of Blacks to John Kerry and his campaign, and the performance of the Black election infrastructure in the Unity '04 Campaign.

Unique Contextual Factors

Terrorism and the War in Iraq

Undoubtedly the tragic events of September 11, 2001, were bound to color the 2004 election. By adopting an aggressive posture toward the al Qaeda organization, and by launching a military operation in Afghanistan that toppled al Qaeda from control of the Taliban regime, President

George Bush established himself as a strong protector of American security. This mantle was to remain a part of his image even though he proceeded to shift the focus of American military operations in the Middle East to a war against Saddam Hussein. The unclear political rationale for this shift, as well as questionable aspects of the war's conduct, colored the ebb and flow of the president's approval ratings among the American people throughout the campaign season and up to election day.

During 2003 President Bush averaged a 60 percent approval poll rating in all Gallup polls. In January of 2004, however, a CBS News poll found George Bush's approval rating at 45 percent—down from a 60 percent rating in December of the previous year, following the capture of Saddam Hussein—and 57 percent of Americans believed that things were worse. While less salient issues such as temporary work permits for illegal immigrants and building a permanent space station on the moon had contributed to his slide, the war in Iraq was most material, with 51 percent of respondents answering "No" when asked, "Was the Iraq war worth the cost?" Another sounding by a New York Times/CBS News poll found considerable anxiousness in the public over the state of the economy. These factors were to continue to keep the president's approval rating under 50 percent, except for a brief rise in April. Bush's ratings went down again because of the Abu Ghraib prisoner scandal in Iraq, remaining lower than 50 percent, until he received a modest "bounce" after the Republican convention, moving to above 50 percent. Shortly afterward, Bush declined to under 50 percent again and remained there until the election, causing widespread speculation of a potential defeat, since no previous president had been reelected with a favorable rating under 50 percent.

If the Iraq war and the economy were playing a role in the job approval ratings of the president, they also affected the attitude of the Black community toward him, as Bush's job approval rating among Blacks fell from 20 percent in January 2004 to 12 percent in May. Most Blacks felt that the war was decidedly wrong because they believed that it lacked a sufficient rationale and was therefore illegal. This belief was intensified by the view that Blacks were paying a disproportionate sacrifice for its conduct. The comments of Senator Kendrick Meek (D-FL) are pertinent.

They [Blacks] come into the military looking for jobs and wanting to serve their country. Our nation's history shows that African

Americans have been willing to fight for their country. But today many ask, what is the motivation behind the fight.[1]

Although most members of the Congressional Black Caucus (CBC) voted to give the president authority to pursue a military option if it became necessary, they were anxious about the issue of disproportionate sacrifice. Congressman Charles Rangel (D-NY) introduced a bill in March of 2004 to re-institute the draft, raising the point that those members of Congress who made the law to initiate military action did not have sons or daughters in the military and if they did, they would be reluctant to approve it. Rangel also believed that excessive Black casualties would occur because of the disproportionate presence of Blacks in the military (20 percent of all services). And although Rangel was roundly criticized for this view, by February of 2004 the Black casualty rate in Operation Iraqi Freedom was 14.3 percent, as indicated by data from the Center for Research on Military Organization at the University of Maryland.

In addition, there was considerable resentment that the economic resources being used to reconstruct Iraq might have been—and indeed should have been—applied to problems in the United States. The resentment this fostered among Blacks drove their opposition to the Iraq war to the highest level in the nation, with 73 percent of Blacks (in polling by Cornell Belcher) disagreeing that the war was worth the casualties, 63 percent agreeing that the U.S. should pull out altogether, and 77 percent agreeing at least somewhat that President Bush intentionally misled the country as to America's entry into the war. The depth of such feelings was explained by David Bositis of the Joint Center for Political and Economic Studies. "To these voters, money is not being spent on health care, education, on jobs . . . now you have double-digit unemployment and the income growth that took place in the last half of the '90s disappeared."[2]

The Impact of the Economy

The second most dynamic issue in the campaign was the performance of the economy. Black voters chose the state of the economy, and employment specifically, as a priority issue. Although many Americans agreed that the nation was on the "wrong track," this proved to be less of a political resource for electoral mobilization than moral values and the war on terrorism. Traditionally, the economy has an explanatory power as far as Blacks are concerned, and Susan Welch and Lorn Foster have identified strong economic motivation as an important source of Black voter turnout in the 1984 election. It has long been noted that Blacks favor such measures as increased job training and access, and growing the economy for higher wages in order to thwart the poverty and unemployment that have had a disproportionate impact on their socioeconomic status.

Blacks are sensitive to the economic motivations for political participation, and see it as an equivalent to civil rights, a sensitivity vested in their low socioeconomic condition relative to whites. From a period of substantial economic growth in the last half of the 1990s, and with the advent of the Bush administration, the unemployment rates for Blacks began to increase. Illustrative of this trend is the fact that the nation moved from a 3.7 percent unemployment rate in February of 2001 to 5.5 percent in February of 2002. This caused Black unemployment to grow from 7.5 percent in February 2001 to 10.2 percent in February of 2002 and 11 percent in March of the same year.

Black unemployment under the Bush administration rose dramatically from Clinton administration levels, and by 2004 still maintained its high levels, causing the poverty rate to rise from 20 percent in the late Clinton years, to 24.4 percent by August of 2004. Overall in 2003, 1.3 million more Americans slid into officially defined poverty.

Belief that the policies of the Republican party contributed to this slide was common among Black legislators. The chairman of the Congressional Black Caucus (CBC), Rep. Elijah Cummings (D-MI), took an opportunity to comment on the president's visits to the urban centers of Philadelphia and Detroit by saying that "because of the President and the Congressional Republicans' economic policies, and their unwillingness to work with Democrats, our great country remains mired in an economic quagmire of which . . . they have no plan for a way out."[3] His observations were augmented by those of Rep. Chaka Fattah (D-PA), who expanded on this notion.

> While President Bush is welcome in Philadelphia, the economic damage of his tax cuts, fewer jobs and more debt, are unwelcomed. Without these tax cuts, we could invest more in education, health care, and affordable housing. Our nation's budget has moved from a surplus to more than a $450 billion deficit. Mr. President, our

community and our country would be better served by the simple assertion of truth, that a $100 tax cut for the average citizen coupled with massive tax cuts for the rich does no good for our struggling economy.[4]

In August of 2004 CBC chair Cummings noted that conditions had not improved and that even though conditions continued to decline, the president would not change his economic policies. Cummings strongly asserted that "therefore, I believe that in order for our economic picture to change for the better, our leadership in the White House and Congress must also change."[5] The poor state of the economy and the negative attitude of Blacks toward the Bush administration were a strong motivation for Blacks to vote in the upcoming election. The traditional pre-election poll of the Black community by the Joint Center for Political and Economic Studies found that 74 percent of Blacks thought that America was on the "wrong track" compared to 54 percent of whites, and that "Employment/Economy" was the top priority issue for Blacks but a second priority issue for whites. This view was supported by Black pollster Ron Lester, who confirmed that the president's standing among Blacks had only worsened since he took office because of issues that included the state of the economy and Bush's handling of the crisis in Haiti where his administration had participated in the overthrow of Haiti's popular president Jean-Bertrand Aristide. The voting record of Republicans in Congress was negatively evaluated by the NAACP, which issued its annual legislative report card in February of 2004. The report card showed that most of the Republicans in the House of Representatives (228) and all the Republicans in the Senate had earned a grade of F on issues of concern to the NAACP.

The Bush Result

As a broader rationale for Blacks' attitude toward Bush than the issues suggested by Lester, the general record of the Bush administration—in both the content of its public policy agenda and its relationship toward Black civil rights and civil rights organizations—was widely perceived negatively. I will briefly summarize this record to show the continuity that the Bush administration shares with other Republican administrations in failing to appeal to the Black community.

In September of 2004 the U.S. Commission on Civil Rights issued a report that summarized the civil rights record of the Bush administration. The report was comprehensive in its treatment of issues concerning the environment, as well as issues affecting minorities, the disabled, women, and immigrants. This report indicated that the Bush administration was deficient in its public support of civil rights, the commission having found that 157 of the administration's public statements on the issue of civil rights contained only 27 substantive proposals, most of which dealt with faith-based concerns. President Bush referred to discrimination as a problem evident in the fact that religious organizations were often prohibited from accepting and using federal funds. Ironically, he therefore pressed to allow religious organizations themselves to practice a form of discrimination by their hiring of individuals of the same faith to work in these federally funded programs. Such discriminatory hiring practices appear contrary to the spirit of Title VI of the 1964 Civil Rights Act, which prohibits discrimination in the use of federal funds. In any case, added to the lack of the Bush administration's public support for civil rights issues was the fact that in every agency charged with upholding basic civil rights laws, administration funding requests between FY01–02 and FY02–03 did not keep pace with inflation, resulting in a net decrease in funding.

Blacks formed their attitudes toward the Bush administration from these cues and others such as the administration's high-profile conflict with the civil rights community over the appointment of conservative judges such as Janice Rogers Brown, Miguel Estrada, and Charles Pickering to the federal bench. An especially contentious conflict occurred over the appointment of Charles Pickering, a Mississippi judge whose background included a highly controversial decision rendering leniency toward a white defendant convicted of burning a cross on the lawn of the home of an interracial couple. Senate Democrats blocked the Pickering nomination but Bush, in an election year, bypassed the Senate with a recess appointment.

A powerfully symbolic act was the Bush administration's approach to an affirmative action case before the Supreme Court that involved the University of Michigan. The solicitor general was instructed by the White House to define the admission requirements of the university as a quota system. One organization that was especially upset by this action was the NAACP, creating a scenario that pitted the nation's most symbolically important civil rights organization against the U.S. government in open conflict. In the aftermath of the Florida voting scandal, the

NAACP had been highly critical of the manner in which George Bush had taken office. Many viewed this as the reason why Bush rejected an invitation by the organization to speak at its July 2004 convention. The NAACP president, Kweisi Mfume, suggested that Bush treated Blacks like "prostitutes" by claiming that he wanted the Black vote but refusing to attend the NAACP's annual convention. When the Bush administration offered Secretary of Education Rod Paige as a speaker for the NAACP convention, the organization rejected Paige, preferring the president. In this context, the speech to the NAACP convention by Board Chair Julian Bond drew national attention and was roundly criticized by conservative activists who charged that the organization had become partisan. In his speech, Bond said that the organization met while the nation was pursuing "an unwise war of occupation [which] continues in Iraq without reason or necessity . . . [The war is] not about weapons of mass destruction, but . . . crass obstruction of the truth," and, "blacks are increasingly angry about the economy and the war."[6] Then Bond said,

> The election this fall is a contest between two widely disparate views of who we are and what we believe. One view wants to march us backward through history—surrendering control of government to special interests, weakening democracy, giving religion veto power over science, curtailing civil liberties, despoiling the environment. The other view promises expanded democracy and giving the people, not the plutocrats, control over their government.[7]

The speech was widely construed by the media as calling for the ouster of President Bush, and on October 8 the Internal Revenue Service sent a letter to the NAACP inquiring whether the board of the organization had authorized Bond to make statements in opposition to George W. Bush's campaign for the office of the presidency. This action was regarded by Bond as politically motivated and as having a chilling effect on the organization and on his First Amendment rights.

The Second Ballot Scenario

Evolving Black Support for John Kerry in the Primaries

John Kerry's dramatic victory in the Iowa caucus and the New Hampshire primary established his lead for the Democratic nomination, and by early February his position appeared to satisfy many Democrats who desired the quick nomination of a candidate in order to begin to compete with incumbent George Bush. Kerry was preferred by 43 percent of Democrats in one poll, compared to 18 percent for his closest rival, Senator John Edwards. Kerry had also increasingly won over Blacks, but the vote was split during the primaries between John Edwards, a Southerner, the Reverend Al Sharpton, Ambassador Carol Moseley Braun, and Kerry. After the primaries, the Black vote coalesced around Kerry as a June poll indicated that whereas whites supported Bush by 53 percent, Blacks supported Kerry by 81 percent. At the same time, the Kerry campaign was criticized because few minorities were a part of his inner circle or exercised any leadership role in the campaign. The Kerry campaign appeared to lack sufficient understanding of the necessity to effect a rapid transition from the kind of campaign structure with which he had won the nomination to a structure that was capable of mobilizing the large national constituencies that were the base vote of the Democratic party. Rep. Jesse Jackson Jr. expressed this view when he said, "I am concerned about diversity, but more importantly, I am concerned about the experience in that diversity—senior policy people who know people from one end of the country to the other."[8] Rep. James Clyburn, who had played a vital role in Kerry's South Carolina campaign, said, "He is generally surrounded by white folks, and sure that concerns me."[9] Kevin Gray, Black Democratic political operative, said, "There's no message, no organizing aimed at Black people. It's not like Kerry stands for anything; Black people are voting against Bush."[10] Others, such as representatives of the National Council of La Raza and Julian Bond of the NAACP, said that the lack of Kerry's staff diversity could be a reflection of the strength of his basic commitment to diversity as president.

Kerry had enlisted the support of key members of the CBC such as Chair Rep. Elijah Cummings (D-MI), Rep. Harold Ford Jr. (D-TN), Rep. Greg Meeks (D-NY), and Rep. Stephanie Tubbs Jones (D-OH). The Kerry campaign gave Rep. Jones a key role as liaison with the Democratic National Committee, important in view of the fact that the state of Ohio had a Black secretary of state and a Black lieutenant governor, both of whom were Republicans. But despite the fact that the campaign added Marcus Jadotte (Florida coordinator of the Edwards campaign) to a prominent post, the team still lacked vital connections to important constituencies within the Black community. Rev. Al Sharpton and others defended Kerry, Sharpton saying that he had experienced two one-on-one meetings with Kerry and had his personal cell phone number.

Perhaps this was the reason why as late as October there were still observations by the press and pollsters alike that Kerry had failed to "energize" the Black vote. Indications of the reason for this failure may be found in a BET/CBS poll taken in mid-July of 2004 in which only 27 percent of respondents were "enthusiastic" about Kerry's candidacy, while most were "satisfied" (58 percent). In the same poll Kerry also earned high marks for such characteristics as "shares your priorities" at 64 percent, "is highly intelligent" at 63 percent, "would appoint Black cabinet members" at 66 percent, and had "more soul" than Bush at 64 percent. But Blacks were doubtful about whether things would get better if Kerry were elected (better, 47 percent; same, 45 percent; worse, 3 percent). The reason for this might be traced to the fact that while 9 percent felt that Bush was concerned with their top issues, Kerry did only moderately better than Bush at 26 percent on this measure.[11]

In response to the fact that his outreach was considered poor, Kerry began to appear in Black churches, asking directly for their vote and warning of the possibility of a repeat of the 2000 Florida disenfranchisement tactics, while pledging to make sure that every vote was counted. In addition, in late September Kerry bolstered his outreach to Blacks by inviting Rev. Jesse Jackson Sr. to become a senior adviser to his campaign.

The CBC had tried to bolster the Kerry campaign by attempting to convince independent candidate Ralph Nader to withdraw his candidacy. In the 2000 campaign Ralph Nader's presence in the election in Florida, which was decided by 537 votes, had attracted 98,477 votes, most of which, analysts agreed, would have gone to Al Gore if Nader had not been in the race. Rep. Sheila Jackson Lee framed the purpose of the meeting with Ralph Nader in terms of the oft heard theme that "this is the most historic election of our lifetime, and it is a life or death matter for the vulnerable people we represent. For that reason we can't sacrifice their vulnerability for the efforts being made by Mr. Nader."[12] With the polls showing the 2004 election to be just as close, the Nader candidacy became a factor again.

On June 21 all thirty-nine members of the CBC met with Ralph Nader in what was described as a "testy meeting," with CBC members passionately presenting Nader with the view that he could again tip the race to George Bush, and that if he valued his friendship with Blacks, he should withdraw. Nader refused to withdraw, causing Chairman Cummings to conclude, "It became abundantly clear to us that this was about Ralph Nader and we were sorely disappointed."[13]

Enhancing Leverage: The Unity '04 Campaign Mobilization

While the Kerry campaign was one focus of activity, nonpartisan registration and get-out-the-vote activity mounted by citizen organizations was an important ingredient in stimulating turnout in the Black community. This activity fulfills the broader objective of civic political participation and builds an infrastructure that allows for the participation of a great number of groups and individuals in coalition.

The Black Civic Culture of Elections

The participation of Black civil society in the election process is not much different from that of any other community, except perhaps for the role of the Black church. Even there, however, the field has been more than leveled by the entrance into elections of the religious Right, which followed the coming of the Moral Majority in the 1970s. The culture of politics that fostered participation in the civil rights movement by ordinary people, a broad range of leaders, and civic organizations has resulted in the socialization of the electoral arena, a socialization that includes a powerful motivation based on personal sacrifice. The motivation that results from the sacrifices of death, jail, and various forms of inhumane treatment exists as a moral reservoir that encourages each generation of Blacks to participate in the Democratic process, and this reservoir is more powerful than even the political tenets that created the political system itself.

The Black civic culture of political participation has traditionally involved a range of organizations that included the NAACP, the National Rainbow Coalition, the Southern Christian Leadership Conference, the Coalition of Black Trade Unionists, the National Urban League, the National Council of Negro Women, the Congressional Black Caucus Foundation, and other organizations as mentioned in chapter 2. But among these there was also an interlocking directorate that featured the Black Leadership Forum and the National Coalition on Black Civic (formerly Voter) Participation (NCBCP). In the 2004 election cycle this infrastructure expanded. It began with the Black church and those specialized organizations devoted to elections such as the NCBCP and went on to include the entertainment sector in the form of hip-hop artists who had their own special attraction for youths. I will comment on each of these sectors of the Black election infrastructure in the 2004 election.

The National Coalition on Black Civic Participation

The NCBCP created the Unity '04 campaign, the basis of which was the membership of 165 organizations that agreed to adopt the Unity '04 logo and theme for their own operations and to mobilize their membership to register and vote, either in their organizational framework or in the geography of their residential location. Not all of the parent organizations were Black—People for the American Way, for example—and others, such as the United Auto Workers of America or General Motors Corporation, had Black caucuses as the focus of their participation. Ethnic communities were represented (the Caribbean People International Collective), along with statewide organizations (the Ohio Coalition on Black Civic Participation) and citywide coalitions.

Preparing for 2004

Some of the programs that the coalition used in 2004 were seeded in 2002, both as a result of what had happened in 2000 and in preparation for 2004. That year, 2002, the coalition worked in sixty cities, and evidence of its presence was widely reported. "Over 200 youth hit the streets of Maryland, 250 volunteers were deployed in Atlanta, and delegates encouraged thousands of churchgoers to vote early in Florida, as part of the National Coalition on Black Civic Participation Unity 2002 Get-Out-the-Vote Campaign."[14] The programs featured all the elements of a campaign: sound trucks blaring messages, high-profile personalities such as Blair Underwood, Bill Cosby, and Angela Bassett to attract potential participants, door-to-door canvassing, barbershop visits, literature distribution, and phone banks. The coalition also tested a "Protect Your Vote" system that featured a telephone hotline to a legal center where lawyers or law students could assist voters in clarifying their rights and voting status. The coalition made a strong pitch for youths through a program known as Black Youth Vote in which students from schools that included the Atlanta University Center in Atlanta, Georgia, and Howard University in Washington, DC, took the initiative to reach their peers.

The 2004 Campaign

For the 2004 election the NCBCP retained its 2002 form and activities and doubled its membership. Its kick-off for the campaign occurred in January with simultaneous press conferences in Washington, DC, and Atlanta, Georgia, with the Georgia Coalition for the Peoples' Agenda, a major regional affiliate in the South headed by Rev. Joseph Lowery, a founder of the Southern Christian Leadership Conference with Dr. Martin Luther King Jr. Headed by Marc Morial, former mayor of New Orleans and the newly elected head of the National Urban League, the second largest civil rights and social service organization in the Black community, the Unity '04 campaign was characterized by local press as "a grassroots, motivational voter empowerment initiative of African American leaders" who "outlined strategy to mobilize the Black electorate—made up of over twenty million registered voters."[15] In February the nine Black Greek-letter organizations reaffirmed their membership in the Unity '04 campaign at the Pan-Hellenic Council Conference in Atlanta, Georgia. By this time, the meetings of the coalition were hosted and attended by Dr. Dorothy Height, the venerable head of the National Council of Negro Women, at the organization's headquarters in Washington, DC.

The Protect Your Vote Project

A critical feature of 2004 was the Protect Your Vote project that was spearheaded by the Lawyers' Committee for Civil Rights Under Law, headed by Barbara Arnwine. Attorney Arnwine reaffirmed that "Election Protection was created in the wake of the 2000 election fiasco in order to prevent voter disenfranchisement from being repeated in future elections."[16] This project distributed a flyer, "You Have the Right to Vote," to counter the widespread feeling created by *Gore v. Bush* that there was no constitutional right of citizens to vote, and also distributed a "Voters' Bill of Rights" that the Help America Vote Act had recommended be posted at polling stations. The key activity of the Protect Your Vote project, however, was a national nonpartisan hotline (1-866-our-vote) by which citizens could access legal assistance to vote. As indicated above, the system was tested in the 2002 campaign, and by 2004 the NCBCP, partnering with legal organizations such as the NAACP Legal Defense Fund, the Advancement Project, People for the American Way, the National Black Law Students Association, and the American Civil Liberties Union was able to field nearly fifteen thousand lawyers by the time of the November elections. These lawyers were an important addition to the virtual groundswell of other legal and civic organizations that would file cases to protect voting rights.

These organizations had much to do in the 2004 election cycle. With the vote purges that were required by state law taking place in states such as Florida and Louisiana, their task was to insure that eligible voters remained on the rolls.

Voter Registration and High Turnout States

The coalition was not free to select its own targets of mobilization because new funding sources dictated that its work be performed in preselected battleground states. The definition of such states varied with the analyst, but generally included a list of states where the 2000 election was close between Al Gore and George Bush and where the polling in 2004 indicated that Democrats and Republicans were still competitive. Table 7.1 below shows those states where the difference between the presidential candidates was close in 2000, and where the unregistered Black vote was larger than the margin of difference. Such calculations

Table 7.1   Difference between the Gore and Bush Vote in the 2000 Election by the Margin of Victory, Black Registration and Voting, and the Unregistered Black Population

State	Gore	Bush	Difference/%	BVAP[a]	Unregistered/%
Florida	2,912,253	2,912,790	537/.01	1,169,000	549,000/47.3
Missouri	1,111,138	1,189,924	78,786/3.3	439,000	149,000/24.3
Ohio	2,183,628	2,350,363	166,735/3.6	907,000	317,000/35.7
Tennessee	981,720	1,061,949	80,229/3.9	654,000	229,000/38.6
Arkansas	422,768	472,940	50,172/5.4	329,000	132,000/40.0

Source: Calculations provided by the author from: Jeff Trandahl, "Statistics of the Presidential and Congressional Election of November 7, 2000," clerk of the House of Representatives, June 21, 2001; U.S. Bureau of the Census, "Reported Voting and Registration of the Total Voting Age Population, by Sex, Race, and Hispanic Origin, for States," November 2000, table 4a, Bureau of the Census, U.S. Department of Commerce, February 27, 2002.
[a] Black voting age population.

often served as a guide for partisan organizations which then factored in the contribution of the Black vote. As a nonpartisan organization, the NCBCP utilized as a basic criterion those states that had the highest number of unregistered Blacks, and those that had experienced low turnout in 2000, some of which were battleground states and some of which were not. A list of states where the coalition worked can be seen in table 7.2. This listing of priority "Tiers" depended upon factors that included strength of funding, staff availability, and number of organizations in the state. Tier 1 included the battleground states of Arkansas, Michigan, Ohio, and a range of Southern states, a pattern repeated in Tiers 2 and 3.

For the second straight presidential election cycle, the targeting strategy of the Democratic party nominee and of the party itself conceded the South as a region where Republicans dominated, with margins of victory by Republican candidates in the double digits. Nevertheless, the South was and continues to be the base of Black voting strength, constituting in 2004 at least half of the Democratic party vote in the primary elections in some states and as much as one-quarter or more in the general elections in states that included Alabama (25 percent), Georgia (25 percent), Louisiana (27 percent), Maryland (24 percent), Mississippi (34 percent), North Carolina (26 percent), and South Carolina (30 percent), and the District of Columbia (54 percent). Many organizations in the Black infrastructure, including 527 organizations like Voices for Working Families, established units in the states of North Carolina, Florida, Georgia, Texas, and Louisiana, where units of the mobilization's "civic culture" organizations were located.

Table 7.2   Selected Voter Registration and Turnout States by Priority of Numbered Tiers, for the National Coalition on Black Civic Participation

Tier 1	Tier 2	Tier 3
Alabama	Arizona	California
Arkansas	Florida	Indiana
Georgia	Nevada	Maryland
Illinois	Pennsylvania	New Mexico
Louisiana	Mississippi	New Jersey
Michigan	South Carolina	New York
North Carolina	Virginia	Tennessee
Ohio	Wisconsin	District of Columbia

Source: "Feel the Power," Overview of the Unity '04 Empowerment Campaign, brochure, National Coalition on Black Civic Participation, Washington, DC, January 2004.

The Black Youth Vote

One of the goals of Black Youth Vote and other organizations such as Rock the Vote (MTV) has been to increase the rate of participation in the political process by youths in the 18–35-year-old group. This group constitutes 40 percent of the eligible electorate, but while their elders voted at the rate of 55 percent in 2000, the turnout of this age group was 35 percent. Young Blacks have closed the registration and voting gap with white youth, which makes their turnout rates very similar. An evolving strategy since the early 1990s has been to appeal to youths in general through the medium of their cultural leaders, and hip-hop artists became a major focus of this enlistment. In 2004, young Blacks expressed strong feelings about the war in Iraq, the difficulty of obtaining employment, and the fact that convicted felons could not vote, especially in the state of Florida. In a focus group in Florida, involving 18–24-year-olds, one participant said,

> In 2000 ex-cons couldn't vote. I was an ex-con who voted for four years. But when Jeb Bush became Governor, they took my rights away . . . sent me a letter saying, "we observe that you were convicted of a felony . . . therefore you can't vote." Kendrick Meek [(D-FL)] helped reinstate me. I know some people who are not going to vote. But me, I will vote because it may determine who will be the next president.[17]

Still other youths reflected the feeling of a participant in the same focus group who said, "I ain't seen no change . . . It'll make me vote when I see change . . . My one vote is not going to make any difference." In this group it was clear that young people were amenable to the leadership of hip-hop and rap artists, not only in music and clothes, but in the field of civic participation as well.

One of those to answer this call was Russell Simmons, a successful New York music promoter and entrepreneur. As a promoter of hip-hop music and its entertainers, he often defended hip-hop against charges by Black leaders, such as Dr. C. DeLores Tucker, head of the National Congress of Black Women, that the values hip-hop promoted were misogynist, violent, and disrespectful to basic values of the Black community.

One response to this dialogue was the creation of the Hip-Hop Summit, sponsored by Russell Simmons as an action forum and eventually an organization that he piloted as early as 1998. In January 2001 the Summit brought together an unprecedented group of 300 musical artists, congressional representatives, and influential civil rights leaders from the NAACP, the Southern Christian Leadership Conference, the National Urban League, the Nation of Islam, the Schomburg Center for Research in Black Culture, and Rock/Rap the Vote. On the Summit's agenda was lobbying Congress to defeat a bill by Senator Joseph Lieberman (D-CT) that would censor hip-hop lyrics, working with the CBC to support candidates for office, and opposing racial profiling. Simmons rejected the charge that the Summit had been initiated because of the threat of the Lieberman bill and maintained that the idea had been discussed for some time in his sector of the industry.

The Summit was minimally active in the 2002 election, but eventually focused on the 2004 presidential election, and in 2003 it created a political action committee headquartered in New York City, with field offices in Los Angeles and Washington, DC, with the objective of "taking back responsibility." The Summit entered the 2004 election as a nonpartisan, voter registration, get-out-the-vote organization that held events featuring entertainers in various cities. For example, a major conference attracting five thousand youths and Black leaders was held by the Hip-Hop Summit Action Network in Newark, New Jersey, in May of 2004. In August an event in St. Louis featuring Nelly, Jadakiss, Rev Run, D12, Lazy Bone, and Remy Martin attracted an equal number of attendants as the Newark conference, and the event's organizers announced they had thus far registered one hundred fourteen thousand people to vote. Another conference was held at Howard University in Washington, DC, to coincide with the annual CBC Weekend. Congresswoman Maxine Waters (D-CA) had long been a patron of the group, and she worked to provide a forum for understanding rap and hip-hop activities and aspirations, and to establish a relationship between the leaders of the industry and Black political leadership. A Howard University panel that discussed the critical factors that motivated youth voting addressed such issues as the need for greater educational resources, an end to the incarceration binge, opposition to the war in Iraq, and the need for universal health care. These meetings were a prelude to a monthlong, ten-state, hip-hop bus tour in October sponsored by the Summit and America Coming Together, and modeled after the Freedom Rides that sparked the 1960s civil rights movement. A "Wake Up Everybody"

CD was produced and widely distributed. It played in many media markets.

In mid-July, another major music producer, Sean "P. Diddy" Combs began a group, Citizen Change, that was similar to the Summit. Citizen Change marketed the eye-catching theme of "Vote or Die." Combs and Simmons, together with Rock the Vote and Project Vote, led a historic increase in youth voting that included equally historic growth in the Black youth vote. The Center for Information and Research on Civic Learning and Engagement at the University of Maryland estimates that youth voting increased by 9.3 percent over 2000, yielding 4.6 million more votes in the 18–29-year-old group. The turnout rate in 2000 was 42.3 percent, and that increased to 51.6 percent in 2004, a figure that for the first time approached the adult overall turnout rate of 56 percent. The Maryland center's report illustrates that at 64.4 percent the turnout was particularly strong in the battleground states where most of the political resources were focused on attracting all voters. Black youths, who constitute 15 percent of all youths, registered an increase between seven hundred thousand and one million in turnout.

Blacks and the 2004 General Election

The Strength of the Black Turnout

The general turnout of all voters had been expected to be the highest ever, given the passion that fueled this election, and the Joint Center for Political and Economic Studies estimated that this would result in more than three million new voters. Although overall turnout increased slightly from 2000 to 58.6 percent of the eligible population, it was not higher than the 1968 level. Black voter turnout continued to close the gap with white voter turnout, moving from 2.9 percent less than whites in 2000 to 1.4 percent less in 2004. What can be said is that the factors discussed above, such as the unique context of the election, the Black infrastructure, and the youth vote, collectively contributed to the very substantial increase of 25 percent in the Black vote and matched the increase in the total vote. The 2004 election cycle featured a campaign strategy focused on what were perceived to be battleground states and, as has been traditional, Black voter turnout was greatest there, averaging 58.7 percent in those contested states with significant Black populations (Arkansas, 56.4; Florida, 58.9; Michigan, 65.9; Missouri, 51.9; Nevada,

62.8; Ohio, 62.5; Pennsylvania, 88.0; Wisconsin, 80.1). The largest proportion of campaign resources was spent in those states as a result of multiple candidate visits, significant political-party spending and coordination with the campaign, and the voter registration and get-out-the-vote activities of nonpartisan organizations. In comparison, the average turnout in those states with significant Black populations but which were not heavily contested was 56.8 percent, or approximately 2 percent lower than the turnout in the contested states (Alabama, 59.1; California, 38.5; Georgia, 50.9; Illinois, 41.5; Kentucky, 69.8; Louisiana, 54.6; Mississippi, 55.8; North Carolina, 72.8; New Jersey, 60.5; New York, 42.8; South Carolina, 58.7; Tennessee, 46.0; Texas, 53.8; Virginia, 66.1).

The Ohio Anomaly

Black voter turnout was highest in the battleground states of Pennsylvania, Wisconsin, and Michigan. Given the heavy concentration of campaign resources from all sources in Ohio, it is somewhat of an anomaly that Ohio's Black voter turnout was less than some of the non-battleground states, including Kentucky, North Carolina (where there were contested Senate races), and Virginia. Since no Republican has ever won the White House without winning Ohio, both campaigns paid special attention to the state. In fact, Kerry's visits to Ohio were matched by Bush so closely that as the campaign reached the final few days, both Kerry and Bush were in the state on the same day before the vote. Poll data showed that there was a virtual dead heat in the battleground states of Michigan, Ohio, Wisconsin, and Iowa.

The Black Vote and the Battleground States

Because of the substantial difference in the popular vote between the two candidates (2,731,873 votes), Black influence in this election cycle was minimized. Nevertheless, there were eight relatively close races, where either Kerry or Bush won the state at a level below 55 percent, with John Kerry winning three (Michigan, Pennsylvania, Wisconsin) and George Bush winning five (Arkansas, Florida, Missouri, Ohio, Virginia). In all of these states (see table 7.3), the Black vote was crucial to Kerry's victory. The size of the Black vote was material in the case of the victory for either candidate, especially in states with significant Black populations, and it is clear from the table that without the Black vote John

Table 7.3   Black Vote Influence by the Kerry/Bush Vote Difference, 2004

State	Kerry/Bush Difference	Estimated Black Vote	Elec. Vote
Arkansas	102,952	158,326	6
Florida	381,147	911,014	27
Michigan	164,243	628,182	17
Pennsylvania	128,869	737,907	21
Ohio	118,775	562,528	20
Total			91

Source: "National Pool Exit Poll," www.cnn.com/ELECTION/2004/pages/results/states/ OH/P/00/epolls.0.html; Network.ap.org/dynamic/files/elections/2004/general/national/president .html.

Kerry would have lost Michigan and Pennsylvania, while Black voter turnout in Arkansas and Ohio made these races much closer than they might have been otherwise. It should be noted that Black turnout in both Arkansas and Ohio was rather modest by the standards of states like Pennsylvania and Wisconsin.

The South Ignored

One of the debilitating factors in the exercise of the Black vote is the fact that the battleground strategy devalues Black voting power by ignoring the South, except for the state of Florida. And although table 7.4 below indicates that George Bush won all of the Southern states, the margin in several of those states was not out of Kerry's reach. The table points our

Table 7.4   The 2004 Presidential Election Results of Selected Southern States and the Potential Influence of the Black Vote (B = Bush, K = Kerry)

State	% B/K Vote	Black Vote	% Registration − %Turnout	B/K Diff.	Swing
Arkansas	54/45	156,418	27.1	102,521	51,261
Florida	52/47	911,014	22.1	377,216	188,609
North Carolina	56/44	885,942	29.5	426,778	213,389
Tennessee	57/43	291,755	16.3	348,761	174,381
Virginia	54/45	648,479	25.0	266,216	133,109

Source: Author's calculations based on data from: "National Pool Exit Poll," www.cnn .com/ELECTION/2004/pages/results/states/OH/P/00/epolls.0.html; Network.ap.org/dynamic/ files/elections/2004/general/national/president/html.

way to a simple assumption: with Kerry losing several Southern states by numbers in the mid-40 percent range, the addition of an achievable number of voters could have resulted in Democratic victories. It shows that the difference between the candidates in the 2004 presidential contest in the South was not so insurmountable but that with some effort additional voters could have been added to the Black voter base to make the Democrats competitive. The difference between the percentage of voter registration and voter turnout in these states indicates that there was much room for the addition of new voters, and that the raw vote difference could have been made up by a reachable number of voters, in most cases by the addition of new voters to offset the total, or by shifting half of the total from one candidate to another.

The Black Infrastructure and Turnout

The Unity '04 Campaign

In mid-October the Unity '04 campaign of the NCBCP held a press conference and announced that the coalition had registered just over one million new voters. And on November 4 the coalition announced that three million new voters had come to the polls, nearly one million of those voters youths.

Key communicators such as Black Entertainment Television, Radio One, and Tom Joyner of the *Tom Joyner Morning Show* were affiliated with the Unity '04 campaign and received more than thirty thousand calls in the month of August before the election, registering more than fifty thousand new voters. Beginning his partnership with the Unity campaign in 2002, Joyner has become a major force in political messaging for Blacks with an audience that is estimated to be over eight million. Also joining the Unity '04 team was the National Association of Black Owned Broadcasters. The coalition partnered with nonpartisan organizations as well to disseminate nonpartisan get-out-the-vote advertisements.

Blacks and 527s

The efforts of groups like Steven Rosenthal's organization America Coming Together (ACT) were effective in many places as the purveyors of new techniques of voter registration and turnout in the general election and in the Black community where outside groups with paid can-vassers worked to turn out the vote. The efforts of ACT were particu-larly effective in Pennsylvania where, by mid-July of 2004, eighty-six thousand additional people had been registered with the assistance of Rep. Chaka Fattah (D-PA), an African American member of Congress. Professional organizers from the Service Employees International Union in New York assisted ACT in Pennsylvania and produced one of the highest turnout rates (88 percent) ever achieved by Blacks nationally.

Nevertheless, some Black leaders who were participants in the Black election infrastructure of Unity '04 objected to Rosenthal's at-tempt to usurp the direction, intensity, and method of Black organiza-tions on the grounds that his efforts had not been effective. In fact, as we have seen, Black voters had effectively closed the gap with white vot-ers in both registration and turnout with the methods they had utilized in the past. Moreover, taking the meaning of "political participation" at its broadest, the value of the participation of Black organizations in the civic life of their communities is important beyond the narrow objective of winning an election. The unsolicited and invasive manner in which Rosenthal deployed his canvassers often promoted conflict in states such as Florida and Ohio, and may have contributed to the less than spectac-ular turnout results in those areas compared to others.[18]

Part of the proof of this assertion is the fact that other 527 organi-zations that worked in the Black community were received enthusiasti-cally because their approach was to hire canvassers from the community and to reach agreements on a division of labor with other organizations in the community rather than foster a competitive edge. Voices for Working Families, an organization funded substantially by organized labor, was active in eight states, some of which overlapped with the Unity '04 campaign, but their relationship with the coalition was harmo-nious. As a result, Voices for Working Families was able to account for 10 percent of the entire number of new registrations in the core Black communities of cities such as St. Louis, Philadelphia, Detroit, Miami, and Cleveland.

The Influence of Black Churches

For one of the few times in a presidential election campaign, Republi-cans targeted Black churches, beginning in February of election year with a meeting in Washington, DC, that honored Black History Month with a forum and dinner featuring Black ministers' wives in a special "First Ladies Summit." At that meeting, Republican National Committee Chairman Edward Gillespie emphasized the $300 million that Bush had promised to churches for prisoner re-entry programs, and said that "in order to confront poverty and family disintegration, and resist attacks on traditional values, President Bush has sought many ways to tap the moral leaders in America's communities."[19] Gillespie continued, "And now President Bush wants to help you," referring to another promise Bush had made to provide money for marriage and abstinence programs in an expanded discussion on an issue that emphasized the Republican party's position.

> We believe "marriage" is the legal union of one man and one woman. We must pursue whatever policy is necessary to protect this institution, including a Federal Marriage Amendment to the United States Constitution. Americans want to see changes in our tax code . . . schools and . . . our health care system, but there is no public clamor to change the definition of marriage.[20]

Gillespie pointed to Senator John Kerry's opposition to the Defense of Marriage Act, passed in 1996 and signed by President Clinton, that denied federal recognition of same-sex marriages and gave states the responsibility to legislate the issue. This cultivation of Black ministers, who might have been recipients of financial assistance from the administration, and who agreed with President Bush's stand proposing a constitutional amendment banning gay marriages, might have played a role in the result of a poll by the Joint Center for Political and Economic Studies in October of 2004 that showed a 100 percent increase in the level of support for Bush among Blacks between 2000 and 2004.

A sign that mainstream Black churches in Kerry's home state were sensitive to the issue of gay marriage occurred in February when the Black Ministerial Alliance of Greater Boston, the Boston Ten Point Coalition (a leading factor in the faith-based program), and the Cambridge Black Pastors Conference issued a statement that said in part, "Each of the (religious) traditions we represent has long upheld the institution of marriage as a unique bond between a man and a woman."[21] When asked about this issue at a forum in Boston, commemorating the twentieth anniversary of his 1984 campaign, Rev. Jesse Jackson noted that he knew "the pain of being unequal" that was experienced by gay persons, but expressed doubt that this issue would be a dominant one in the 2004 election campaign.[22] His view reflected the general strategy of the Democratic party to devalue same-sex marriage as a voting issue. In the fall general election, however, the expectation that Black support for Bush might rise by 100 percent over the 2000 level was not realized, though there was a slight rise in Black voter support for George Bush from 9 percent in 2000 to 11 percent in 2004. Nevertheless, if 11 percent was the national average level of Black support for Bush, a look at specific states reveals a somewhat different picture: Oklahoma, 28 percent; California, 18 percent; New Jersey, 17 percent; Pennsylvania, 16 percent; Ohio, 16 percent; South Carolina, 15 percent; North Carolina, 14 percent; Florida, 13 percent; and Virginia, 12 percent. This higher than average level of support for Bush in several states requires further discussion. One reason for higher Black support for Bush in Florida was enunciated by a Democratic leader in South Florida who said, "Bush didn't take the county [Palm Beach] but he went to the heart of the black community, our churches, with his faith-based initiatives, [and] got some of them to vote for him."[23] And in Miami's Liberty City, another Democratic leader echoed this, saying, "This is the first time Republicans have made an honest appeal to us. They spent dollars in our neighborhood. This is the first time I ever heard black radio ads by Republicans. They came with a strategy that worked."[24] Additional anecdotal testimony that referenced these themes came from a Black female Democrat in Jacksonville who voted for Gore in 2000. "All the days of my life I've been a Democrat, but I voted for Bush because I believe he is a Christian. I admire him because he's not for gay marriage and he's pro-life. He's strong in his morals."[25] No doubt this kind of impact made a difference in a state such as Ohio where, although the Black Republican vote declined over 2000, it still represented nearly 100,000 votes, a crucial number when the difference between Bush and Kerry was certified at only 118,775 votes on December 13, 2004.

On the other hand, Black churches were subject to pressure from the Internal Revenue Service to moderate their political activities. The First Baptist Church of College Hill in Tampa, Florida, received a letter from the IRS asking the minister to explain why the church had provided an opportunity during its regular service for candidates (Janet Reno accompanied by actor Martin Sheen in the 2002 election; the Reverend Al Sharpton in 2004) to make statements to the congregation. Although some of these letters were generated by Americans United for Separation of Church and State, a liberal watchdog organization, church members still found them intimidating and wondered why the political activities of white Evangelical churches, such as nearby Idlewild Baptist Church, which invited political activists, printed candidate fact sheets, and held political forums, were overlooked. It should be added that conservative churches, such as those led by well-known Southern Baptist pastors Ronnie Floyd and Jerry Falwell, also received such letters, and Falwell remarked that they were intimidating as well.

It is undeniable that such use of the IRS had a chilling effect on Black churches, perhaps more pronounced than on white Evangelical churches, as it was obvious that many churches moderated their political activities in the 2004 election cycle. One response to such measures is indicated by the comments of Rev. Albert T. Wilkins of Morningstar Baptist Church in Pasco, Washington, who said, "It seems the Black church, and not just in the South, has retreated from its historic role. There seems to be an incredible level of ambivalence toward politics."[26] In fact, Rev. Jackson noted to this writer that for the first time in addressing church members, he was faced with a written "disclaimer" spoken by the minister of the church before his address. The urgency of this matter led the bishops of the African Methodist Episcopal Church to issue a call to parishioners all over the country to come out to vote.

Continuing Tactics of Disenfranchisement

The 2004 election ended with considerable suspicion and recrimination, and a distrust of the electoral process somewhat similar to that following the 2000 election, but obviously not as intense. Indeed, in terms of the national attention it generated in the aftermath of the 2004 election due to a number of allegations of voter irregularities, Ohio assumed, though to a lesser extent, the role that Florida had in the 2000 elections. The Ohio secretary of state J. Kenneth Blackwell, an African American Republican, rebutted the Florida analogy, but his own actions generated considerable controversy. For example, he worked to refuse to allow provisional ballots to be cast in precincts other than where a voter legally resided; he issued a directive on the weight (eighty-pound stock) of paper voter registration forms; and he was cited by a district court for not instructing thirty-four thousand felons that they had the right to vote. As a result of these acts, he became the focus of numerous lawsuits as well as demonstrations by Black leaders and the organizations that support fair elections.

Another tactic involved the Republican party recruiting thousands of election monitors, who were paid $100 per day, to challenge the credentials of potential voters at polling stations in battleground states where Democratic party and 527 voter registration was heaviest. One opinion writer chastised the Republican party for its ballot security program of stationing "thugs" at polling stations to intimidate minority voters in a scenario that the writer called "voting while Black."[27] This view runs counter to the claim of Republicans that they were only fighting voter fraud, and it should be considered in the light of a larger government program in which Attorney General John Ashcroft asked state and local law enforcement officials to target voter fraud and ferret out other election crimes in the massive voter registration campaigns that were occurring. Many observers pointed to the lack of balance in such programs if the nation's highest law enforcement official, the attorney general, was not working as vigorously to insure the right to vote, and they saw this as an indication that the project had a distinctly political motivation.

Leverage Politics and the General Election Result

For most Black Americans, the conclusion of the 2004 election that reelected George Bush to the presidency was a disaster. But Black voter turnout, while it did not break records, had substantial and positive result: it reflected one of the highest increases in modern times, eradicated the voter turnout deficit with white voters, contributed to the expansion of the CBC from thirty-nine to forty-two members, and elected Barack Obama from Illinois to be another Black member of the U.S. Senate. Had John Kerry won, Blacks were poised to exercise a relatively normal form of leverage to realize Black interests, but one that I have described as dependent. It depended upon reminding Democratic party leaders that the Black vote had played a substantial role in their candidate's victory and upon this basis, hoping for sufficient policy returns. In short, Blacks would have been able to make claims on the administration, based on the currency of having been a loyal and significant part of the Democratic party electoral coalition—a claim, however, that could have been made by other elements of the Democratic party's constituency as well. This would place Black leaders and through them, their community, in the weak position of hoping and trusting that Kerry would reciprocate. In the wake of Kerry's defeat, there are at least two counterintuitive results that might be considered. First, in a Kerry administration Blacks may have had difficulty in attracting his attention to solid issues affecting the Black community. Kerry stated many times that he followed the centrist tradition of the Bill Clinton era, an era in which economic gains were substantial, but in which social policy gains were minimal if not retrogressive. Second, there is the issue of who controls the Black vote, an issue that was created by the new 527 organizations, based outside the Black community, which attempted to control and direct political resources for turning out the Black vote in contravention of the mature Black get-out-the-vote infrastructure. Yet the impact of their success in Black turnout was severely reduced by the more successful turnout of white Evangelicals.

A consequence of the foregoing is that if Kerry had won, the absence of a unified Black agenda, as a result of the failure of the politics of Black agenda-setting, would have worked to the detriment of Blacks. The politics of Black agenda-setting in this context was primarily the traumatization of the Black community by the Iraq war, the lack of jobs, and the poor performance of the economy. Because the removal of George Bush from the presidency became the most highly charged issue, no group of political leaders took responsibility for the construction of a set of issues or demands upon which leverage politics might have been based. Such responsibility came from outside the sphere of official Black politics, when a group of social activists in Boston and in Chicago held hearings and drafted Black-agenda documents, but these documents were all but forgotten and never injected into the election. Kerry, then, would have been in a much stronger position to exercise a weak accountability approach to the Black community even though its vote would have been critical to his victory.

Third, in the positive appeal to the Black church by Republicans with policy, money, and mobilization, there is some evidence that the Republicans are becoming competitive. Democrats did not compete as well either through or for the mobilizing power of the Black church because of relatively weak political resources of policy, money, and mobilization, in contradistinction to the Republicans. Given the greater position of the Democratic party not only in terms of tradition, but in terms of time, money, and Black leaders available, this failure of the Democrats constituted a serious flaw in their political strategy in the 2004 election cycle.

Nevertheless, the weakening of the base of the Black church as a vehicle for political mobilization expresses a weakening of the cultural base of the unity of the Black community, and not just in terms of the narrow function of its role in voter turnout. This weakening cultural base could have a much larger impact on the Black community than simply in terms of elections. It could signal that large segments of the Black infrastructure are unavailable for political mobilization work, and it could also signal the emergence of a serious ideological conflict within the Black community over the priority of issues that have not been hitherto regarded as central to Black political behavior. Eventually, the question must be answered whether the inroads into the Black church made by Republicans reflect a real crisis of value priorities within the Black community, or whether it is a political effect, manufactured by the attention and resources given to some Black church leaders by Republicans in the 2004 campaign cycle.

8

The 1965 Voting Rights Act: Leveraging the Power of the Black Vote

The Impact of the Black Vote

Motivation or Structure?

There is a relationship between the status and enforcement of the Voting Rights Act and the use and effectiveness of leverage politics by Black leaders. As such, the proper use of the Voting Rights Act to protect and enhance voting rights affects the opportunity for Blacks to achieve maximum political participation on the national level. Some analysts, such as Curtis Gans, head of the Committee for the Study of the American Electorate, believe that the key to expanding the vote in America does not reside in the structural processes of voting, but in the motivation to vote. This position comports well with my view that the most important increases in Black voter turnout in presidential elections were registered when a powerful motivation to vote was expressed in the form of greater than usual political mobilization that created a "social movement" dynamic in the political system. Note the stark difference between the presidential campaigns of the Reverend Jesse Jackson and the Reverend Al Sharpton. Both appealed directly to the mobilization of Black voters, but yielded markedly different results, largely because the Jackson campaigns occurred in a period in which the locus of a political movement was within the Black community, while the Sharpton campaign found Blacks reacting to passionate forces outside of the Black community. What this suggests is that, like social movements, the high levels of motivation that undergird strong voter mobilization in the political system cannot be sustained. In the instances where mobilization cannot be sustained, there must be an electoral system with the structural integrity to promote fair political participation and to allow the achievement of various ends by all of the citizens who participate, and by Black voters in particular.

In this work I have framed the Voting Rights Act as the structural dimension that, in the expanded universe of electoral reform that resulted from the National Voter Registration Act and the Help America Vote Act, now works to enable Black political behavior to have an impact on the national political system of elections and to generate the power resources that lead to effective bargaining for principles, goods, and services. That bargaining, I have asserted, is comprised of opportunities presented by a "two ballot scenario" in which the Black vote acts as a resource in the primary elections and in the general elections. This focus on the Voting Rights Act at the national level, rather than on its coequal concern with local districting, is important because a great deal of politics—very often its most authoritative aspects—is national. The interrelationship between the national and local levels often means that what happens in the politics that decide the distribution of resources at the national level affects the limits of what it is possible to accomplish at the local level.

Having posited the relationships above, this work also recognizes that the political fortune of any theory of politics is influenced by the context within which it exists. In this historic era, a strong conservative movement has assumed nationalistic features and now dominates the political system by dominating each of the existing national political institutions—the House, the Senate, and the White House—and it has even influenced decisions of the Supreme Court.

This conservative movement regulates the access of progressive sectors of society to the political system, and does so through its impact on the electoral system. Conservative governance has promoted strong actions vested in such measures as deep cuts in the federal budget, the privatization of public resources, and the initiation of war. These actions have cumulatively fostered strong passions, and the resultant action and reaction are reflected in the dueling moves of the Democratic and Republican parties as well as in the intense politics of elections. Politics is important to both sides because it exists as the gateway through which factions enter government and elect those who seek to implement or change the prevailing ideology.

Black politics exists substantially within the Democratic party as a subordinate racial political system. Therefore, the activities of Blacks as a constituency of that party have a direct bearing upon whether or not Black interests are respected by the party leaders in that system, in government, and in the process of election. I have suggested that leverage is the strategic tool that Blacks have used to gain power within the Democratic party. This work has been a discussion of that theory, with equal attention given both to the role of the Voting Rights Act in facilitating the size and shape of the Black vote and to the methods utilized to achieve that vote.

Because Black politics is part of a subsystem of politics, it is affected by the prevailing politics of the two major parties: the issues and currents of ideology that flow from the political culture and the nature of the electoral warfare the parties deploy to contest for power. Leverage strategies, therefore, may generally be rendered less effective by the nature of that warfare as they were in the 2004 election cycle. Nevertheless, the last twenty years of elections that I have summarized in this work are useful in understanding what elements are important in perfecting the leverage strategies that must be used by Blacks or any other culturally cohesive minority with a similar socioeconomic status in American society. Since the 2004 election is where I end this summary of Black political strategies in presidential elections, I will use it as a way to make some concluding observations on the way in which the Voting Rights Act might facilitate leverage politics in the future.

The Power of Black Turnout in 2004

The Black turnout rate of 57 percent in the 2004 elections was not the highest in modern times, but it was historic in having virtually matched white turnout. It contributed strongly to the national popular vote for John Kerry, and it would have probably ensured a Kerry victory in Ohio had all the votes been counted. There were seven states where Black voter turnout exceeded the percentage of Blacks in the eligible voting age population, and three states where the Black vote statewide contributed the margin of victory to a Senate Democrat. One way then to assess the strength of Black voting in a state is to use the degree to which Black turnout exceeds Black representation in the population.

Notwithstanding structural problems, and even in view of the fact that Black turnout in 2004 increased 25 percent over 2000, it is possible to reach the conclusion that leverage strategy failed both at the primary election level and in the general election. This conclusion does not prevent the researcher who is concerned with strategy from reaching a co-equal conclusion that for leverage strategies to be successful, even greater levels of Black voter turnout may be achieved, contributing to the possibility of more effective leverage politics in future elections. It is necessary to continue to demand a version of election reform that protects the Black vote and allows for the maximum participation of the Black community in the political system. This may require a reconsideration of the strategies employed by the Unity '04 campaign with respect to the character of campaigning itself, the mechanics of voter registration and voter turnout, and the places in the country where such activity is conducted.

Improving Leverage Strategies

Electoral Reform

The election of 2004 was challenged in a number of states on the basis of substantial claims that the voting systems in critical states yielded results that were incompatible, not only with the National Pool Exit Poll that was done on election day but with a wide variety of post-election studies. One such study, conducted by the Election Protection Coalition, found 1,100 irregularities in voting machines on election day.[1] Other groups challenged that the voting machines used at some polling stations in Oklahoma and Florida were programmed with software that was written to handle a certain number of votes and then begin to count backward. Many of the discovered irregularities were found in Ohio, as in a suburb of Columbus where a machine recorded 4,258 votes for President Bush, in a place where only 638 people voted. Additional information on voting irregularities may be found at the websites of the following organizations: the Center for Voting and Democracy, People for the American Way, the ACLU, the Leadership Conference on Civil Rights, and the Lawyers' Committee for Civil Rights Under Law. These organizations have also formed a collective website: www.civilrights.-org. The fact that the great balance of such discoveries were found to have favored the reelection of George Bush gave substantial impetus for challengers to pursue their claims.

Nevertheless, the Caltech-MIT Voting Technology Project said that "huge improvements were made" in voting systems and that as a result, hundreds of thousands more votes were counted.[2] This was echoed by numerous election officials in Maryland, Georgia, California, Nevada, and other states that reported that voting went relatively smoothly and without much error. This positive result, however, might be seen in the context of a potentially skewed result for the incumbent. One study by a research team at the University of California at Berkeley, a study that was not specifically focused on such anomalies, indicated that the effect of electronic voting favored President Bush. Utilizing election data, demographic data, and voting machine type data, researchers found that

> electronic voting raised President Bush's advantage from the tiny edge he held in 2000 to a clearer margin of victory in 2004. The impact of e-voting was not uniform, however. Its impact was proportional to the Democratic support in the county, i.e., it was especially large in Broward, Palm Beach, and Miami-Dade. The evidence for this is the statistical significance of terms in our model that gauge the average impact of e-voting across Florida's 67 counties.[3]

Members of the House of Representatives and community organizations in various states called for recounts in states such as Ohio before the certification of election results. But despite the prevalence of voting irregularities, John Kerry (as Al Gore in 2000) decided to concede defeat to George Bush rather than to challenge the result, although he had pledged on the campaign trail to "have every vote counted."

Insofar as the Voting Rights Act has been the engine of Black voter turnout, it is a tool to utilize to make leverage politics more effective. It is emerging as an important tool for increased participation, and one that enables the techniques and methods of turnout to produce results. The resolution of massive electoral violations of the rights of Blacks and minorities has thus far been addressed by a version of electoral reform that is heavily weighted on the side of fixing voting equipment and reforming material aspects of the electoral system. However, many of the problems that Blacks faced in Florida and Ohio stemmed from intentional racial discrimination in the administration of voting systems, a problem that new machines will not fix. This suggests that after the 2004 election there should be a new round of amendments to the Help America Vote Act (HAVA), that these amendments should take into consideration the participation of those who potentially may be harmed by structural impediments of the system, and that they should include and encourage those individuals, as election officials, to participate in its correction. In other words, the encouragement of diversity in the management of voter systems in the states is a fair fix of the potential for race, ethnic, and age discrimination.

The problems of having fair access to the ballot and of having one's vote counted constitute a new frontier in voting rights enforcement designed to protect Blacks. For example, it is curious that no case was filed to limit or prohibit the activity of vote challengers at the polling stations, when the intent of these challengers was to disproportionately challenge the credentials of Black voters. Some state laws give vote challengers unusual access to the process of voting, allowing them to operate inside polling stations and thereby producing a possible result of voter intimidation. This flies in the face of efforts to strengthen the legal federal right to vote and to enhance subsidiary voting rights laws such as the Voting Rights Act, HAVA, and the National Voter Registration Act, and it complicates the relationship of these acts to the facilitation of the right of Blacks to vote and to have their vote counted, when considered as a resource for leverage politics. In view of that, I concluded the previous chapter with some serious reservations about the utility of leverage politics in the 2004 elections. What, besides greater federal oversight of the right to vote, could improve the leverage position of Blacks in future presidential elections?

There will no doubt be substantial changes in the political process of presidential elections with the implementation of HAVA requirements both at the national and state levels (remembering that states have obtained waivers until 2006 to implement HAVA provisions). These requirements include new definitions by the Federal Election Commission with regard to the nature of 527s and their role in the political process, amendments to HAVA itself by Congress as a result of the 2004 election, the recommendation of the HAVA Commission, and actions of the courts that will decide questions such as whether the Voting Rights Act is pertinent in regulating the behavior of states with regard to felon disenfranchisement. All of these elements will, to some extent, affect the environment within which Blacks attempt to utilize leverage politics.

Campaigning

One could argue that the strong motivation of Blacks to vote in 2004, being driven by a consuming desire to remove President George Bush from the White House, created a special focus on this election from the outset that overrode the normal process of campaign agenda-setting. Although this motivation devalued the process of Black agenda-setting, it stimulated Black support for John Kerry in the primaries more than it did in any other part of the Democratic party constituency and drove high levels of voter registration and turnout in the general election. What is not clear is the extent to which or the manner in which Black turnout was achieved, and whether this will facilitate or inhibit Black campaigning in the future. Will a Black presidential campaign, or a campaign mobilized by Black voter registration and get-out-the-vote organizations that transfers the energy of citizens into a politics that legitimizes their interests, or both, become the new character of Black political participation in presidential politics?

There is a difference between Black participation in campaigns that are partisan in character and in those organizations that are ostensibly nonpartisan. But the practical fact of Black politics is that they end up at the same place because of the overwhelming support of the Black community for Democratic presidential candidates. Nevertheless, it is important to reaffirm the basic function of the campaign for Blacks as a community: the campaign is an indirect vehicle through which the community attempts to achieve power—translated as effective attention to its national policy agenda.

It was the achievement of a modicum of power, and the ability to make or participate in authoritative decisions about the livelihood of Blacks and their communities, that was the original motivation to achieve full participation in the political system. In *Black Power* by Stokely Carmichael and Charles Hamilton, the authors labor to make a distinction between the colonial forms of politics under which Blacks lived both in Africa and America and modern forms of politics that foster self-determination.

> The point is obvious: black people must lead and run their own organizations. Only black people can convey the revolutionary idea— and it is a revolutionary idea—that black people are able to do things for themselves. Only they can help create in the community an aroused and continuing black consciousness that will provide the basis for political strength . . . They must achieve self-identity and self-determination in order to have their daily needs met.[4]

191

The ability of the Black political infrastructure to contribute to the creation of political leverage for the Black community is dictated by its ability to successfully engage in the process of campaigning under conditions in which it is able to exercise control or self-determination with respect to the deployment of a strategy designed to maximize Black voting. As a cultural organization, the Black political infrastructure is dependent on valuing cues of self-identity and basing its appeal to political participation on the identity of those it seeks to mobilize. As we have seen, the capability of the Black infrastructure, as represented by the Unity '04 campaign, is dependent upon decisions made in the wider context of politics. It includes a complex set of actors: candidate organizations reflecting the strategies of the Democratic, Republican, and independent parties; the new political organizations known as 527s; organizations within the Black community such as the Congressional Black Caucus; and regulators of the political process, such as the Internal Revenue Service and the U.S. attorney general.

Given the fact that Black voting power was only partially mobilized in the 2000 and 2004 elections, let me reiterate that ceding the South to the Republican party is a questionable strategy, as questionable as would be the Republican party ceding the industrial belt to the Democrats. Richard Nixon understood the potential congruence of the Democratic and Republican parties in the realm of conservative politics, and he knit together an economic and social conservatism that became a potent political electoral force in 1972. In the early twenty-first century, the Democratic party has the same responsibility to break the solid Republican lock on the South by adding to the Black base those white voters whose interests are perceived to be similar to Democratic interests, or whose demands of the Democratic party can be met to their satisfaction without endangering the interests of other parts of the Democratic constituency.

Expanding Leverage: Multicultural Politics

Increasingly, the civic culture of Blacks must take into consideration the maturing Hispanic vote in presidential elections. In 2004 there were approximately five thousand Hispanic elected officials, 92 percent of them Democrats. With the size of the Hispanic electorate expected to grow substantially, the Democratic party began to reach out to this community as early as 2002 with a substantial financial program to attract their vote to John Kerry. The key person in this campaign was Bill Richardson, a popular Latino candidate for governor of New Mexico in 2002, former Clinton administration secretary of energy, and former U.S. ambassador to the United Nations, who said of his run for governor, "I made a decision [to run] after I saw the size of the check Terry McAuliffe wrote to the New Mexico Democratic party."[5] Richardson went on to win that election, and in 2004 he established his own 527 organization, Moving America Forward Foundation, which raised millions of dollars for the Kerry campaign.

A movement that links Black voting power with that of Hispanics, its closest cultural minority, could yield substantially increased political power for both groups. One fact that will have a profound effect upon American politics is that by 2025 thirteen states will have populations comprised of Hispanics, Blacks, and Asians that, given present voting trends, will have a substantial impact on American elections. The socioeconomic status of Hispanic immigrants is similar to that of Blacks, and it is clear that the nature of the political representation that Hispanics

Table 8.1   Black and Hispanic Population by Electoral Vote (% of the state)

State	Blacks	Hispanics	% Total	Electoral Votes
New Mexico	1.9	42.1	44.0	5
Texas	11.5	32.0	43.5	34
Mississippi	36.6	1.4	38.0	6
California	7.0	32.4	39.4	55
Georgia	28.7	5.3	34.0	15
South Carolina	29.5	2.4	31.9	8
Florida	14.6	16.8	31.4	27
New York	15.9	15.1	31.0	31
Louisiana	28.3	2.4	30.7	9
Alabama	26.0	1.7	27.7	9
Illinois	15.0	12.3	27.3	21
New Jersey	13.6	13.3	26.9	15
Virginia	29.6	4.7	24.3	13
Total				248(46%)

Source: U.S. Bureau of the Census, "Black or African American Population for the United States, Regions, and States and for Puerto Rico: 1990 and 2000," table 2, U.S. Bureau of the Census, Census 2000 and Redistricting Data Summary File, table PL1; "Hispanic Population by Type for Regions, States, and Puerto Rico: 1990 and 2000," table 2, U.S. Bureau of the Census, Census 2000 Summary File 1.

will seek will be concerned with a pattern of issues similar to those pursued by the Black population, and will be focused on a concern with fairness in treatment and in the distribution of resources. Moreover, the trends in question have an even more profound meaning when one considers their possible effect upon statewide offices and in presidential elections. The influence of people of color in the thirteen states where Black and Hispanic populations constitute over 25 percent of the total state electorate can be seen in table 8.1. These states accounted for 248 electoral votes or 46 percent of the Electoral College total in 2004. The predominant regions of impact were the southern and southwestern parts of the United States, with New Jersey, New York, and Illinois being the geographic exceptions. This results in a coalition in which Latinos are strongly represented in the southwestern states of California, New Mexico, and Texas, while Blacks are strong in the states of the Deep South. But even in the South, Hispanic voters are growing. The potential political power of Hispanics and Blacks in a framework of multicultural politics is real, but such factors as a lag in citizenship attainment by Hispanics, their comparatively low rate of voting behavior, and the failure of Blacks and Hispanics to consolidate coalition politics will delay this eventuality for some time.

Nevertheless, Hispanic turnout in 2004 represented a very substantial increase of 9 percent over the 2000 level, achieving a respectable 8 percent share of the total vote. Because of the split in the Hispanic vote (Bush, 44 percent; Kerry, 53 percent; and Nader, 2 percent, the highest of any Nader vote in the country), the swing potential of the Hispanic vote will make it more competitive. The irony is that such competition may divide the Hispanic vote more than the more coherent Black vote, making the Hispanic vote less of a factor in winning elections for the candidates it supports. This potential of the Hispanic vote to split between the two major parties could establish competition for a marginal share of the vote by both major political parties, the result of which would be to neutralize the vote for Democrats while adding to the total vote base of the Republicans. The most important determination of the value of such a result, whether or not it flows from a strategy, is whether it serves Hispanic interests in the policy system. If Republicans do not reciprocate with social policies that accrue to the benefit of the Hispanic community, the net effect of such an electoral result would appear to be contrary to the basic interests of Hispanics.

Here it should be observed that the Hispanic vote is also vulnerable to the same forces, such as moral values issues, that have allowed Republicans to make some inroads into the Black vote. In fact, the reduction in the Hispanic vote for Democrats in the 2004 election from 67 percent in 2000 to 53 percent in 2004, as indicated in table 8.2 below, may have occurred because the Hispanic population, being predominantly Catholic, was responsive to the negative publicity to which John Kerry, also a Catholic, was subjected when some of the leaders of the Catholic church called upon their members not to support his candidacy.

Aside from the Hispanic community, although both Hispanics and Asians tend to vote for Democratic candidates less often than Blacks, the possibility of a coalition with the Asian community finds some potential in that Asians have been trending toward the Democratic party in increasing measure since 1992. It is obvious from the data on the various votes of minority groups between 2000 and 2004 (see table 8.2) that while the Black share of the vote has increased modestly to 11 percent, and Asians have remained stable at 2 percent, the explosive growth of Hispanics has doubled their share of the vote in one election cycle. However, as the Black and Asian vote contribution to the Democratic candidate remained relatively stable, the Hispanic Democratic vote dropped substantially in 2004 as indicated. The growth in the Asian contribution to Democratic candidates has been the most significant over time, nearly doubling since 1992.

It should be understood that the mere observation that there will be increased numbers of immigrants is only important as public policy makers take into consideration issues that involve the distribution of resources. This question is also qualified by the decision of some groups, Hispanics in particular, to define their identity in relation to the prevail-

Table 8.2 Proportion of the Black, Latino, and Asian Votes for the Democratic Presidential Candidate, 1992–2004

	% Share of the Vote		% Contribution to Democrats			
	2000	2004	1992	1996	2000	2004
Blacks	10	11	83	84	90	88
Latinos	4	8	61	72	67	53
Asians	2	2	31	43	54	56

Source: National Pool Exit Poll, 2004; Gerald M. Pomper, *The Election of 2000* (Chatham, NJ: Chatham House, 2001), 138.

ing patterns in America. For instance, the indigenous pattern of racial formation in America suggests that since Hispanics can be any race, some will choose to be Black and some white. In the Race and Ethnic Standards for Federal Statistics and Administrative Report (1977) prepared by the Office of Management and Budget, 18 percent of Hispanics, when afforded the opportunity to respond to questions with respect to both race and Hispanic origin, indicated that they were white, and that figure grew to 47 percent in the 2000 census, with only 2 percent identifying as Black. What will be the political behavior of Hispanic racial groups? Will they identify with the already established voting patterns of Blacks and whites? What will be the voting pattern of any residual group that identifies itself as only "Hispanic"?

One very important aspect of politics is the probability that there will be a new round of social change movements among various immigrant groups as they seek to achieve their place in American society. For any further changes to occur, nonwhite immigrant groups especially will have to mount movements of social change to signal the nature of their agenda and to mobilize their vote within the electoral system—or in other ways—in order for the political system to respond.

What can be concluded is that in most cases, immigrant population interests will enhance a direction already mapped out by other groups in terms of public policy in areas that deal with the acquisition of the means to become full citizens. There will also be some dimensions consistent with the cultural values of these groups and their need for expression, and as their numbers increase this will add a different effect to American politics. Much of this potential impact, however, is dependent upon the construction of more effective coalition-building among immigrant and domestic groups that share socioeconomic characteristics. In this sense, the direction of Asian political participation, being slightly more Democratic than Republican in 2004, indicates that Asians may contribute to coalition potential in some states and thus to the presidential vote in a similar manner to that of Blacks and Hispanics.

Potential Conflict in the Democratic Party Constellation

In the postmortem of the defeat of John Kerry in the 2004 presidential election there are the seeds of substantial future conflict within the Democratic constellation that comprises the party itself, its various constituencies, its presidential candidates, and its allies in the 527 community. This conflict will flow from the attempt by Democrats to position their party to win elections, without sufficient regard to the legacy of the party and its constituency. Since 1992 the response of the party to the prevalence of a rightward-leaning electorate has been to reposition itself toward a centrist politics. This has been regarded as copycat conservatism by many within the party's liberal and progressive wing. Thus, in the 2004 elections the intrusive politics of voter registration and get-out-the-vote campaigns by the 527s and the new competitive status of the Black church provided openings for a widening fissure between Blacks and the Democratic party, a fissure that began with the symbolic Sister Souljah incident in 1992.

The nature of this division between the interests of the Democratic party's black constituency and its white leadership should be seriously considered, since it was visible enough to motivate two Black candidacies in the 2004 elections. And despite the fact that Al Sharpton's campaign, although addressed directly to this issue, was not viable in political terms, his campaign continued to raise this issue as one that was and is resident in the thoughts of many of the party's most loyal Black supporters. The question may be: Under what conditions will the Democratic party change from a position that is tolerated by Blacks to one that causes even more serious changes in Black political behavior? Three factors arose in the 2004 election cycle that may have a bearing on this question.

Rosenthal: Defeated by Micropolitics

Steve Rosenthal, CEO of the 527 organization America Coming Together (ACT), claimed to have registered 85,000 new voters in Ohio, while the associated America Votes coalition claimed to have registered 215,000 new voters with the help of some African American organizations. If half of the 300,000 new voters went to the polls, they would have accounted for 150,000 votes, a reasonable assumption, since in 2003 Rosenthal found in a Pennsylvania test of his methods that 44 percent of recently registered voters went to the polls. Assuming that half of the 150,000 new voters were Black, that would amount to about 75,000 new Black voters.[6] The estimated total number of Black voters in the state of Ohio, however, was about 600,000 and the increase over the 2000 election was about 150,000. It may be safely said that this coalition might have accounted for half of the new Black voters, but the main body of 525,000 Black voters was a product of their civic culture—a result of the self-determined behavior of individuals as well as of the push/pull effect of their organizational structure.

In this sense, while the methods of voter registration and turnout by ACT have been referred to as "revolutionary," it is highly questionable whether the intrusion of a nonindigenous and non-Black army of canvassers who left Post-it notes on the doors of people urging them to vote was at all the most effective strategy. Matt Bai says, in speaking of the people he met while observing ACT on election day in Ohio, that the "outsider" status of Rosenthal's army had a certain cachet and consisted of "thousands of volunteers from New York, New England and California [who] chose to work for the organization in Ohio instead of [for] the Kerry campaign; among them, I met a book editor from Manhattan and a massage therapist from Santa Barbara."[7] In fact, such volunteers may have had only a marginal effect on the Black vote in critical states. In that case, one does not know whether, in the vote targets established by ACT, the activity of ACT was decisive or whether the motivation of Blacks was so strong that it rather than ACT affected the turnout.

Moreover, although the combined efforts of every organization involved yielded a substantial increase in voters, the brilliance of the strategy of emphasizing turnout in heavily Democratic areas was also questionable in that its exclusiveness contributed to the Democratic loss of the state. To the question as to why an increase in nominally Democratic voters was not enough, the answer is that Republicans were exceedingly adept at capitalizing on their own electoral advantage in the "red" areas of the Ohio counties, especially in the new demography of "micropolitan" residential areas. These areas, recently defined by the Census Bureau as areas with populations between ten thousand and fifty thousand, are associated with a "core-based statistical area," or a much larger population complex, and are becoming a typical place of residence for commuters in edge suburban or exurban communities. Residents of these micropolitan areas were the targets of Republican campaigning in large cities all over the country.

Jennifer Palmieri, spokeswoman for the Kerry campaign in Ohio, said that the activity of Republicans in those areas was not visible and that Democrats were caught by surprise. When it became visible, it resulted in "conservative voters rising up out [of] the hills and condo communities in numbers [we] never knew existed. They came in droves. We didn't know they had that room to grow. It's like, 'Crunch all you want—we'll make more.' They just made more Republicans."[8] Then Palmieri said something very interesting:

> From the time of FDR, and "especially" after '00, Dems operated in the premise that they were superior in numbers, if only because their supporters lived in such concentrated urban communities. If they could mobilize every Dem vote in the industrial centers—and in its populist heartland as well—then they would win on math alone. Not anymore. GOPers now have their own concentrated vote, and it will continue to swell. Turnout operations like ACT can be remarkably successful at churning out the votes that exist, but turnout alone is no longer enough to win a national election. The Democrat who wins will be the one who changes minds.[9]

Donna Brazile, a Black party activist who ran the field operation for Al Gore's 2000 presidential campaign, said in a postelection analysis that the Democratic party had to lay a new foundation from top to bottom. "Don't get me wrong, I am still for Head Start, job training programs and the Children's Health Insurance Program, but in this day and age, running will not win elections."[10] This position, if adopted by the Democratic party in response to the view of Palmieri, will widen the already visible fissure in the party and will itself threaten the motivation of a vital segment of the party constituency that it needs to win elections.

If the micropolitan areas that defeated the Rosenthal strategy become the new contested zones of politics, the immediate implication for minority populations may be that urban inner-city areas will become less of the focus of battleground strategies by Democrats. And while this may resolve the issue of the interference of groups like ACT with the civic culture of Black political participation, it may create other problems, such as the fact that in order to successfully compete in such micropolitan areas, Democrats will have to espouse policies that are acceptable to voters in those areas, voters whose interests are sharply divergent from those of urban inner-city residents. And it may also exacerbate the financial resources problem of turnout in the inner city. These issues may be mitigated to some extent by the fact that the micropolitan political strategy for Democrats may become a reasonable expenditure of political capital as Democratic voters move into these areas over time.

Who Controls the Black Vote?

Much of the lack of respect and the treatment Blacks receive from the Democratic party, and which motivates the feeling and the fact that Blacks are being taken for granted, resides in the failure of Black leaders to bargain using the resource of the power of the Black vote. This presupposes that Blacks must control their own vote. In fact, this supposition is questionable. The control of the Black vote resides somewhere among the competing interests of Blacks themselves, the Democratic party operation, the president's campaign operation, and now, the new 527 political organizations. The failure both to clarify who controls the Black vote and to bid seriously for that control weakens the attempt to bargain.

The major question, therefore, is whether Blacks are able to control their own vote without the necessary campaign finances to do so. The ability of 527s to raise substantial funds outside of the control of either the Democratic party or a presidential candidate's campaign organization makes the 527s an independent player, especially if those resources are not shared. Key to this equation is the behavior of organized labor, which poured substantial funds into 527 operations in 2004. Organizations such as the Service Employees International Union (SEIU) have a large minority membership but have not invested proportionate resources in the control of Black voting organizations.

The Democratic party raised substantial sums of money in 2004 but did not subsidize operations that gave Black organizations the institutional strength to perform registration and get-out-the-vote operations in their own communities. This is important because there is the clear issue of the political accountability of the Democratic party to its Black constituency, an accountability based on the stunning record of past victories by Democrats that would not have occurred except for the Black vote.

But the white leaders in the Democratic party are not all to blame. Black political leaders inside the party apparatus traditionally have only episodically made strong and effective demands that the party's campaign resources be used in minority communities. One factor that undergirds Black leaders' consent to this treatment is their fear that if the party is pushed too far to the left, it will become uncompetitive and Black interests will suffer as a result. Evidence of this is that although Howard Dean initially excited the liberal wing of the Democratic party by offering a strong alternative to centrist politics, his brutal rejection by the party leadership was not countered by the Black political establishment.

The Black political leadership has succumbed to a politics of "positioning." During the primary and caucus season of the 2004 elections, most of the members of the Congressional Black Caucus, for instance, endorsed different candidates in an attempt to position themselves to exercise individual leverage. The emergence of strong individualism rather than collective strategies has, however, contributed to a reticence on the part of Black political leaders to aggressively push the party to dignify the interests of their national constituency, resulting in their being relegated to "appendage politics." Appendage politics is a descriptive term for dependent leverage, the accommodation of Black leadership to the party's rightward shift on the grounds that there is no valid option other than to adjust to decreasing policy returns in exchange for their constituency's political participation.

This paradigm should be exchanged for another that suggests that Black political leaders should exercise leverage politics for the basic interests of their constituents and compromise only when they must. Posing a strong alternative will be the only way to create bargaining situations that have the effect of pulling the Democratic party toward the desired policy goals of Black political leaders.

In a larger sense, the entire Democratic party should also practice this form of leverage. Americans are amenable to political education through public debate over clear differences in policies and by aggressive campaigning toward those ends, as Republicans have clearly shown. But the quality of the debate suffers if strong positions are not presented on both sides, and if resources are not provided as a foundation to support the promotion of those positions.

In response to this state of affairs, there should be a serious evaluation by Blacks of their role and position within the Democratic party. They should summon the courage to confront the truth that the route to positive outcomes from the political process for Blacks, as for any other group, is not lodged only in their ability to vote in substantial numbers, but also in their ability to see that their vote is respected in the process of party campaigning and governance. The route to the restoration of respect is through tough bargaining. Because of the erosion of that respect, Blacks must now work to determine an effective strategy based on independent leverage. Their strategy must place Black interests first and allegiance to the Democratic party in a neutral position relative to all other possible options, treating that allegiance only as a mechanism to achieve those interests.

Moral Issues and Black Political Vulnerability

Another important issue has to do with the base of Black civic culture and its relationship to politics, as implied in the role of Black religious organizations. The most prominent among the various analyses of the reason John Kerry lost the 2004 election is the view that the Religious Right was better mobilized by the Republican party and turned out to vote in greater numbers, especially in the micropolitan areas. The antidote, many believe, is to compete in the politics of moral values more effectively. Steve Rosenthal acknowledged that all of the turnout levels in Ohio were exceeded, and he couldn't think of an additional thing that could have been done to boost the vote. Then he concluded, "The shortcoming in some ways is that the national Democratic Party has built this values wall between itself and a lot of voters out there, and the Republicans took advantage of it."[11]

There is some evidence that trends in the opposite direction. For example, the National Pool Exit Poll illustrates that those who voted for George Bush said "terrorism" was their highest priority, at 86 percent, with 80 percent saying "moral values" were most important. With respect to all voters, if one adds their concern with terrorism (19 percent) to the war in Iraq (15 percent), these far outstrip the moral issue (22 percent). With respect to religion, while Bush attracted only 3 percent more of the Protestant vote than he had in 2000, he earned 5 percent more of the Catholic vote and 6 percent more of the Jewish vote. Overall, 23 percent of the voters in this poll were white Evangelical/Born-Again voters and 78 percent of these voted for Bush, but only 8 percent of respondents said that religious faith was Bush's most important quality. Finally, of all voters who considered the abortion issue, 55 percent thought that it should be either "always" or "mostly" legal, and 42 percent thought it should be illegal. These results lead me to conclude that the religious conservative vote was not important for the impact of its moral values on the election, but for its strategic value as a group that was mobilized disproportionately to others. In any case, there will be a debate about the effectiveness of using values as the prism through which a party's issues are framed, due to the public perception that both features are important.

Some of the religiously motivated vote included Black Christian conservatives. In the previous chapter we saw that the programmatic Republican approach to a sector of the Black church was important in fostering an increase in Black support for George Bush in the presidential election in several states. At the same time, it weakened the support for John Kerry and unearthed a level of competition not hitherto experienced in modern times. If this pattern continues (and the prospect is that it may, given that George Bush has won a second term), it may cause serious internal conflict within the Black community over issue priorities. The nature of this conflict may intensify and become highly subjective within the Black community if the pattern persists and Black Bush supporters receive rewards and resources for their work that are not matched by the Democratic party. The result could be a further drift of Black religious conservatives in that direction, accompanied by heightened acrimony from Black religious liberals and political leaders for their behavior.

The question of interpreting public issues through a moral prism is one that has been a unique part of the Black experience, and it was a critical aspect of the leadership of Dr. Martin Luther King Jr. His focus on racial discrimination, poverty, and war as moral issues lent to these issues a public credibility and a force that effectively challenged opponents to see the ways in which the Black struggle for justice, as a movement associated with the acquisition of basic citizenship rights, was consistent with the best traditions of America. To the extent that the Democratic party has distanced itself from these traditions, it may have yielded the moral high ground to a conservative brand of moral interpretation that is now the basis of a narrowly focused public policy agenda, especially in the social realm. The problem here is that some Black ministers have exchanged this prophetic tradition of the "social gospel" for a conservative doctrine that favors financial reward, materialist preoccupation with large institutional structures, and a fundamentalist interpretation of social life that affects their political identity and behavior.

This internal division, now at a relatively minor level, may pose a threat to the ability of Blacks to exercise leverage politics by weakening the effectiveness of the turnout mechanism in the Black community and by weakening their unified support for one candidate. The result of such weakening is that the Black vote may pose even less of a vital constituency to the Democratic party in the future because it may contribute less to the winning margin of Democratic candidates and it may, therefore, attract even less attention by party leaders to an issue agenda of substantial need.

The question then becomes, given that the increased Black support for Bush must still be considered moderate. Is there the possibility of a serious Black Republican constituency emerging that could play a substantial role in campaigning, in a manner that Black Republicans have yet to demonstrate, or that the Republican party has yet to encourage? There is also the question of whether the restoration of a powerful moral interpretation of social needs might effectively counter the growth of such a Black conservative force. It is a lesson that possibly Blacks could teach the Democratic party and perhaps restore its attractiveness to voters in the process.

Black Participation in Presidential Elections

The issue of whether structure or motivation promotes Black voting should be resolved in favor of both as the discussion above suggests. The Black agenda should encourage Blacks to participate, and the structure of the political system should allow individuals to vote and ensure that their votes are counted in an effective manner, as envisioned by the Voting Rights Act. As I have stressed, however, voting alone is often not sufficient to obtain the maximum results from Black political participation. It will take leadership to exercise the leverage gained through the performance of the Black vote. In this case, such leadership takes the form of either a Black presidential candidacy or the leadership of the Black civic culture working through coalitions to effect voter registration and turnout. Below, I will briefly describe my conclusion with respect to the potential of both.

The Black Presidential Candidacy

One possible primary conclusion about the nature of the Black candidacy is that there are circumstances under which the Jackson model is relevant, and if it is properly implemented, the model establishes the political resources whereby effective leverage may take place. The Jackson model yielded significant returns to the Black community in terms of political elements in the Democratic party, electoral gains in lower levels of politics, and subsequent policy considerations in the Clinton administration. The conditions necessary for Jackson's success had to do with the motivation of the Black electorate to participate, based on a direct relationship to the desire to foster change in a presidency that posed a threat to the interest of Blacks; the leadership of Rev. Jesse Jackson in the form of a presidential campaign vehicle with a powerful voter registration and election mobilization operation in the primary elections; and the structure of a Black civic culture, in the form of Operation Big Vote, that was able to mobilize voters to participate in voter registration and turnout in the primary elections.

By contrast, the campaign of Rev. Al Sharpton took place in the context of a number of elements that detracted from his campaign. First was the existence of an administration that posed such a severe threat to the interests of the Black community that it motivated the Black electorate to consider electability rather than leverage politics as a prime value to govern their candidate support in the primary and general elections. In other words, the context depends on the nature of the opposition as well as on the plausibility of the candidate in order for Blacks to deliver the majority of their support.

Second, with respect to the attraction of the Black candidate, many Blacks objected to Rev. Sharpton's candidacy for reasons relevant to his personal history, a point that we have covered. The Black community was, therefore, not united on his candidacy, and their division was enhanced by the presence in the race of Ambassador Carol Moseley Braun. Therefore, the second condition depends upon the acceptability of the candidate to the Black community and the subsequent unity of the community with respect to the candidate.

Third, there was strong opposition to the candidacy of Rev. Sharpton, outside of the Black community, by the Democratic party leadership and the media, partly because his candidacy was devoted to changing the centrist direction of the party. The media provided constant opposition to his candidacy based on his previous record of having participated in protest movements and various causes of social justice that they considered racially divisive and did not see as a qualification for presidential leadership. Thus a further condition for a credible candidacy is a modicum of public support beyond the Black community that allows for equal entrée of the Black candidate to the public arena.

Fourth and finally, the Sharpton campaign did not have the requisite financial resources to mount a successful appeal to the Black voter and to others because its structure and organization were compromised.

In addition, the lack of such resources as finances and expertise led Sharpton to make questionable alliances with individuals whose credibility was questioned, and which led some potential Sharpton supporters to question his credibility in return.

Any campaign in the future may or may not be able to implement the Jackson model successfully, based on whether it possesses the basic elements and meets the conditions outlined above.

Participation Strategy: Two Campaigns

In a review of both the 2000 and the 2004 presidential campaigns in which Blacks were predominantly involved, it is obvious that insofar as the Democratic party conceded the South (except for Florida) to Republicans, they also conceded the base of Black voting power. Therefore, a strategy has to be designed that presupposes a campaign that is configured to maximize *national Black registration and turnout* in the general elections. There should be a national Black campaign that has at least two critical elements.

The first of these elements is the development of a national mobilization (similar to the Unity '04 campaign of the National Coalition on Black Civic Participation) in the presidential elections of selected states with high Black populations. In these states, the maintenance of and an increase in Black registration and turnout is the objective. In some areas, such a strategy will combine with the Hispanic community to create additional voting power and thus, the prospect for the increased leverage of both groups.

The second element of a national Black campaign is one that might, in some ways, be consistent with a so-called battleground state strategy by which the Black vote might contribute to making the difference between candidates. This may or may not be able to be effected through the Unity '04 campaign, given the nature of campaign finance laws that clarify the relationship between organizations with 501(c)(3) tax exempt status, 527 organizations, organizations that work directly with the presidential campaigns, and those that are able to accept financial resources from a political party. I have not attempted in this work to wander into this thicket, since it is a contested area that will subsequently be amended by Congress, addressed by the Federal Election Commission, and altered by the working of the Help America Vote Act. Such aspects of a national Black campaign should be operationalized along these lines when and where possible.

Finally, given the previous sentiment about the complexity of the agents involved in shaping the process of political participation in elections, there is a necessity for greatly enhanced training mechanisms related to the process of voting. These mechanisms should address the use of various kinds of machines, the dissemination of information on voter rights, the availability of information on polling stations and their operations, the availability of knowledge about various resources (such as Election Protection) that can assist voters in general and on election day, and the acquisition of funding resources through HAVA and other sources of electoral resource support. The fierceness of political competition and the attendant challenges to the qualifications of voters and their knowledge of the political process require that Black voters become more knowledgeable about this process.

Black Civic Culture

It is the aim of Black political participation in elections to effect fundamental objectives that contribute to the freedom of Blacks in the twenty-first century. Engagement with the political system is not only a power activity; it presupposes and therefore helps in building civic culture. In this sense, regardless of whether turnout targets are met, there is a value in participating in the process as a learning opportunity, and in using the control and implementation of political resources as an aspect of enhancing self-determination. Because it is the key to leveraging political power in the systems of elections and policy making *by Black leaders,* the control of Black political resources should not be abdicated. If some entity outside of the Black community controls the resources possessed by Blacks, the outside entity, rather than Black leaders, will be in a position to spend or not spend those resources in these systems.

Future Stakes of Leverage

The 2004 campaign posed the question of what returns, given the substantial role that the Black vote played in the election, would accrue to the Black community. Leverage politics is at stake. At this writing, there are no top Black Democratic party leaders in the House of Representatives even though the time to have a Black minority or majority leader, caucus chair, or whip has long since passed. And even at the state level, there is the embarrassing fact that the two top Black officials are Republican lieutenant governors in Ohio and Maryland. If Black Democratic leaders cannot gain such positions, then their ability to translate their constituents' voting power into public policy is even more severely limited.

The answer to the questions raised above may depend upon the nature of the crisis of Black political participation. The continuing crisis of Black political participation is not merely the threat posed to new interpretations of the Voting Rights Act by the courts and the machinations of those in the conservative movement—it is the unfinished enforcement of the Voting Rights Act of 1965 as a tool to facilitate the full enfranchisement of Blacks as participants in a political system of national elections.

Notes

Chapter 1

1. Alexis de Tocqueville, *Democracy in America* (New York: Vintage, 1954), 100.

2. Linda K. Kerber, "The Meanings of Citizenship," *Journal of American History*, vol. 84, no. 3 (Dec. 1997), 836.

3. Frederick Douglass, "What the Black Man Wants" (speech given at the annual meeting of the Massachusetts Anti-Slavery Society, Boston, Massachusetts, April 1865), in *Let Nobody Turn Us Around: Voices of Resistance, Reform and Renewal*, eds. Manning Marable and Leith Mullings (Lanham, MD: Rowman & Littlefield, 2000), 125–31.

4. Ira Berlin, Barbara J. Fields, Steven F. Miller, Joseph Reidy, and Leslie S. Rowland, eds., *Free at Last: A Documentary History of Slavery, Freedom, and the Civil War* (Edison, NJ: Blue & Gray Press, 1997), 499.

5. Berlin et al., *Free at Last: A Documentary History of Slavery*.

6. Clayborne Carson, ed., *The Autobiography of Martin Luther King, Jr.* (New York: Warner, 1998), 107–8.

7. Carson, *Autobiography*, 109.

8. Lynda T. Wynn, *Tent Cities of Fayette and Haywood Counties (1960–1962)*, Tennessee State University, www.tnstate.edu/library/digital/tent.htm (accessed December 15, 1995).

9. Alabama Department of Archives and History, *Selma-to-Montgomery, 1965 Voting Rights March*, www.alabamamoments.state.al.us/sec59det.html.

10. Lawrence Guyot, interview from the *Oral History Project*, University of Southern Mississippi, September 7, 1996.

11. Robert Jackall, "Bureaucracy and Moral Casuistry," *Quarterly Review* (Winter 1987–1988), 47.

12. Charlie Cobb, interview from the *Oral History Project*, University of Southern Mississippi, October 12, 1996.

13. John Lewis, interview from the *Voting Rights Oral History and Documentation Project*, Moorland-Spingarn Research Center, Howard University, November 11, 1995, 4.

14. Beasley and Harlow, "Voices of Change," *Lexington Advertiser,* May 16, 1963, 89.

15. Howell Raines, *My Soul Is Rested* (New York: Putnam, 1977), 25.

16. U.S. Commission on Civil Rights, *Political Participation*, report, May 1968, 11–17.

17. Carson, *Autobiography,* 248.

18. Carson, *Autobiography,* 271.

19. President Lyndon Baines Johnson, "President Lyndon B. Johnson's Remarks in the Capitol Rotunda at the Signing of the Voting Rights Act," speech given August 6, 1965, Lyndon Baines Johnson Library and Museum, U.S. National Archives and Records Administration.

20. President Lyndon Baines Johnson, "To Fulfill These Rights," commencement address given June 4, 1965, at Howard University, Lyndon Baines Johnson Library and Museum, www.lbjlib.uTexas.edu/Johnson/archives.hom/speeches.hom/650604.asp.

21. President Lyndon B. Johnson, "To Fulfill These Rights."

22. Joint Center for Political and Economic Studies, *Blacks and the 2000 Democratic National Convention* (Washington, DC, 2000), 6.

23. John Lewis, interview from the *Voting Rights Oral History and Documentation Project*, 16.

24. National Urban League, *State of Black America 2004*, 2004 Executive Summary, press release, March 4, 2004 (covers 15–34 in the published text).

25. Lucius J. Barker and Mack H. Jones, *African Americans and the American Political System*, 3rd ed. (New York: Prentice Hall, 1994), 71.

26. Barker and Jones, *African Americans.*

Chapter 2

1. Gerald Pomper, *The Election of 1988: Reports and Interpretation* (Chatham, NJ: Chatham House, 1988), 52.

2. Susan Tifft, "Push Toward the Presidency: A Black Convention Urges Jesse Jackson's Candidacy," *Time,* August 8, 1983.

3. Joseph L. Wagner, "Labor Day Picnic Tradition Has Become an Institution," *Plain Dealer,* Cleveland, Ohio, September 7, 2004, 1.

4. Frederick Harris, "Something Within: Religion as a Mobilizer of African-American Political Activism," *Journal of Politics,* vol. 56, no. 1 (February 1994), 63.

5. Cited in Allen D. Hertzke, *Echoes of Discontent: Jesse Jackson, Pat Robertson, and the Resurgence of Populism* (Washington, DC: CQ Press, 1993), 122.

6. Hertzke, *Echoes of Discontent*, 131.

7. C. Eric Lincoln and Lawrence H. Mamiya, *The Black Church in the African American Experience* (Durham, NC: Duke University Press, 1990), 227.

8. "The Public Influences of African-American Churches: Contexts and Capacities," A Report Submitted to the Pew Charitable Trust by the Public Influences of African American Churches Project, Directed by Dr. R. Drew Smith, The Leadeship Center, Morehouse College, Atlanta, GA, 2002, 3.

9. Bayard Rustin, *Down the Line: The Collected Writings of Bayard Rustin* (New York: Quadrangle, 1971), 345.

10. Rustin, *Down the Line*, 349.

11. Melvin Maddocks, "Labor's Love Lost, or Whatever Became of Samuel Gompers?" *Christian Science Monitor*, Boston, June 10, 1988, 19.

12. Kenneth B. Noble, "Labor-Jackson Connection in the City Strengthens Both," *New York Times*, April 18, 1988, A17.

13. E.J. Dionne, "Unions Make Major Gains in '88 Politics," *New York Times*, June 5, 1988, 1.

14. Ronald Walters, *Black Presidential Politics in America* (Albany, NY: SUNY Press, 1989), 169.

15. Ronald Smothers, "The Impact of Jesse Jackson," *New York Times Magazine*, March 4, 1984, 41.

16. Charles Henry, *Jesse Jackson: The Search for Common Ground* (Oakland, CA: Black Scholar Press, 1991), 21.

Chapter 3

1. Bill Clinton, *My Life* (New York: Knopf, 2004), 364.

2. The Hotline, "Jackson: Clinton Disavows DLC Director's Slight," *National Journal*, www.politicsonline.com/coverage/hotline/h980930.htm (accessed April 22, 1991).

3. David Mills, "Sister Souljah's Call to Arms: The Rapper Says the Riots Were Payback. Are You Paying Attention?" *Washington Post*, May 13, 1992, B1.

4. Clinton, *My Life*, 411.

5. Jack Germond and Jules Witcover, *Mad as Hell: Revolt at the Ballot Box, 1992* (New York: Warner, 1993), 303.

6. Germond and Witcover, *Mad as Hell*, 394.

7. Germond and Witcover, *Mad as Hell*, 257.

8. Gerald Pomper, ed., *The Election of 1992: Reports and Interpretations* (Chatham, NJ: Chatham House, 1993), 62.

9. Pomper, *Election of 1992*.

10. *Richmond Times-Dispatch*, "Coleman Faults Wilder Presidential Bid," May 6, 1991, 9.

11. The Hotline, "Poll Update—Gallup: Non-candidate Cuomo Outpolls Dems Running," *National Journal*, www.politicsonline.com/coverage/hotline/h980930.htm (accessed September 23, 1992).

12. The Hotline, "Poll Update—Gallup"; see also Michael Hardy, "Wilder Challenges President," *Richmond Times-Dispatch*, October 26, 1991, 1.

13. John F. Harris and Donald P. Baker, "Wilder Trying to Polish His Tarnished Image: Presidential Bid Rusted Governor's Armor," *Washington Post*, March 23, 1992, C1.

14. Ronald Smothers, "Beyond the Jackson Bid: Some Gains for Blacks," *New York Times*, July 1, 1984, 16.

15. Gerald Pomper, ed., *The Election of 1996* (Chatham, NJ: Chatham House, 1997), 198.

16. Pomper, *Election of 1996*.

17. The Hotline, "Poll Update—HBO/Joint Center: Blacks—Clinton 43%, Perot 14%, Bush 13%," *National Journal*, www.politicsonline.com/coverage/hotline/h980930.htm (accessed July 9, 1991).

18. David Bositis, "A Watershed for the Black and Hispanic Vote," *The Record*, December 11, 1996.

19. U.S. Bureau of the Census, "Reported Voted and Registered by Race, Hispanic Origin, Sex and Age: November 1964 to 1968" (Washington, DC, July 19, 2000); the Committee for the Study of the American Electorate reports the following numbers: 1994—38.79%; 1998—36.06%, or a difference of 2.73%. Committee for the Study of the American Electorate, "Final Post Election Report: Notes and Summary Chart" (Washington, DC, February 2, 1999).

20. Richard Benedetto, "Polls Paint Picture of Who Voted, and How," *USA TODAY*, November 4, 1998, 18A.

21. Committee for the Study of the American Electorate, "Final Post Election Report."

22. Thomas B. Edsall and Claudia Deane, "Poll Shows Democratic Gains with Key Voters," *Washington Post*, November 4, 1998, A27.

23. "For Voters, Its Back toward the Middle," *Washington Post*, November 5, 1998, A33.

24. MSNBC Staff and Wire Reports, "Black Vote Key in Democratic Wins," www.msnbc.msn.com (accessed November 3, 1998).

25. Sam Fulwood III, "Blacks Play Pivotal Role in Party Wins," *Los Angeles Times*, November 5, 1998, www.latimes.com.

26. Hector Tobar, "In Contests Big and Small, Latinos Take Historic Leap," *Los Angeles Times*, www.latimes.com (accessed November 5, 1998).

27. Tobar, "Latinos Take Historic Leap."

28. Edsall and Deane, "Poll Shows Democratic Gains."

29. Jean Merl, "Legislative Races Go Mostly to Democrats," *Los Angeles Times,* www.latimes.com (accessed November 4, 1998).

30. "Large Turnout of Black Voters," *Washington Post,* November 4, 1998, A34.

31. Charles Babington, "Glendening Prevails in MD, Sauerbrey Defeated as Democrats Have Strong Showing," *Washington Post,* November 4, 1998, A1.

32. Donald P. Baker, "Democrats Get Out the Black Vote, Door-by-Door," *Washington Post,* November 4, 1998, A35.

33. Babington, "Glendening Prevails."

34. CNN.com, "Election '98," www.cnn.com/allpolitics.html (accessed November 3, 1998).

35. Geoff Earle, "CQ: Conservative Southern Democrats Seek House Seats—and Credibility," *CNN.com,* www.cnn.com/allpolitics.html (accessed October 20, 1998).

36. Rick Brand, "Schumer Topples Senator D'Amato: 'The Battle Is Over' Incumbent Concedes," *Newsday,* November 4, 1998, A3; Deborah Barfield and William Douglass, "Grassroots Boost: African-Americans, Labor Turn the Tide," *Newsday,* November 5, 1998, A55.

37. Charlotte-Mecklenburg voter registrar, by telephone conversation, November 5, 1998; Faircloth said in his campaign that he had invoked the wrath of "Jesse Jackson, Louis Farrakhan, [and] DC Mayor Marion Barry, who shot back that Faircloth's message had "racial overtones"; David A. Vise and Michael Powell, "Faircloth Invokes DC Power Shift in NC Campaign," *Washington Post,* June 4, 1998, D1.

38. Baker, "Democrats Get Out the Black Vote."

39. Baker, "Democrats Get Out the Black Vote."

40. Cook County Government, voting registrar; Edsall and Deane, "Poll Shows Democratic Gains."

41. Flynn McRoberts, "Senator's Defeat Is Her Last Hurrah," *Chicago Tribune,* www.chicagotribune.com (accessed November 5, 1998).

42. *Washington Post,* "Democrats Gain Seats in State Legislatures," November 5, 1998, A46.

43. *Washington Post,* "Democratic Leadership Council Press Conference," November 11, 1998, A35.

44. Tom Edsall, "Democrats Lean Right, Hold On," *Washington Post,* November, 5, 1998, A35.

45. John H. Britton, "Operation Big Vote," *Focus,* vol. 4, no. 9 (August 1976), 4.

46. Black Leadership Forum, national nonpartisan briefing, June 25, 1998, Washington, DC. The Black Leadership Forum is comprised of twenty-

five well-known national Black organizations and is chaired by Rev. Joseph Lowery and directed by Dr. Yvonne Scruggs-Leftwich. The National Coalition on Black Civic Participation is a coalition of eighty-five Black nonprofit associations (representing a variety of aspects of Black life) that is headquartered in Washington, DC, and is headed by Richard Womack, an official of the AFL-CIO. Its main projects are Operation Big Vote, Black Youth Vote, and the Black Women's Roundtable.

47. Britton, "Operation Big Vote," 5.

48. *Washington Afro-American,* "National Civic Coalition Gets Out the Black Vote," November 15, 2002, C10.

49. National Coalition on Black Civic Participation, "25 Years of Making Democracy Work," Washington, DC, 7.

50. The message in the advertisement was, "The Black Leadership Forum, Inc. and Black Entertainment Television, Inc. (BET) urge African Americans to vote on November 3, 1998 for the political party whom you believe will deliver results on: Improved Education, Quality Health Care, Jobs, Affirmative Action, Sentencing Parity for Drug Convictions, Equal Justice for All, Fair Urban and Rural Policies. Lift every voice and vote on November 3 for the party of your choice." Twenty-one Black organizations that were part of the coalition of the Black Leadership Forum signed the advertisement. See *USA TODAY*, October 30, 1998, 5A.

51. See Bill Nichols and Jessica Lee, "Dems Try Last-minute Push to Boost Black Votes," *USA TODAY*, November 2, 1998, 9A.

52. MSNBC Staff and Wire Reports, "Black Vote Key in Democratic Wins," www.msnbc.com (accessed November 4, 1998).

53. A. Philip Randolph Institute, "APRI Plays Key Role in '96 Election," 1998, www.apri.org/Home.htm.

54. Coalition of Black Trade Unionists, "History: A Sleeping Giant Awakens," www.cbtu.org.

55. Coalition of Black Trade Unionists, "PEN 2002: A New Model for Political Participation," www.cbtu.org/pen.

56. Wolfgang Saxon, "Harold Curtis Fleming Dies at 70; Tirelessly Fought for Civil Rights," *New York Times*, September 7, 1992, 20.

57. George Edmonson, "Campaign 2000: Volunteers' Hard Work Pays Off on Election Day," *Atlanta Journal-Constitution*, November 4, 2000, G5.

58. Christopher Dunn, "100,000 Voters Is Goal of Coalition," *Atlanta Journal-Constitution*, June 2, 2002, C1.

59. Doug Payne, "Volunteers Prepare for Voter Drives," *Atlanta Journal-Constitution*, February 8, 2004, C3.

60. Ronald Walters, *Black Presidential Politics in America: A Strategic Approach* (Albany: SUNY Press, 1988), 110–38.

Chapter 4

1. U.S. Commission on Civil Rights, *Political Participation,* May 1968, 60–130.

2. Kathryn Abrams, "Raising Politics Up: Minority Political Participation and Section 2 of the Voting Rights Act," *New York University Law Review,* vol. 63, rev. 449 (June 1988), LexisNexis Academic, www.lexisnexis.com.

3. Abrams, "Raising Politics Up."

4. Steven L. Lapidus, "Eradicating Racial Discrimination in Voter Registration: Rights and Remedies under the Voting Rights Act Amendments of 1982," *Fordham Law Review,* vol. 52, LexisNexis Academic, www.lexisnexis.com.

5. Bickerstaff, Heath, Smiley, Pollan, Kever & McDaniel, L.L.P., "Frequently Asked Questions on *Shaw v. Reno*—Racial Gerrymandering," www.votinglaw.com (accessed April 1, 2001).

6. Bickerstaff, Heath, Smiley, Pollan, Kever & McDaniel, L.L.P., "Questions on *Shaw v. Reno*," 2818.

7. Characteristics that define any culturally coherent group abound in the literature of the social sciences and, thus, the elements of ethnicity may also apply to Blacks, as suggested in a recent study of this subject: "a human population with myths of a common ancestry, shared historical memories, one or more elements of common culture, a link with a homeland and a sense of solidarity among at least some of its members." John Hutchinson and Anthony D. Smith, *Ethnicity* (New York: Oxford University Press, 1996), 6.

8. *USA TODAY,* "Polls Paint Picture of Who Voted, and How," November 4, 1998, 18A.

9. Robert Singh, *The Congressional Black Caucus* (Thousand Oaks, CA: Sage, 1996), 145.

10. David Bositis, *The Congressional Black Caucus and the 103rd Congress* (Washington, DC: Joint Center for Political and Economic Studies, 1993), 19.

11. Leslie G. Carr, *"Color-Blind" Racism* (Thousand Oaks, CA: Sage Publications, 1997), 126.

12. Ronald Walters, "Color-Blind Redistricting and the Efficacy of Black Representation," in *The State of Black America 1999* (New York: National Urban League, 1999), 131.

13. Susan Milligan, "New Congress Is Most Diverse Ever," *Boston Globe,* November 6, 2004, A1.

14. See, for example, Bernard Grofman and Chandler Davidson, eds., *Controversies in Minority Voting: The Voting Rights Act in Perspective* (Washington, DC: The Brookings Institution, 1992). See especially the contributions of Abigail Thernstrom, Katherine Butler, Timothy O'Rourke, and Carol Swain.

15. Charles Cameron, David Epstein, and Sharyn O'Halloran, "Do Majority-Minority Districts Maximize Substantive Black Representation in Congress?" *The American Political Science Review,* vol. 90, no. 4 (December 1996), 809.

16. Walters, "Color-Blind Redistricting," 107–36.

17. Charles Bullock, "The South and the 1996 Elections," *PS: Political Science & Politics,* vol. 29, no. 3, 450.

18. Author's calculation. The eleven states of Alabama, Florida, Georgia, Louisiana, Maryland, Mississippi, North Carolina, South Carolina, Tennessee, Texas, and Virginia contributed 12.5 million votes to Robert Dole in 1996 (out of 39.2 million) and 16.3 million votes to George Bush in 2000 (out of 50.5 million votes cast).

19. Earl Black and Merle Black, *The Rise of Southern Republicans* (Cambridge: Harvard University Press, 2002), 213.

20. Black and Black, *Rise of Southern Republicans,* 212.

21. Ronald Walters, *White Nationalism, Black Interests* (Detroit: Wayne State University Press, 2003), 38–66.

22. James H. Kuklinski, Michael D. Cobb, and Martin Gilens, "Racial Attitudes and the 'New South,'" *American Journal of Political Science,* vol. 59, no. 2 (May 1997), 323–49.

23. Kuklinski, Cobb, and Gilens, "Racial Attitudes," 346.

24. Alan S. Zuckerman, Nicholas A. Valentino, and Ezra W. Zuckerman, "A Structural Theory of Vote Choice: Social and Political Networks and Electoral Flows in Britain and the United States," *Journal of Politics,* vol. 56, no. 4 (November 1994), 1029.

25. Committee for the Study of the American Electorate, report (Washington, DC, 2001).

26. David Bositis, *2000 National Opinion Poll: Politics* (Washington, DC: Joint Center for Political and Economic Studies, 2000), 3.

27. *Indianapolis Star,* Library FactFiles, "Election 2000: The Presidency," www.indystar.com/library/factfiles (accessed December 14, 2000). This factfile contains a timeline of events in the legal battle between the two campaigns.

28. NAACP Office of Communications, "NAACP Escalates Efforts to Investigate Voter Fraud," press release, November 7, 2000.

29. Allan J. Lichtman, "Report on the Racial Impact of the Rejection of Ballots Cast in the 2000 Presidential Election in the State of Florida," presented before the U.S. Civil Rights Commission, *Voting Irregularities in the Presidential Election of 2000 in Florida,* June 2001.

30. Lichtman, "Report on the Racial Impact of the Rejection of Ballots Cast."

31. John Mintz and Dan Keating, "A Racial Gap in Voided Votes," *Washington Post,* December 27, 2000, A1.

32. The Sentencing Project (with Human Rights Watch), "Losing the Vote: The Impact of Felony Disenfranchisement Laws in the United States" (October 1998), table 3; The Sentencing Project, "Disenfranchisement of Felons by State and Correctional Status" (October 1998), 9.

33. The Civil Rights Project, "Democracy Spoiled," Harvard University, report, 2001.

34. Greg Palast, "Florida's 'Disappeared Voters': Disenfranchised by the GOP," *The Nation*, www.gregpalast.com (accessed February 5, 2001).

35. Guy Stuart, "Databases, Felons, and Voting: Errors and Bias in the Florida Felons Exclusion List in the 2000 Presidential Election" (Faculty Research Working Paper Series, John F. Kennedy School of Government, Harvard University, September 2002), RWP02-041.

36. Stuart, "Databases, Felons, and Voting," 6.

37. Ann Louise Bardach, "How Florida Republicans Keep Blacks from Voting," *Los Angeles Times*, www.latimes.com (accessed September 26, 2004).

38. Abby Goodnough, "Disenfranchised Florida Felons Struggle to Regain Their Rights," *New York Times*, www.nytimes.com (accessed March 28, 2004).

39. Gary Fineout, "State: Purge Felon Voters on List," *Miami Herald*, www.miamiherald.com (accessed May 6, 2004).

40. *Johnson v. Bush*, U.S. District Court Southern District of Florida, April 2003.

41. Jay Weaver, "Ex-felons Seeking Voting Rights Get Trial," *Miami Herald*, www.miamiherald.com (accessed December 20, 2003).

42. Tony Mauro, "Supremes May Consider Convicted Felons' Voting Rights," *Legal Times*, www.law.com (accessed November 5, 2004).

43. Linda Greenhouse, "Supreme Court Declines to Hear Two Cases Weighing the Right of Felons to Vote," *New York Times*, www.nytimes.com (accessed November 9, 2004).

44. The Sentencing Project, "Felony Disenfranchisement Laws in the United States" (Washington, DC, October 1998).

45. *George W. Bush, et al., Petitioners v. Albert Gore, Jr., et al.*, 531 U.S. 98, 121 S.Ct. 525 (2000).

46. *Bush v. Gore*.

47. *Bush v. Gore*.

Chapter 5

1. People for the American Way and the National Association for the Advancement of Colored People, "The Long Shadow of Jim Crow: Voter Intimidation and Suppression in America Today," September 2004.

2. Kathleen Gray, "Remark Sets Off Election Fervor," *Detroit Free Press,* October 13, 2004, 1.

3. People for the American Way, "Long Shadow of Jim Crow."

4. People for the American Way, "Long Shadow of Jim Crow."

5. Associated Press, "Jesse Jackson Warns DNC about GOP," August 13, 2000.

6. Alicia Montgomery, "Jesse Jackson Questions Florida Voting," *Salon .com,* www.salon.com (accessed November 8, 2000).

7. BBC News, "Jackson Leads Florida Re-vote Protest," www.bbc.co.uk (accessed November 10, 2000).

8. Steve Bousequet, "Democrats at Rally Promise to Even the Score in 2002," *Miami Herald,* January 21, 2001, 6B.

9. CNN.com, "Election Reform Rally Held in Tallahassee, without Jesse Jackson," www.cnn.com (accessed January 20, 2001).

10. Jackie Calmes, "Election-Reform Proposals Pop Up All Over the Country," *Wall Street Journal,* February 5, 2001.

11. Calmes, "Election-Reform Proposals Pop Up."

12. Frank Davies, "A Push for Election Reform Floridians' Gripes on 'Debacle' of '99 Heard by House Group," *Miami Herald,* February 28, 2001, 3A.

13. Davies, "A Push for Election Reform."

14. HAVA, Title III, Subtitle A, Sect. 302. Provisional Voting and Voting Information Requirements.

15. HAVA, 11.

16. Jeffrey Gettleman, "In Duval County, Views of Vote Process as Different as Black and White," *Los Angeles Times,* December 10, 2000, A28.

17. Lawyers' Committee for Civil Rights Under Law, "Settlement Reached in Florida Lawsuit," www.lawyerscomm.org (accessed September 3, 2002).

18. National Conference of State Legislatures, "U.S. Supreme Court Upholds McCain-Feingold Campaign Finance Law," www.ncsl.org (accessed December 10, 2003).

19. The Fannie Lou Hamer Project and The William C. Velasquez Institute, "The Color of Money," October 2004, 1–4.

20. Amy Keller, "FEC, Nonprofits at Odds over Proposed Changes to Regulations," *Roll Call,* www.rollcall.com (accessed March 4, 2004).

21. See, for example, Harold Myerson, "Numbers Game," *The American Prospect,* March 2004, 11; Corey Dade, *Atlanta Journal-Constitution,* May 21, 2004, 4A; Susan Milligan, "Democrats Turn to Black Voters for Donations," *Boston Globe,* January 30, 2004, A1. The latter article describes a meeting that took place in Charleston, South Carolina. Sponsored by wealthy African American lawyer Willie Gary, the conference was designed to develop a plan to fund Black infrastructure operations.

Chapter 6

1. Ronald Walters, *Black Presidential Politics in America* (Albany, NY: SUNY Press, 1988).

2. Michael Powell, "Unafraid of Speaking Out, Moving to a National Stage," *Washington Post*, June 29, 2003, A1.

3. Nedra Pickler, "Sharpton Brings Diversity, Controversy to Democratic Presidential Field," Associated Press, March 3, 2003.

4. Heather Mac Donald, "Al Sharpton Just Won't Let Wounds Heal," *Wall Street Journal*, www.wsj.com (accessed August 31, 2000).

5. Reverend Al Sharpton, "Racism," www.blackelectorate.com (accessed December 30, 2002).

6. Mike Glover, "Sharpton: Major Media Dismiss Him," Associated Press, www.msnbc.com (accessed August 25, 2003).

7. Seth Gitell, "Al Sharpton for President," www.thephoenix.com (accessed March 10, 2003).

8. National Public Radio, "The Reverend Al Sharpton," *The Morning Edition*, interview on June 13, 2003.

9. National Public Radio, "Reverend Al Sharpton."

10. Reverend Al Sharpton, "I'm Running to Revive and Reclaim Our Democracy and to Make America 'a More Perfect Union,'" Reverend Al Sharpton's Top Ten, platform statement.

11. Mark J. Penn, "The Democratic Party and the 2004 Election," convention of the Democratic Leadership Council, Washington, DC, July 28, 2003.

12. U.S. Bureau of the Census, "Voting and Registration in the Election of 2000," Bureau of the Census, Department of Commerce, 2002.

13. Tim Whitmire, "Sharpton Urges Blacks to Support His Campaign," Associated Press, Charlotte, NC, August 7, 2003.

14. *Washington Post*, "Comes Now the Rev. Sharpton," editorial, January 22, 2003, A14.

15. Dan Balz, "Sharpton Launches Run for Presidency: Candidate Cites Advocacy of Disaffected," *Washington Post*, January 22, 2003, A1.

16. DLC letter, July 31, 2003.

17. "Remarks of Al From to the 2003 DLC National Convention," July 28, 2003, Washington, DC.

18. "Remarks of Senator Evan Bayh to the 2003 DLC National Convention," July 28, 2003, Washington, DC.

19. Jim VandeHei, "Lieberman: The Democrats' Centrist," *Washington Post*, www.washingtonpost.com (accessed August 19, 2003).

20. Carol Moseley Braun, "In Her Own Words," excerpt from Carol Moseley Braun's stump speech, *Washington Post*, July 13, 2003, A6.

21. Martin Schram, "Mondale Seen Hurt by Black Nominee," *Washington Post,* June 22, 1983, A5.

22. David Broder, "Is Jesse Jackson?" *Washington Post,* December 14, 1983, A23.

23. Walters, *Black Presidential Politics,* 52–84.

24. Black Entertainment Television, "Presidential Candidate John Kerry Opens Door for Rival Sharpton to Address Democratic National Convention," *Nightly News* interview on May 3, 2004, www.bet.com.

25. Jonetta Rose Barras, "Nice Try, Reverend, but We're Past That Brand of Politics," *Washington Post,* February 22, 2004, B1.

Chapter 7

1. Nancy Pelosi, Office of the House Democratic Leader, press release, March 17, 2004.

2. Terry M. Neal, "Bush, Blacks and Iraq," www.washingtonpost.com (accessed May 20, 2004).

3. Congressional Black Caucus, "Detroit and Philadelphia Feel Pain of Bush Administration Economic Policies," press release, www.house.gov/cummings/cbc/cbcpress (accessed July 24, 2003).

4. Congressional Black Caucus, "Detroit and Philadelphia."

5. Elijah E. Cummings, "The July Employment Report: More Disappointing News for Millions of Americans Looking for Work; African American Unemployment Soars to Almost 11 Percent and Job Growth Drastically Below Forecast," press release of the Congressional Black Caucus, www.house.gov/cummings/cbc/cbcpress (accessed August 6, 2004).

6. Julian Bond, "2004 NAACP Convention Speech," Philadelphia Convention Center, Philadelphia, PA, July 11, 2004, 18.

7. Bond, "2004 NAACP Convention Speech."

8. CNN.com, "Kerry Camp Makeup Criticized," www.allpolitics.cnn.com (accessed April 29, 2004).

9. Jodi Wilgoren, "Some Blacks and Hispanics Criticize Kerry on Outreach," *New York Times,* www.nytimes.com (accessed April 30, 2004).

10. *LA Weekly,* "15 Weeks and Counting: Black Power(less)," www.laweekly.com (accessed July 23, 2004).

11. BET/CBS News Poll, "African Americans and the 2004 Vote," July 6–15, 2004.

12. Ted Barrett, "Black Democrats Hold Heated Meeting with Nader," www.cnn.com (accessed June 22, 2004).

13. MSNBC.com, "Congressional Black Caucus Presses Nader: Indepen-

dent Refuses to Quit Presidential Race," www.msnbc.com (accessed July 22, 2004).

14. *Washington Afro-American*, "National Civic Coalition Gets Out the Black Vote," Washington, DC, November 15, 2002, C10.

15. David Stokes, "'Feel the Power,' Black Voters," *Atlanta Inquirer*, January 17, 2004, 1.

16. Eliza Barclay, "Analysis: Voting Groups Avoid 2000 Mix-ups," *Washington Times*, www.washingtontimes.com.

17. Author's notes, as participant and observer in a Focus Group (youths aged 18–24, 25–35), at Focus Miami, sponsored by Voices for Working Families, August 4, 2004, Miami, FL.

18. The author participated in debriefing sessions with Unity '04 field directors and in other settings where complaints were voiced about the tactics of ACT both before and after the election.

19. "Statement by RNC Chairman Ed Gillespie on Black History Month," Republican National Committee press release, February 5, 2004, Washington, DC.

20. "Statement by RNC Chairman Ed Gillespie."

21. Marcella Bombardieri, "Jackson Wary of Same-Sex Rift," *Boston Globe*, February 17, 2004, B1.

22. Bombardieri, "Jackson Wary of Same-Sex Rift."

23. With special reference to Florida, see also Gregory Lewis, "Bush Makes Inroads with Black Christian Voters," *Sun-Sentinel*, www.sun-sentinel.com (accessed November 11, 2004).

24. Lewis, "Bush Makes Inroads."

25. Martin C. Evans, "Gay Marriage Gained Bush Black Votes," *Newsday*, www.newsday.com (accessed November 5, 2004).

26. Ira J. Hadnot, "Some Black Churches Ambiguous about Political Action," *Dallas Morning News*, www.dallasnews.com (accessed July 30, 2004).

27. Harold Myerson, "The GOP's Shameful Vote Strategy," *Washington Post*, October 28, 2004, A25.

Chapter 8

1. Grant Gross, "Group Records More Than 1,100 E-voting Glitches," www.computerweekly.com (accessed November 3, 2004).

2. NewScientists.com, "Success Claimed for US E-voting Machines," www.newscientists.com (accessed November 4, 2004).

3. Michael Hout, Laura Mangels, Jennifer Carlson, and Rachel Best, with the assistance of the University of California at Berkeley Quantitative Methods

Research Team, "Working Paper: The Effect of Electronic Voting Machines on Change in Support for Bush in the 2004 Florida Election" (University of California, Berkeley, November 2001).

4. Kwame Ture and Charles Hamilton, *Black Power: The Politics of Liberation* (New York: Random House, 1992), 46.

5. John Mercurio, "Democratic Party Reaches Out to Hispanics," *CNN .com*, www.cnn.com (accessed August 9, 2002).

6. Matt Bai, "Who Lost Ohio?" *New York Times Magazine*, November 21, 2004, 68.

7. Bai, "Who Lost Ohio?"

8. The Hotline, "Postmortem: How Ohio Was Won (and Lost)," *National Journal,* 5, www.politicsonline.com/coverage/hotline/h980930.htm (accessed November 17, 2001).

9. The Hotline, "Postmortem."

10. Donna L. Brazile, "In Rebuilding Party, Democrats Need to Start from Scratch," *Roll Call,* www.rollcall.com (accessed November 4, 2001).

11. Bai, "Who Lost Ohio?" 74.

Bibliography

Books

Barker, Lucius J., and Mack H. Jones. *African Americans and the American Political System*. 3rd ed. New York: Prentice Hall, 1994.

Black, Earle, and Merle Black. *The Rise of Southern Republicans*. Cambridge, MA: Harvard University Press, 2002.

Carr, Leslie G. *"Color-Blind" Racism*. Thousand Oaks, CA: Sage, 1997.

Carson, Clayborne, ed. *The Autobiography of Martin Luther King, Jr.* New York: Warner, 1998.

Clinton, Bill. *My Life*. New York: Knopf, 2004.

Germond, Jack, and Jules Witcover. *Mad as Hell: Revolt at the Ballot Box, 1992*. New York: Warner, 1993.

Grofman, Bernard, and Chandler Davidson, eds. *Controversies in Minority Voting: The Voting Rights Act in Perspective*. Washington, DC: Brookings Institution, 1992.

Henry, Charles. *Jesse Jackson: The Search for Common Ground*. Oakland, CA: Black Scholar Press, 1991.

Jackson, Jesse, Jr., and Frank Watkins. *A More Perfect Union: Advancing New American Rights*. New York: Welcome Rain, 2001.

Lincoln, C. Eric, and Lawrence H. Mamiya. *The Black Church in the African American Experience*. Durham, NC: Duke University Press, 1990.

Marable, Manning, and Leith Mullings, eds. *Let Nobody Turn Us Around: Voices of Resistance, Reform, and Renewal*. Lanham, MD: Rowman & Littlefield, 2000.

Pomper, Gerald. *The Election of 1988: Reports and Interpretations*. Chatham, NJ: Chatham House, 1988.

———. *The Election of 1992: Reports and Interpretations*. Chatham, NJ: Chatham House, 1993.

———. *The Election of 1996*. Chatham, NJ: Chatham House, 1997.

Raines, Howell. *My Soul Is Rested*. New York: Putnam, 1977.

Rustin, Bayard. *Down the Line: The Collected Writings of Bayard Rustin*. New York: Quadrangle, 1971.

Sharpton, Al. *Al on America*. New York: Dafina, 2002.

Singh, Robert. *The Congressional Black Caucus*. Thousand Oaks, CA: Sage, 1996.

Ture, Kwame, and Charles Hamilton. *Black Power: The Politics of Liberation*. New York: Vintage Books/Random House, 1992.

Walters, Ronald. *Black Presidential Politics in America*. Albany: SUNY Press, 1989.

Supplementary Reports

"Activities of the Voting Rights Project, 1998–2001," Voting Rights Project, Lawyers Committee for Civil Rights Under Law, Washington, DC, www.lawyerscomm.org.

"Al Sharpton: Top Contributors," 2005 cycle, Center for Responsive Politics. www.opensecrets.org.

Campaign Finance Documents of Former Senator Carol Moseley Braun, U.S. Federal Election Commission, August 2004.

"Election Reform," Summary, Collins Center for Public Policy, 2001, Miami, Florida.

"Has NAACP Taken Sides in the Presidential Campaign? Black Conservatives Say Revoked Invitation to Bush Official Implies Partisanship." Press Release, The National Center for Public Policy Research, September 10, 2004, www.nationalcenter.org.

"Help America Vote Act," Civil Rights Division, Voting Section, U.S. Department of Justice, Washington, DC.

Panel Presentation, American Enterprise Institute, Washington, DC, October 19, 2004.

Political Participation, U.S. Civil Rights Commission, Washington, DC, May 1968.

"Redefining Rights in America: The Civil Rights Record of the George W. Bush Administration, 2001–2004." Staff Draft for the Commissioner's Review, Office of Civil Rights Evaluation, U.S. Commission on Civil Rights, September 2004, Washington, DC.

Report, Unity '04 Strategy Meeting, Summary Notes, August 31, 2004. Also, Richard Muhammad, op. cit.

"Revitalizing Democracy in Florida," The Governor's Select Task Force on Election Procedures, Standards and Technology, Tallahassee, Florida, March 1, 2001.

"Standards for Defining Metropolitan and Micropolitan Statistical Areas," *Federal Register,* Vol. 65, No. 249, Office of Management and Budget, December 27, 2000, 82232.

"Status Report on Probe of Election Practices in Florida during the 2000 Presidential Election," U.S. Civil Rights Commission.

"The Color of Money: The 2004 Presidential Race," The Fannie Lou Hamer Project and the William C. Velasquez Institute, October 2004.

"The Joint Center for Political and Economic Studies 2004 National Opinion Poll," October 19, 2004, Joint Center for Political and Economic Studies, Washington, DC.

"The Long Shadow of Jim Crow: Voter Intimidation and Suppression in America Today," Report, National Association for the Advancement of Colored People, Baltimore, MD, September 2004.

The State of Black America 1999. New York: National Urban League, 1999.

"Voter Intimidation and Suppression by Republicans," People for the American Way, Democratic Wings, archives. www.democraticwings.com. See also "RNC in Blatant Violation of Court Consent Decree, Says Advancement Project," *Tullahoma News,* October 27, 2004. U.S. Newswire.

"Youth Turnout Up Sharply in 2004," November 3, 2004, the Center for Information & Research on Civic Learning & Engagement (CIRCLE)," School of Public Policy, University of Maryland, College Park.

Index

Page numbers in italics indicate tables.

About the Author

Ronald W. Walters is professor of government and politics and director of the African American Leadership Institute at the University of Maryland in College Park. He is a well-known national political analyst and helped run Jesse Jackson's presidential campaign in 1984. He is the author of many books on African American politics, including *Black Presidential Politics in America*, winner of the Ralph Bunche Award of APSA, and *White Nationalism*, covered by C-SPAN. Ron Walters appears frequently on major network television, in national newspapers, and other outlets and was a featured commentator throughout the 2004 election season. He writes a weekly syndicated column for the National Newspaper Publishers Association, appears regularly in *Ebony* and *The Nation*, and lives in Silver Spring, MD.

AMERICAN POLITICAL CHALLENGES
Larry J. Sabato, *Series Editor*

The American political process is in trouble. Although we witnessed a movement toward specific electoral reforms in the aftermath of the 2000 election debacle and in the run-up to 2004, the health of our political system is still at risk. Recent events have altered the political landscape and posed new challenges, and reforms are much needed and wanted by the American public. Diligence is required, however, in examining carefully the intended and unintended consequences of reforms—such as BCRA—as we look toward the 2006 elections and beyond.

Series Editor Larry J. Sabato of the University of Virginia Center for Politics is a leading political scientist and commentator who has clear ideas about what needs to change to improve the quality of our democracy. For this series, he taps leading political authors to write cogent diagnoses and prescriptions for improving both politics and government. New and forthcoming books in the series are short, to the point, and easy to understand (if difficult to implement against the political grain). They take a stand and show how to overcome obstacles to change. Authors are known for their clear writing style as well as for their political acumen.

Titles in the Series

Chesapeake Bay Blues: Science, Politics, and the Struggle to Save the Bay
Howard R. Ernst

The Pursuit of Happiness in Times of War
Carl M. Cannon

The Presidential Nominating Process: A Place for Us?
Rhodes Cook

Freedom Is Not Enough: Black Voters, Black Candidates, and American Presidential Politics
Ronald W. Walters

Attack the Messenger: How Politicians Turn You Against the Media
Craig Crawford